D1741771

GROUP ANALYSIS IN THE LAND OF MILK AND HONEY

NEW INTERNATIONAL LIBRARY OF GROUP ANALYSIS
Series Editor: Earl Hopper

**Recent titles in the NILGA Series
(for a full listing, please visit www.karnacbooks.com)**

GROUP ANALYSIS IN THE LAND OF MILK AND HONEY

edited by

Robi Friedman and Yael Doron

KARNAC

First published in 2017 by
Karnac Books Ltd
118 Finchley Road, London NW3 5HT

Copyright © 2017 to Robi Friedman and Yael Doron for the edited
collection and to the individual authors for their contributions.

The rights of the contributors to be identified as the authors of this work
have been asserted in accordance with §§77 and 78 of the Copyright Design
and Patents Act 1988.

All rights reserved. No part of this publication may be reproduced,
stored in a retrieval system, or transmitted, in any form or by any means,
electronic, mechanical, photocopying, recording, or otherwise,
without the prior written permission of the publisher.

British Library Cataloguing in Publication Data

A C.I.P. for this book is available from the British Library

   ISBN 978 1 78220 356 8

Excerpt from *Between Time. Poems and Prose* by Ofer Lider reproduced by
kind permission of Osnat Lider.

Edited, designed and produced by The Studio Publishing Services Ltd
www.publishingservicesuk.co.uk
email: studio@publishingservicesuk.co.uk

Printed in Great Britain

www.karnacbooks.com

CONTENTS

ACKNOWLEDGEMENTS

This book, co-created by many authors and a whole Matrix, calls for many acknowledgements. First, we would like to extend our gratitude to Earl Hopper, with whom the idea of this book was first created. His support and encouragement helped us to stand up to this challenge. We thank our families for bearing with our investment in the book. We wish to thank the Israel Foulkes Fund, the Israeli Institute of Group Analysis, and anonymous donors, who helped to finance the book.

We are especially grateful to the twenty writers who joined this project and together with us made this dream come true. We are also grateful to Adeela Sharif, who worked on the first English editorial language phase.

We thank our cherished and loved first professional guides in our journey of becoming group analysts: first, Bryan Boswood, Tom Hamrogue, Robin Cooper, Sheila Ernst, and Felix Mendelsohn, who are no longer among us. Then we also want thank Beatrice Hook, Levana Marshall, Veronika Munz, and Gabrielle Rikfind, may they enjoy long and healthy lives, who also came from Europe six times a year, in good and bad times. All of them will be remembered forever by our founding generations.

Finally, we would like to extend our gratitude to the many contributors to the life of our Institute, all volunteers, who invested their energy and love into the management of the IIGA over the years. We consider this book as a present from all of us, the editors and the authors, to our friends, colleagues, and partners.

ABOUT THE EDITORS AND CONTRIBUTORS

Miriam Berger, MA, senior clinical psychologist, supervisor, and group analyst is a former co-Chair of the Israeli Institute of Group Analysis and one of its co-founders. She is the first chief psychologist of Amcha Tel Aviv (treating Holocaust survivors and their families).

Avi Berman, PhD, clinical psychologist, psychoanalyst, and a group analyst, is a member of the Tel Aviv Institute of Contemporary Psychoanalysis and initiator, co-founder, and the first Chair of the Israeli Institute of Group Analysis. He is also co-founder of "Be'Sod Siach"—conflict resolution in Israel.

Hanni Biran, MA, is a clinical psychologist and supervisor, training psychoanalyst, and group analyst. Member of the Tel Aviv Institute of Contemporary Psychoanalysis and member of the Israeli Institute of Group Analysis. She teaches at Tel Aviv University, at Magid Institute, and at the Tel Aviv Institute of Contemporary Psychoanalysis.

Rachel A. Chejanovsky, MA, is a clinical psychologist and group analyst. She is a member of the Israeli Association for Psychoanalytic Psychotherapy and teaches at the Israeli Institute of Group Analysis. She is also consultant to an educational psychologists' team.

Yael Doron, MA, is a rehabilitation psychologist and group analyst. Teaches at the Israeli Institute of Group Analysis, at Haifa University, at the School of Psychotherapy in Rambam Hospital, Haifa, and at the Central School for Social Workers in Tel Aviv.

Robi Friedman, PhD, is a clinical psychologist and group analyst. Co-founder and former Chair of the Israeli Institute of Group Analysis. President of the Group Analytic Society International, he is also the former Chair of the Israeli Association for Group Psychotherapy. He teaches at Haifa University and at the Israeli Institute of Group Analysis.

Shulamit Geller, PhD, clinical psychologist, supervisor, and social psychologist. She is a lecturer in the faculty of Clinical Psychology Graduate Program at the Academic College of Tel-Aviv-Yaffo and a Member of the Israeli Institute of Group Analysis.

Nurit Goren, MSW, is a psychotherapist, supervisor, and group analyst. She is one of the initiators and past convener of the Training Program for Group Analysts in Israel (2004–2012). She was a member of the Israeli Institute of Group Analysis Executive Committee, Chair of the Education Committee of IIGA, and a lecturer and supervisor in the programme. She is a psychotherapy supervisor in "The Psychoanalytic Psychotherapy Programme", in Bar-Ilan University.

Bracha Hadar, MA, is a clinical psychologist, group analyst, and bioenergetics analyst. She is a specialist in body–mind therapy and developed an integrative approach for group work with body work.

Ilana Laor, MA, is a clinical psychologist. Her doctorate thesis will be completed soon. She is a lecturer, supervisor, and a group analyst on the psychotherapy programme at Tel Aviv University, core programme, and the relational track.

Enav Karniel Lauer, PhD, is a clinical social worker, psychotherapist, and group analyst. She is a lecturer at Bar-Ilan University's School of Social Work, and at the Kibbutzim College, Director of the Training Programme at the Israeli Institute of Group Analysis, and supervisor of group and individual psychotherapists.

Joshua Lavie, MA, is a clinical psychologist and group analyst. He is a teacher and supervisor at the Israeli Institute of Group Analysis and one of its founders. He is also a co-founder of the Israeli Journal of Group Psychotherapy, "Mikbatz", and Head of Forum Institute for Psychotherapy in Tel Aviv.

Marit Joffe Milstein, MA, is a psychodramatist, supervisor, and group analyst. She is Chair of the Israeli Institute of Group Analysis. Shiba Hospital Clinic for Eating Disorders. Conductor and lecturer at Mazra hospital, and at the Ministry of Education and the Ministry of Defence.

Eric Moss, PhD, is a clinical psychologist and group analyst and is on the staff of the Israel Institute of Group Analysis.

Gila Ofer, PhD, is a clinical psychologist, psychoanalyst, and group analyst. She is a founding member and past president of the TA Institute of Contemporary Psychoanalysis, a founding member of IIGA, a supervisor and teacher at the Post-Graduate Programme of Psychoanalytic Psychotherapy, TA University, and Editor of the EFPP *Psychoanalytic Psychotherapy Review*.

Ido Peleg, MD, is a psychiatrist and group analyst, and director of an acute open ward in "Mazor" mental health center, Akko. He is a staff member at the Israeli Institute of Group Analysis and teaches at Haifa University and the Professional School of Psychology, Sacramento.

Pnina Rappoport, PhD, is a group analyst, individual, couple, and group psychotherapist. Board member of the Israeli Institute of Group Analysis. She has lectured in many academic institutes in Israel, and internationally. She specialises in treatment of stage fright and fear of relationships.

Ravit Raufman, PhD, is a clinical psychologist, group therapist, and scholar in Hebrew and comparative literature. She is a senior lecturer at the University of Haifa.

Eran Shadach, PhD, is a clinical psychologist, member of the IIGA, and a lecturer in the faculty of Clinical Psychology Graduate Program at the Academic College of Tel-Aviv-Yaffo. He teaches at the school of social work, Tel-Aviv University and is the professional manager of "Reut" Institute for Psychotherapy.

Suzi Shoshani, MA, senior psychologist, group analyst, supervisor individual, couple, and group therapist. She is a former co-chair of the Israeli Institute of Group Analysis (IIGA) (2005–2010), and was the Convener of the Training Program for Group Analysts in the Israel Institute (2010–2016).

Haim Weinberg, PhD, is a clinical psychologist and group analyst. He is the director of a doctorate programme focusing on group therapy and dean of International Programmes at the Professional School of Psychology, Sacramento, CA, USA.

Hagit Zohn, MSW, is a psychotherapist, group analyst, and a supervisor at the IIGA. She is head of the Group Conductors Programme in Kibbutzim College, and co-leads the conductors' programme in IDC Herzlyia. She is a member of the academic board of the programme for psychotherapy in Tel Aviv University.

SERIES EDITOR'S FOREWORD

It is an honour to be able to include in the New International Library of Group Analysis this superb book about the theory and practice of group analysis in Israel and inevitably about Israel itself. As the product of what in group analysis is called the "tripartite matrix", it reflects the constraints and restraints of the contextual society of Israel, the dynamic matrices of its citizenry and its groupings (in particular the Israeli Institute of Group Analysis), and the personal matrices of each of the authors and co-editors. Although individual creativity should be understood in terms of the Western myth of the individual mind, which ignores the power of the social unconscious, there can be no doubt that each chapter is also the product of a personal struggle to integrate psychoanalysis, the study of group dynamics, and social systems thinking.

Written in a second and sometimes a third language, the authors transcend locality in favour of the cosmopolitan perspective inherent in international modern science. Although they are loyal to the demands of their location within the Middle East, they are determined to communicate with colleagues throughout the world. Although they respect the fecundity of their own soil, they are aware that there is often a shortage of milk and honey, at least for some. Standing on any hillside in Israel, and turning north towards Syria and south towards Egypt, overlooking the boardwalks of Lebanon and the beaches of Gaza, one's gaze is interrupted only by the natural curves of the earth's horizon. Moved by a sense of potential and possibility, perhaps even by the hope for peace, one is all too painfully aware of the inability of the peoples of the Middle East to follow the biblical admonition to turn their swords into ploughshares.

The social and personal realities of post-Holocaust/Shoah make life in Israel even more of a challenge than it otherwise would be. Israelis are determined not to be anyone's "sucker", "bar of soap", or "lampshade". Such determination suffuses their lives and their work. This sometimes leads to their disavowal of creative sexuality and the full appreciation of the life-force. After all, in the context of traumatogenic processes across the generations, the search for the feminine is not an easy one. Nonetheless, although tending to work in the fields of conscious interpersonal and intersubjective relationality, and of frustration, aggressive feelings, and aggression, the authors of this book seem to be intuitively aware of what is poetically symbolic in unconscious life. Perhaps this stems from the positive encapsulation of good experience in order to keep it safe and untarnished by exposure to violence.

It is noteworthy that in general group analysts who have contributed to this book eschew those forms of psychoanalysis that privilege innate malign envy over helplessness. This can be seen in their efforts to integrate the perspectives of the forefathers in group analysis in both Europe and in the USA. Our colleagues in Israel are engaged both in analytical work and committed to political action that involves finding just and good enough solutions to social and personal problems. Clearly, they appreciate both the value of insight and the power of outsight.

The Appendix, which provides a brief history of the Israeli Institute of Group Analysis, is especially informative and instructive. It illustrates the vicissitudes of love and hate in socio-cultural-political innovation, seen in terms of the inevitable heritage of conception trauma and birth trauma. In the life of organisations some events and processes are destined to be repeated. Their consequences can be moderated, but only rarely can they be eliminated completely. Constant reflection and working through, usually in group settings, must become an element of organisational life. This requires a great commitment to collective well-being as well as the appreciation of the contributions of individuals to it.

The possibilities of making creative use of traumatic experience is articulated throughout this book, which can be seen in the passion brought to clinical work in groups. Full credit must be given to Robi Friedman and Yael Doron for co-editing these contributions, and for pulling them together into a coherent whole. I wonder whether this activity has been healing and reparative for all concerned. Certainly it has been so for me. Within a few short years of the founding of the Israeli Institute of Group Analysis, its members have taken leading roles in the profession of group analysis. We have all benefited from their efforts, as will the many readers of this book.

Earl Hopper
Series Editor

Introduction

Robi Friedman and Yael Doron

Group Analysis in the Land of Milk and Honey[1] is a collection of clinical essays by group analysts in Israel. We are fascinated by group analysis as a theory, method, and ever-developing body of knowledge for understanding and treating the person, the group, and society. We are delighted to share our work with a wider, international audience.

S. H. Foulkes, the founder of group analysis, was a German Jewish psychoanalyst who, in 1933, sought asylum in England. Working traditionally with individual patients, who lie on the couch and produce free associations, he became curious about how these patients would communicate with one another in a group. He used clinical proof that the proper setting for solving many of an individual person's problems is where these problems originated. He realised that communication operates in groups through complex interpersonal networks. They make it possible for individuals to change by gaining insight into themselves, the relations to and between others, and by having a space in which it would be possible to "play". Foulkes was a revolutionary, insisting on the importance of unconscious and interpenetrating connections among persons and their contextual groupings of various kinds. This transpersonal and transgenerational perspective not only abolishes much of the conceptual separation of the "individual" and his "society", but it also enables us to understand that the group can be the primary therapeutic agent through processes of resonance, mirroring, exchange, and other forms of communication. Transformation and healing by and through relationships with fellow members of a group, including the group therapist (preferably called "conductor", rather than facilitator or leader), makes group analysis unique. The centrality of the group's contribution is seen in the conductor's first task: as the "holder" of the group, he secures it and promotes communication within its dynamic matrix, the total but open network of relations, values, and norms, and patterns of communication.

Editing and writing this book has allowed us—indeed, has required us—to reflect on our lives and work in Israel. The chapters manifest the whole gamut of influences that life in Israel has on group analytic work, from daily survival, episodic violence, animosity with neighbours, to the fantastic national and social growth of our young country. Our book illustrates of the contextual constraints and restraints of the foundation matrix of our society and the dynamic matrix of our Institute. Our cooperation as editors characterises the Israel Institute of Group Analysis, which encourages the integration of both senior and junior members. The more experienced share their extensive clinical experience and particular insights, passing the group analytic baton to younger generations. We think some of the Institute's character, especially the intergenerational relations, necessarily reflect aspects of Israeli society.

The translation of our work from Hebrew into English has proved to be a particularly challenging step. Translating the original Hebrew book (Friedman & Doron, 2015) into this English version has involved so much writing that it almost seems to be a new book, with all the pleasures and pains associated with a new creation. By having to separate from previous meanings attached to our "natural" way of thinking and understanding in our native Hebrew, preparing this English version has pushed us also through a further group process. The patience of our several translators and the editor of the New International Library of Group Analysis was essential. We were all committed to finding a way with words and concepts through which we could express our Hebrew into understandable English. Thus, this co-created book has gone through several transformations and "translations", perhaps in the best sense of the term and the project!

While most of the writers of the chapters live in the large cities of Israel, together we represent considerable socio-demographic diversity. But the participants in our groups, who provide much of the material throughout the book, include an even wider range of ages, social classes, and ethnic diversity. Jews, Arab-Israelis, and Palestinians, as well as immigrants to Israel from all over the world, exhibit a broad spectrum of experiences of trauma, ranging from survivors of the Shoah to soldiers, and a broad spectrum of personal and relational pathologies. However, in Israel, we all live in a "soldier's matrix" (Friedman, 2015).[2]

We do not always appreciate the degree to which our identities as group analysts are, therefore, so similar. As a group, we might even be characterised by a high degree of homogeneity. Our training has been deeply influenced by psychoanalysis, especially by the contemporary relational forms of it. Those of us who have gone through the Israeli school system are also likely to have incorporated the gist of the myths and narratives of the Old Testament. Most of us have had our education in psychology in common, especially at the beginning of our careers. However, through editing these chapters and translating them into English, we discovered a less obvious parameter of our commonalities: in almost all the chapters of this book there is an absence of Eros, and an omnipresence of Thanatos. In thinking more about the literature from several countries, and in the context of our dialogue and work with the Editor of NILGA, we have become aware of the prevalence in our writing of pain, exclusion, humiliation, shame, violence, and aggression at the expense of joy, pleasure, optimism, and "sexuality" in its broadest sense and in its specific sense. We have also become aware of our common emphasis on the importance and security of the therapeutic setting. We are obliged to wonder why.

Reflecting on this phenomenon was not easy, either emotionally or intellectually, because Israel is surely also a land of love and work, and certainly an arena of passion in the fullest sense. We have several possible explanations for what seems to be a shared but unconscious "representation" of this in the work of two dozen group analysts. The preoccupation with Thanatos seems to be a consequence of the authors being citizens of the "soldier's matrix" and their coping with their past and their present traumas. They also pertain to an older than average age cohort with similar war experience. As a group, most of them were also educated under the influence of Kleinian and Bionian psychoanalysis, which emphasises the death instinct, envy, and inter-personal destructiveness. In addition, the present war situation is undeniably dominant, because the struggle in Israel has not only a past, but also a daily impact on the population. Denying and pre-cluding the present "troubles" from consciousness does not suspend their unconscious influence from the authors' matrix. Last, but not least, there is the possibility that in same way the "land of milk and honey" holds something for the Western world, the Israeli Institute of Group Analysis contains the dread and traumas for the world of group analysis. Perhaps this is a matter of the dynamics of survival.

In re-editing the book, we again felt that we were part of a selected group inside a longed for community (the society of the group ana-lysts). We have also become aware of the unique communal matrix from which the various and diverse chapters have been created. At some point during the editing process, we even imagined being ourselves part of a very special large group which was gathering in our fantasy through the course of our work. Re-creating this large group it can be described as follows: in the inner circle of it the two editors and the other twenty authors sit together with the NILGA editor. They are discussing the meaning of "translation" and "editing" in the group analytical sense of these terms, helping each other shift from precept to concept, to ideas, to communicational argument, and from monologue to dialogue, and to discourse. This inner circle is sur-rounded by dozens of chairs, organised in concentric, ever larger circles occupied by members of the Israeli Institute of Group Analysis, who "hold" the inner circle and "contain" the dialogue. They are surrounded, in turn, by colleagues and associates who have con-tributed to our thinking and to the book, specifically.

The next circle of this large group is filled by other members of the Institute, and then by fellow group therapists and friends of the authors, as well as students and supervisees. A special "space" is reserved for our patients, especially those who have been described throughout the book's chapters. There are also members of our fami-lies, who have not only touched our lives, but influenced us, together with other significant persons, in numerous ways. Is it a wish that this large group exists within the context of the international Group Analytic Society and the European Group Analytic Training Institute Network, not to mention other international professional organisations? In this fantasy, we see the dynamic matrix of group analysis and the foundation matrix of Israel containing neighbour-hoods, communities, and our country as a whole. Letting our imagination wander widely and freely, we see how this very space is also timeless. It includes all who have inspired our authors over the generations: poets, writers, playwrights, philosophers, biblical figures, and imaginary characters from literature—all voices in a large, large group, a polyphony which can be read and heard both in and between the lines of the book.

This very special large group represents the "land of milk and honey". It also represents the matrix that contains the Israel Institute of Group Analysis, from which our authors are drawn. Their work is characterised by complex thinking, and the acceptance of different perspectives within an implicitly unified therapeutic approach of group analysis. Cure is a matter of healing, which, in turn, is less a matter of isolated and abstract "knowing", and more a matter of "feeling" and resonating together. Groups are perceived to exist within the context of the community. We believe that, in a way, an entire nation participates in the process of healing. We are united by our love of, and interest in, group work and many of us might even be fascinated by the unique energy of group analysis. It is the place where sensations and feelings transform into words in the presence of others. It is the space in which, together, we can capture the music and dance which exist between letters and us, in which we can turn pages and relationships in a way, which was not possible in any other therapeutic setting.

The book is organised into three parts: theory, practice, and the application of group analysis.

In the theory section, Chapter One, Miriam Berger presents the idea that democratic values such as reciprocity, justice, and fairness are implicit in the philosophy of group analysis. Foulkes' ideas of the group circle, and the importance of communication can be envisaged as a democratic viewpoint on the basis of which an "ethical envelope" is wrapped around the group and its members.

In Chapter Two, Avi Berman asks interesting questions: when we talk about "the group", what do we actually mean? What is the "group entity"? He answers that, as opposed to individual therapy, in group analysis the entire group is the therapeutic agent. Group members communicate through exchange, mirroring, and resonance, and, thus, a unique therapeutic benefit is achieved, but only if the therapist keeps himself from getting trapped in group dyads.

Hanni Biran, in Chapter Three, describes processes in contextual society through the prism of psychoanalysis and group analysis. She analyses the Oedipus myth and connects leadership to the desire to explore the truth. Drawing on the ideas of Bion, she describes different kinds of knowing, offering the type of knowing that a leader must practise in order to be able to handle a traumatic social situation, which demands endless sacrifice.

In Chapter Four, Joshua Lavie writes about Foulkes' revolutionary perspective concerning the Oedipus myth, viewing the Oedipus complex as a process in which all family members experience a regression, not only the child. He describes how Israel sends its children to battle, thus continuing, on the social level, the story of Oedipus and Laius.

Robi Friedman, in "The group analysis of the Akeda: the worst and the best feelings in the matrix" (Chapter Five) describes, through an unconventional analysis of the story of Isaac's binding, the "Akeda", the most terrible process that occurs in groups: the scapegoating and "sacrifice" of a member of the group. He analyses the personal and social aspects involved in the story of the binding, and then presents the parallels with those that are often found in the group—the victim's co-operation, the lack of guilt and shame experienced by the others, and the role of the group leader in such processes.

In Chapter Six, Yael Doron describes a group that re-enacts over and over again in the "here and now" of the therapy group a "friendly fire" attack on one of the participants in the group. She uses a clinical example to examine the concept of the social unconscious and, in particular, the social defence of the "collective black hole": material that is not expressed but denied due to painful shame and guilt, and, thus, unconsciously drive and affect people in the group.

Nurit Goren, in "The 'immune system' and group analysis: communication between 'self' and 'non-self'" (Chapter Seven) describes the phenomenon of a group that attacks itself. She analyses it through the powerful metaphor of autoimmune disease, in which the body, due to a faulty misidentification, attacks and hurts itself. She describes through examples how the group, including its conductor, cope with such attacks and how the group eventually manages to survive and progress.

In Chapter Eight, Ilana Laor uses and explains the key concepts of the relational, intersubjective point of view: recognition, surrender, multiple selves, and the not-me state. These concepts are illustrated by a vignette from her group-analytic group.

The second part of the book focuses on "Practice". Marit Joffe Milstein, in Chapter Nine, "On arrivals and departures in slow-open group analytic groups", deals with the setting of the analytic group. She focuses on the influences of the participants' arrivals and departures during the course of work, and on the challenges brought by these changes for the group and the conductor. She discusses the disruption of the group dynamic and the regression of individuals and the group as a whole, stressing the potential progress that can occur through understanding these movements.

In Chapter Ten, Hagit Zohn explores the group setting by relating to the concept of boundaries in the context of group therapy. She describes how a group of Jewish participants cope with an Arab participant, and how the experience of boundaries is expressed in coping with the turbulent reality outside the room, as well as in the minds of individuals, the group as a whole, and the conductor.

Pnina Rappaport, in Chapter Eleven, describes the issues that emerge in combined treatment, when the patient is in individual and group therapy at the same time, using the same therapist or two different therapists for each modality. She describes how patients with severe personality disorders can especially benefit when their individual therapist also serves as their group conductor.

In "Is there hope for change at my age?" (Chapter Twelve), Bracha Hadar links the issue of group structure with the question of hope for change in old age. She asks whether differences of twenty years in age among group members are likely to enable or to prevent a healing process. She uses a clinical case from her analytic group to demonstrate that there is no age limit for change

In Chapter Thirteen, Eric Moss is concerned with the issue of old age. He shares with us his feelings as an ageing therapist. He describes how psychological theories perceive old age and elderly people, presenting the issues that arise when an elderly patient is introduced into a group. He illustrates how the group can gain from the participation of an older member. He argues that it is important that the leader does not suffer from "age blindness".

Rachel A. Chejanovsky, in Chapter Fourteen, uses a detailed case study to describe a process that occurs when a member of the group uses what she terms "subtle aggression". This behaviour can appear to be gentle, but it permeates and destroys the matrix of the group members. She describes the gentle way in which the group and the conductor work together to cope in such cases.

In "Foreigner in your motherland, foreigner in your chosen homeland: Jewish cultural identity" (Chapter Fifteen), Suzi Shoshani has written a unique chapter in which she uses the metaphor of the "new immigrant" in order to illustrate feelings of alienation and strangeness of the individual in the group. With considerable charm, she draws upon her personal experience as an alien in both her native land and in her chosen homeland, sharing the difficult experiences she endured in both societies.

In the third part, devoted to applications of group analysis, Chapter Sixteen is authored by Shulamit Geller and Eran Shadach, who describe how they use group analytic insights and perspectives in their teaching and supervising of graduate students in psychology. They focus on the concepts of the foundation matrix and the dynamic matrix, ego training in action, and exchange and translation processes.

In Chapter Seventeen, "Working with a multi-cultural group in times of war: three metaphors of motion and mobility" Ravit Raufman and Haim Weinberg describe the complex reality of working with multi-cultural groups at times of war. They use three movement metaphors to describe processes that occurred in their groups during politically and socially complex times in Israel.

Ido Peleg, in Chapter Eighteen, illustrates how a psychiatric ward functions as a dynamic matrix during the supervision of the ward staff. Supervision is a process in which common language is established, one that can connect professionals in different positions and roles in the ward. He uses a powerful vignette to show us how group analytic understanding can support the psychotic group, and encourage new and engaging group dialogue.

In Chapter Nineteen, Enav Karniel Lauer illustrates how an analytic group can build a healing matrix for Holocaust survivors and second generation participants. She illustrates how "mutual recognition"—a key term in intersubjective theory—serves as a therapeutic element that allows the promotion of healing processes within the group, and connects this term to Foulkes' "mirror reaction".

In the final chapter, "The personal, group and social aspects of dreaming", Gila Ofer illustrates the use of dreams in the spirit of group analysis. She distinguishes between three dimensions of dreams and in dream telling: personal, group, and social. She analyses several dreams, including Freud's famous dream of "Irma's injection", and concludes with an illustration of the unique method of the "social dreaming matrix".

The book ends with an Appendix, which is actually a kind of Epilogue to the book, entitled "The co-creation of the Israeli Institute of Group Analysis: notes from the Archives", by Avi Berman, Miriam Berger, and Joshua Lavie. They describe the efforts and hardships of the first attempts to bring together and educate Israel's leading group therapists in conducting therapeutic groups analytically. They then recount the history of the Institute from its foundation in 2001, with the mission of promoting group-analytic therapy, including training group analysts until today.

Notes

1. All names and identifying details of the participants mentioned in the various chapters have been changed and disguised to protect confidentiality. The book is written in masculine form, but relates to both genders.

2. The matrix is the society, its culture and total communication. "The matrix is the common shared ground which ultimately determines the meaning and significance of all events" (Foulkes, 1964, p. 292) or our shared mind.

    The soldiers' matrix is a society in or after war, which enlists everyone into different but rigid and fixed roles. The soldiers' matrix habitus seems to contain rejection and annihilation anxieties and desires for glory. Soldiers represent the matrix in the shared mind.

References

Foulkes, S. H. (1964). *Therapeutic Group Analysis*. London: Karnac.

Friedman, R. (2015). A soldier's matrix: a group analytic view of societies in war. *Group Analysis*, *48*(3): 239–257.

Friedman, R., & Doron, Y. (Eds.) (2015). *Group Analysis in the Land of Milk and Honey*. Kiryat-Bialik: Ach.

PART I
THEORY

The "ethical envelope" of the analytic group: some thoughts about democratic values implicit in group analysis

Miriam Berger

In this chapter, I present some reflections on the democratic values implicit in group analysis and in its clinical praxis. They can be envisioned as a kind of collective holding, cloak wrapped around the group, which I define as an "ethical envelope". It represents an ethical covenant between group members and relates to basic human concerns such as reciprocity, justice, fairness, and caring. It transcends any given personal or social qualities and is woven into the matrix of the group analytic culture, whether consciously or unconsciously.

The presence of such an envelope is implicit in Foulkes' writing and in the way he perceives maturity, mental health, neurosis, and cure. It is sometimes conveyed indirectly through some ideas such as the group circle or the importance of the capacity for communication. However, a closer reading is required in order to understand that his approach is, indeed, grounded in a democratic worldview.

I suggest that acknowledging explicitly the values that are implicit in the "ethical envelope" can be curative; it deepens the therapists' understanding and enhances their emphatic capacities.

Democracy and psychoanalysis

The interconnectedness between psychoanalysis and democracy is not to be taken for granted. Traditionally, psychoanalysis shuns value-laden terminologies, since it prefers to be considered as a neutral, impersonal study of human psychic reality. Issues such as transparency, justice, equality, or lawfulness are perceived as being too "political", or too "external" and, therefore, could interfere with the purity of its scientific findings. It is believed that the real work of psychoanalysis should focus on the inner dynamics of the individual (Altman et al., 2004; Frosh, 2011).

A quick search through the PEP (Psychoanalytic Electronic Publishers) database reveals that the word "democracy" does not appear in the writings of Freud even once. Klein, for example, does not refer to this concept at all, and Bion mentions it only twice, in his book *Attention and Interpretation* (Bion, 1970, p. 127).

Relational psychoanalysis does relate more often to the impact that the social context has on the personal lives of people; however, ethical and moral concerns are still referred to with caution and reluctance (Benjamin, 1997). Years of involvement with supervision and teaching have convinced me that therapists who declare themselves to belong to the relational approach tend to protect the therapeutic relationship from social reality and seal the therapy room from its "intrusions", just as their more traditional colleagues do. Referring to "real realities" such as status, gender, age, ethnic origins, or the like is immediately suspected of superficiality or defensive denials. Therapists tend to see patients' accounts about facts—about who did what to whom—as material that is "too concrete" for psychoanalytic processing. It raises fears of being too far away from the "pure gold" of psychoanalysis. ("This is not psychoanalysis" is a well-known slight in professional circles.) Although relational theorists acknowledge the importance of the environment in shaping the human psyche, they still consider the inner personal dynamics as the key to affect change. Consciously or unconsciously, clinical discourse tends to avoid, or even ignore, the social context.

Even today, nearly sixty years after the publishing of his seminal papers, Winnicott is still unique in his radicalism when he poses an explicit question about the meaning of the word "Democracy" in the nursery and relates it explicitly to issues such as morality, responsibility, and mutual concern as vital qualities of maturity and of mental health. (Winnicott, 1986).

The absence of socio-political realities from psychoanalysis and an apparent lack of interest in exploring their dynamic meanings deserves a discussion in its own right. Needless to say, political attitudes can be charged with intense feelings and motivate extremely destructive behaviours. Sometimes, it seems that social reality is just too large for the lens of the psychoanalytic microscope. As said, this sharp distinction (not to say splitting) between the individual and society is supposed to ensure the purity of psychoanalytic enquiry, to safeguard the scientific truths ascribed to it. It appears that the "noise" of life might pose a threat to the silence needed to "hear" the soul; hence, we are called upon to eliminate that "noise", with its infinite complexity, and seal the therapy room from outside intrusions. Supposedly, this enables us to focus our attention on what is more relevant: the workings of the inner personal world and its dynamic processes.

The individual and society: continuities and discontinuities

I would like to state from the beginning that I disagree with the above dichotomies between inner and outer realities. I consider that group analytic ideas offer a basis for bringing together the individual and society. The struggle to repair the sense of continuity between the personal and the social is one of its core issues, both theoretically and clinically; it is perceived as a central human developmental task.

Nevertheless, group analysis itself does not relate directly and explicitly to social issues too often. Foulkes, the founder of group analysis, does mentions "democracy" occasionally. One such example is worth mentioning as it contains a rather ground-breaking statement (for those days), which expresses explicitly the democratic humanistic vision inherent in Foulkes approach.

> The widest view will look upon (analytic) group therapy as an expression of a new attitude towards the study and improvement of human inter-relations in our time. It may see in it an instrument, perhaps the first adequate one, for a practicable approach to the key problem of our time: the strained relationship between the individual and

> the community . . . Perhaps someone taking this broad view will see in it the answer in the spirit of a democratic community to the mass and group handling of Totalitarian régimes. (Foulkes, 1946, p. 51)

Although such a claim is quite rare in Foulkes' writings, I suggest that group analytic framework is imbued with universal democratic values; it creates a space in which each member has a right to develop his own unique individuality and to have a say in issues that matter; it can be defined figuratively as "democracy training in action".

Different facets of these ideas have been explored and illuminated by a number of group analysts, including Brown (1998), Dalal (1998), De Maré (1975), Hopper (2000, 2003), Nitzgen (2001), and Weegmann (2014); they support the view that group analysis is embedded in the wider context of a liberal democratic culture. Following their ideas, I shall briefly discuss some of its key principles and argue that they represent an ethical/moral dimension which I define as an "ethical envelope"; the ability to acknowledge it as part of the shared reality of group members can promote a democratic culture in one's relationship with self and others.

It should be noted that the curative factors, along with the ideas they are derived from, are all interconnected and define each other. I present them separately, only for the sake of clarity.

Before that, I would like to mention the fact that I use the notion of "democracy" in a most simple way without exploring its meanings and complexities. In ancient Greece *demos* meant "people" and *krátos* meant "power"; thus, democracy entails granting power to the people, or endorsing the "rule of the people". It defined a form of government in which all citizens have an equal right to voice their opinions and influence decisions that affect their lives. Thus, democracy aims to establish a social reality, where differences ("otherness", in our modern discourse) are acknowledged without domination, coercion, subjugation, or exclusion. In other words, democracy struggles to establish a base for the ability to reach mutual agreements about issues that matter; to achieve a consensus about urgent human concerns without resorting to violence and without excluding the subjective, unique voice of anyone. Democracy strives to constitute an inclusive culture; much akin to the aims of group analysis.

The "basic law" (1): a "democratic ego" in action

The "matrix" is a central concept in Foulkes' writing; it denotes his idea that man's life is social through and through, that he can develop his individuality only in a context of relationships with others.

> The Matrix is the hypothetical web of communication and relationship in a given group. It is the common shared ground, which ultimately determines the meaning and significance of all events and upon which all communications and interpretations verbal and non-verbal, rest. This concept links with that of communication. (Foulkes, 1984, p. 292)

The matrix can be perceived as a founding mould, which contains several significant principles.

First and foremost is the "basic law" of group dynamics, which Foulkes regarded as key to his approach. This "law" depicts his claim that the human capacity for co-operation and reciprocity is the most significant resource for personal and social growth. This capacity outlines the pathways to recovery and defines the healing effect group members have on each other:

> The deepest reason why patients . . . can reinforce each other's normal reactions and wear down and correct each other's neurotic reactions, is that collectively they constitute the very norm from which, individually, they deviate, (Foulkes, 1948, p. 29)

What does this mean and in what way is the "law" connected to the creation of a democratic culture?

As I understand it, Foulkes believed that group members jointly constitute a framework from which each of them carves out his unique subjectivity and defines his own personal identity. One can envision this process as a fabric that group members weave together and from which each of them cuts out his own personal cloths. Thus, the entire group creates a communicative network, a vocabulary, a common language imbued with attitudes and norms that become part of it.

The formation of these norms is a live and evolving process that gives meaning to the relationship of each participant with himself and others; it is carried out through continuous negotiations about mutual understanding, recognition, and self-realisation. Each participant, including the conductor, has an impact on the nature of this communicative network. In this sense, the group really becomes a Greek democracy in which ". . . all citizens have an equal right to voice their opinions and influence decisions that affect their lives". As previously said, this network creates a base on which each one develops his individuality; at the same time, it is also an open dynamic process that expands into new experiences and connections, which constitute ever-changing new contextual configurations. This circular thinking, in which cause and effect are intertwined, is built into the thinking of group analysis and characterizes the therapeutic process of the group.

The "basic law" (2): the "negative matrix" in action

Following the above thoughts, I suggest that this "basic law" has an underside which is less explored by Foulkes: as mentioned, the group creates together, out of itself, the norms from which its members shape their unique identities. At the same time, it also creates a network of prohibitions and restrictions, which become norms in their own right. Thus, the group constitutes rules and regulations of "do's" and "don'ts" and imposes them on its members, consciously or unconsciously. Both kinds of norms (the "do's" and the "don'ts") join forces to delineate the boundaries of legitimacy and saneness, on the one hand, and shaming and exclusion on the other. Each group member contributes unknowingly his share in sanctioning some moves, while proscribing others. As a rule, any norms of belonging inevitably also define non-belonging. Thus, the group network of communications also contains an antithetical pole, which I define as a "negative matrix"; it consists of prohibitions that are conveyed by unconscious processes and communicated implicitly through the interactions between group members. From this perspective, members cause each other (unknowingly) the very same relational wounds that closed them off defensively in the first place. Paradoxically, group members might, at times, seek a cure from the same malady they inflict on others. Weegman (2014) discusses the nature of this paradox at length, and posits the existence of a "negative matrix" in history and social sciences (2014, pp. 103–119).

Mitchell (1997) said that if we want to be part of the solution, we have to agree to be part of the problem; this idea catches the essence of the complexity inherent in the therapeutic relationship, which is asymmetrical, yet reciprocal to its very core. As I see it, this relational paradox pertains to Foulkes' "basic law" as well, since it adds a dimension of ethical depth to the group analytic perspective or to the psychoanalytic perspective in general.

The emotional vulnerabilities of group participants and their defensive closing off of dissociations are part of the group's communicative network, no less than their wish for healing and growth. For better or worse, the desire for change and the defensive manoeuvres against it are both part of its matrix, just as they are part of human relations in general. Paradoxically, when the vulnerabilities of group members, painful or pathological as they might be, are played out on the stage of groups' interactions, they provide an opportunity for transformation into personal strength. The multi-directional relationships in the group create an incredibly rich field for enactments, which, in turn, enable more productive processes of healing to evolve.

The relevance of the concept of "enactment" to the development of an "ethical envelope" is a subject that deserves a study in its own right; I will mention just briefly that the ability of group members to cure each other implies that they will become "infected" with each other's "sickness"; while seeking relief for their problems, they become inevitably each other's problems (including the conductor). It is a mutual entanglement that happens unconsciously, automatically, and uncontrollably. The continuous processing of such interactions in the group, which are defined as "enactments", could eventually mature into the ability to participate more fully in "subject relations" (Kennedy, 2000.) From my point of view, the readiness to struggle with the difficulties and emotional pain imbued in this process, along with a willingness to bear its pains for each other in the group, constitutes democratic values and deepens the "ethical envelope" the group is enwrapped with.

The "I" and the "we": continuity in action

Foulkes' idea that the individual, the "subject", is a dynamic social construct is not self-evident; it was quite radical in its day. I will present some of the salient points which stem from it while using the "I and the "we" as symbols of personal *vs.* social realities.

1. The definitions of "I" and "we" are not a fixed entity; according
    to group analysis, they are continuous processes shaped by
    the contributions of each group member and determined by the
    specific context that prevails at any given time in the group.
2. There is a continuum between the "I" and the "we". The indi-
    vidual and society are two sides of the same human reality, rather
    than positioned as dichotomous to each other.
3. The existence of dichotomies between inner and outer realities is
    indicative of emotional difficulties that seek healing; the analytic
    group offers a space where this healing can take place.[1]

The "basic law" emphasises the central role of creating a
communicative network in the group: its aim is to contain otherness,
to defend against exclusion, and to promote a process of inclusion. It
should be emphasised that the collective network is woven out of individual voices; outlandish as they might be, they still have to be heard,
acknowledged, and to count. Consensus is not achieved through the
ruling of the majority at the expense of silencing the minority. Rather,
it means that each group participant is relevant and contributes his
specific understanding to the process. In other words, the power of the
group depends on the ability of each participant to develop his own
unique subjectivity, and *vice versa*. Thus, the achievement of reciprocity and continuity between the "we" and the "I" is an essential part of
the therapeutic process.

Following the above understanding, the "basic law" contains
several democratic values that postmodern discourse is concerned
with: categories of knowledge are man-made and, therefore, open for
change by man; they should be considered as social constructs, rather
than truths engraved in stone, or innate characteristics defined as
"human nature". Categories such as status, race, gender, nationality,
religion, or age are negotiable and changeable. Therefore, any person,
at any point in time, can have a say and make a difference. Thus,
Foulkes' "basic law" represents his hope, indeed his vision, that
people can cure each other and create a culture of mutual caring. This
idea is also supported by Friedman (2005).

The connectedness between the well-being of the "I" and the "we"
can be illustrated by envisioning the group as a bunch of strangers
who have inherited a fortune which can be used only if they join

forces: they are fortunate, since they have become an emotional resource for each other and since their inherited wealth grows through their co-operation (Beukenkamp, 1958).

The group circle: transparency in action

Transparency is considered to be a significant part of the democratic culture. Bearing this in mind, we can see Foulkes' rationale for the group circle as aimed at achieving transparency: "This (circle) leaves nothing to hide behind, so that members . . . 'talk' . . . even during silent periods of the session. The therapist is one of the circle and equally vulnerable to the eye" (Foulkes & Anthony, 1990, p. 63).

The circle symbolises the importance of inclusion, belonging, and participation. Seeing each other is a reciprocal process that increases members' vulnerabilities, but, at the same time, might decrease the neurotic alienation they suffer from. The movement of joining others in the circle can be likened to the process of moving from repression to awareness. Therefore, the circle signifies a symbolic cure against the disease of exclusion, a release from neurotic confinement, from defensive hiding, and from isolation (Berger, 2012).

The group circle prevents mystification; it encourages members to share their difficulties and needs directly and explicitly; it is an invitation to be honest and truthful and struggle openly for the right to become a subject among subjects (De Maré, 1975).

The "hall of mirrors": human commonality in action

Foulkes perceived the group as a "hall of mirrors". He defined "mirror reactions" as a major therapeutic factor: each person sees himself in the other and *vice versa* (Foulkes, 1984). Thus, mirror reactions function as navigators for finding a safe route in the stormy waters of members' inner and outer realities. The idea that group members reflect each other's inner selves emphasises their interdependence and essential need for each other; it is, in itself, an acknowledgment that each individual counts and that relationships matter.

Foulkes' description speaks for itself:

A person sees himself—often a repressed part of himself—reflected in the interactions of other group members. . . he also gets to know himself . . . by the effect he has upon others and the picture they form of him. (Foulkes, 1984, p. 110)

Since every point of view is as valid as any other, mirroring processes can be perceived as a system of checks and balances that limit the ability of any single participant to control the agenda of the group; accordingly, the conductor has no monopoly on knowledge or wisdom. The multi-directionality of mirror reactions protects the group from forming rigid hierarchies; it gives every single member a chance to make a difference. Thus, one of the implications of the group as "a hall of mirrors" is that access to power can be distributed equally between all members at any given moment. It provides a "horizontal axis" for exploring dynamic processes (Foulkes & Anthony, 1990, p. 42).

According to Foulkes, the "horizontal axis" is a necessary addition to Freud's "vertical axis"; it stands for seeing the interactions that occur in the group in real time as not less meaningful than the in-depth explorations that characterise Freudian analysis.

In any case, group analysis strives to connect the "depth" and the "surface" to form one continuum. It claims that perceiving them as two sides of the same coin is essential in order to grasp the complexities of human relationships more fully and to strengthen a sense of human commonality. It is a vision that contributes to the humanisation of the therapeutic relationship (Pines, 1998).

Exchange: diversity in action

Foulkes defines "exchange" as one of the group specific therapeutic factors. It is a process of meeting with otherness, difference, and separateness. The continuous interactions between diverse viewpoints can stimulate growth and eventually turn into a collective resource. Group members share a large range of experiences, emotions, dreams, and thoughts with each other. However, interactions may easily turn into angry clashes which cause pain, evoke shame, or indignity. The ability to be with each other authentically depends on one's readiness to tolerate emotional difficulties. Hence, creating a shared reality is born through a continuous effort to bear with each other, to open up to the other's vulnerabilities, expectations, pain, or joy.

Foulkes is consistent in his belief in the curative value of reciprocity defined as exchange:

> Very soon . . . members of the group will . . . see that just as they tell someone else what they think or feel about him, they must also tolerate being told the same sort of things. They . . . discover the mutual benefit of such communications. They come to realize that the person who makes an observation speaks as much about himself as he speaks about the other person, and that by pointing out something whether correctly or incorrectly, to another person, he helps the latter's self-knowledge. (Foulkes & Anthony, 1990, p. 82)

It is clear that Foulkes perceives the difficulties inherent in tolerating diversity as an opportunity for growth, a potential resource; thus, "exchange" in the analytic group can strengthen the capacity for mutual concern, for "brotherhood", and for empathy. It becomes part of the "ethical envelope" group members weave together and wrap around themselves.

The conductor: the orchestration of playing together.

Foulkes prefers to look for therapeutic solutions *in* the group itself and not in the interpretative wisdom of its conductor. From his perspective, the work of the conductor is to maintain the group setting, to ensure it is a safe space, and to facilitate the flow of free group associations. It follows that the major therapeutic resource is the active participation of members and their readiness to be there for each other. This view is emphasized by replacing the term "leader" with that of "conductor": he ". . . follows the process . . . but I don't know in the least what the music is which will be played" (Foulkes, 1990, p. 292). Interpretations and insights are not imposed on the group from the outside, by some supreme authority represented by a "leader". Rather, each member contributes his personal knowing to the collective pool, which can enhance the healing capacities of the group. This conceptual framework reduces the risk of infantilising patients and attributing maturity or wisdom to the conductor only. It conveys the message that everyone is responsible for everyone else's wellbeing. Thus, the analytic group acts as a simulator that enables its members to practise their ability for "subject relation" in real time.

Foulkes' repeated emphasis on the patient as an independent, sovereign agent who is responsible for his actions defines the therapeutic relationship as a relationship between equals. It is part of the striving to democratise the psychoanalytical culture and to enhance its humanistic spirit.

The analytic group: praxis of belonging

Foulkes believed in the central importance of belonging as a basic human need; he offered the analytic group as a reparative space through which the suffering of non-belonging can be healed:

> The first and foremost aspect with which group psychotherapists are usually concerned and according to which they form their concepts is that of belonging, of participation. Being a respected and effective member of the group, being accepted, being able to share, to participate, to belong is the basic constructive experience in human life. No health is conceivable without this. (Foulkes, 1990, p. 155)

For Foulkes, the alienation of man, his estrangement from his community, was perceived as the mother of all diseases. Isolation, dissociation, and lack of communication cause profound mental pathology. The neurotic man is trapped in his private world, lost in the web of his projections. In the group, he can undergo a process of normalisation that releases him from the restrictions his history has forced him into; gradually, he joins the collective communicative network and becomes part of it. In other words, the deviant neurotic becomes a unique subject who can participate as an equal in a shared reality with others; pathological dichotomy between inner and outer realities gives way to a sense of continuity. Thus, continuity and belonging are curative; they dissolve dissociations and assist members in coming out from their neurotic isolation.

The analytic group: an ethical envelope

In this context (and following Levinas), I would like to relate to the concept of justice and assign it a special place among the therapeutic factors. The need to belong to a just, lawful society is an essential component of being human. I argue that the analytic group creates a space in which this fundamental need for justice receives recognition.

Each group member has been scarred by injustice and each seeks acknowledgement for the injuries that were inflicted on him by wrongdoing. These injuries require public recognition for the process of healing to take its course. Hence, the group acts as a symbolic town square that can grant this needed recognition. The readiness of group members to witness each other's suffering, to validate the reality of wrongdoing, whether they were victims or perpetrators, is a major factor in the healing process. Group members participate in a process of mutual reparation, even though they are often required to make amends for wounds that were caused by others. Their very readiness to be there creates norms of lawfulness, caring, and fair-ness.

In this context, one should keep in mind that Foulkes sees the objections to group analysis as stemming mostly from the unwillingness of the community to take responsibility for the welfare of its members. This refusal legitimises a culture of indifference and encourages an attitude of "every man for himself". The emphasis that group analysis places on interdependence, mutuality, and reciprocity indicates that the "ethical envelope" is a vital part of the healing process (Foulkes, 1990, p. 225).

Following the above remarks, I suggest that the analytic group offers "an incubator" for the development of a "democratic ego"; it creates a frame in which the "I" and the "we" can thrive together without dichotomies.

The recovery process that takes place in the analytic group can be recapitulated as follows: the pathological need of group members to hold each other as hostages to their neuroses makes room for their ability to accept responsibility for their actions and to be bound by a mutual commitment to each other's wellbeing (Billow, 2015). The dynamic processes in the group aim to enhance personal relevance and constructive participation in community; they cultivate a democratic culture and present a vision of a heterogeneous society that welcomes difference and sees in it the only way for thriving personally and socially without violence.

Note

1. This is a brief remark about a major subject: that breaks in continuity point to the existence of dissociated traumatic experiences in the life of the group.

References

Altman, N., Benjamin, J., Jacobs, T., & Wachtel, P. (2004). Is politics the last taboo in psychoanalysis? *Psychoanalytic Perspectives*, 2: 5–36.

Benjamin, J. (1997). Psychoanalysis as a vocation. *Psychoanalytic Dialogues*, 7: 781–802.

Berger, M. (2012). The dynamics of mirror reactions and their impact on the analytic group. In: J. Kleinberg (Ed.), *The Wiley-Blackwell Handbook of Group Psychotherapy* (pp. 197–217). London: Wiley-Blackwell.

Beukenkamp, C. (1958). *Fortunate Strangers. An Experience in Group Psychotherapy*. New York: Rinehart.

Billow, R. M. (2015). *Developing Nuclear Ideas: Relational Group Psychotherapy*. London: Karnac.

Bion, W. R. (1970). *Attention and Interpretation: A Scientific Approach to Insight in Psycho-Analysis and Groups*. London: Tavistock.

Brown, D. (1998). Foulkes' basic law of group dynamics 50 years on: abnormality injustice and the renewal of ethics. *Group Analysis*, 31: 391–420.

Dalal, F. (1998). *Taking the Group Seriously: Towards a Foulkesian Group Analytic Theory*. London: Jessica Kingsley.

De Maré, P. (1975). The politic of large groups. In: L. Kreeger (Ed.), *The Large Group: Dynamics and Therapy* (pp. 145–158). London: Constable.

Foulkes, S. H. (1946). On group analysis. *International Journal of Psychoanalysis*, 27: 46–51.

Foulkes, S. H. (1948). *Introduction to Group-Analytic Psychotherapy: Studies in the Social Interaction of Individuals and Groups*. London: William Heinemann Medical Books.

Foulkes, S. H. (1984). *Therapeutic Group Analysis*. London: Karnac.

Foulkes, S. H. (1990). *Selected Papers: Psychoanalysis and Group Analysis*. London: Karnac.

Foulkes, S. H., & Anthony, E. J. (1990). *Group Psychotherapy. The Psycho-Analytic Approach* (2nd edn). London: Karnac.

Friedman, R. (2005). Disorders heal each other in group analysis: a relation pathology perspective. Accessed at: www.funzionegamma.edu.

Frosh, S. (2011). The relational ethics of conflict and identity. *Psychoanalysis, Culture and Society*, 16: 225–243.

Hopper, E. (2000). From objects and subjects to citizens: group analysis and the study of maturity. *Group Analysis*, 33: 29–34.

Hopper, E. (2003). *The Social Unconscious: Selected Papers*. London: Jessica Kingsley.

Kennedy, R. (2000). Becoming a subject: some theoretical and clinical issues. *International Journal of Psychoanalysis, 81*: 875–892.

Mitchell, S. A. (1997). *Influence and Autonomy in Psychoanalysis*. Hillsdale, NJ: Analytic Press.

Nitzgen, D. (2001). Training in democracy, democracy in training: notes on group analysis and democracy group analysis. *Group Analysis, 34*: 331–347.

Pines, M. (1998). *Circular Reflections: Selected Papers on Group Analysis and Psychoanalysis*. London: Jessica Kingsley.

Weegmann, M. (2014). *The World within the Group: Developing Theory for Group Analysis*. London: Karnac.

Winnicott, D. W. (1986). Some thoughts about the meaning of the word 'Democracy'. In: *Home Is Where We Start From. Essays by a Psychoanalyst* (pp. 239–260). New York: W. W Norton.

CHAPTER TWO

What is the "group entity"[1] in group analysis?

Avi Berman

> "... the group uses its own resources ... The members of the group ... are engaged actively in the therapeutic process and they are not merely 'recipients' of treatment as they so very much wish to be"
>
> (Foulkes & Anthony, 2003, p. 82)

A few years ago, I was invited to supervise group therapists in a large public clinic. All the group therapists were also dedicated and experienced individual therapists, as is customary in these clinics. I soon discovered that the groups were relatively small, and, despite an abundance of patients and long waiting lists, the groups were diminishing. I realised that the patients in groups at this clinic had expressed dissatisfaction, and often requested individual therapy rather than group therapy.

In the supervision group, we were trying to decipher the reason for this. The group therapists told the supervision group what had taken place in the group meetings, and then we found time for a reverie of personal associations of the other supervision group members (Berman et al., 2000). The patients in these groups were generally hardworking people, exhausted from life crises and long struggle. Some of them came from poor families and continued to experience poverty and economic and existential anxiety in the families which they built. There were men who could not bear the burden any more, so it was carried by the women instead. There were women who had to bear the consequences of their neglected and now grown children, after years of over-working away from home. Most of them needed medical help. For some of them, the group was designed to help avoid further hospitalisations due to brief psychotic episodes.

Our cumulative experience shows that in some of the mental health clinics, including those that deal with treatment of severe post traumatic burnout, group therapy is a key factor in rehabilitation and recovery. Foulkes said that one of the insights that inspired him to found group analysis was his experience as an intern in a psychiatric hospital. During his night shift, he sat with patients and saw how a spontaneous interaction between them created a rehabilitation processes. What explains the absence of therapeutic success and dissatisfaction of the patients with their treatment? In the supervision group, we tried to find the answer to this question. Following reports of what had taken place in the group meetings, we heard a reverie of personal associations of the other members (Berman & Berger, 2000).

It was clear that the therapists felt compassion towards the patients in their groups and aimed to give their best to each of them. Usually, the group meeting opened with a distress call from a particular patient who managed to talk first: "Yesterday I heard a motorcycle's backfire. It was like an explosion and all the trauma of the attack came back to me." The conductor immediately responded with an expression of empathy. The participant grasped this lead and described in detail the tough week he experienced. "My wife is not feeling well again. I told her to see a doctor but she doesn't want to, and she is also mad at me." A conversation between him and the conductor ensued, for about half an hour. The conductor turns to the other participants and invites them to respond. The participant who talked first receives two short responses, then the two other participants demand the conductor's attention. One of them, and sometimes each of them, gain it. Usually, at the end of such a meeting, one of the participants requests individual therapy or a referral to a psychiatrist for medication.

One of the female therapists in the supervision group said that a female participant in her group does not speak at all. She simply stares at the conductor from the moment the meeting begins. Her silent distress call is painful and powerful, and the conductor has difficulty looking away from her to turn to other participants, also waiting for her attention.

It seems that the conscious and unconscious wish of the participants is to establish a preferred dyad with the conductor as a form of an archaic wish for idealised relations with a parent. The patient–therapist dyad known to us from individual psychotherapy does not help and probably interferes with the creation of the group. The group is based on a system of participants' relations and not on dyads. To be precise, the only possible dyads in the group are ever-changing dyads, which suspend the wish for a patient–therapist's preferred relations. In this sense, the group replaces the personal.

In group analysis, the entire group is the therapeutic agent. The group is the therapist. The first role of the conductor is to help the participants to create the interaction between themselves and, thus, to form a group.

We can understand a participant's wish for a preferred dyad with the conductor: he is in distress, he feels lonely. He comes to the group with a prolonged sense of deprivation of attention. He wishes for empathy. Instead, he meets a group of "needy" strangers. He feels that the chance of having his needs fulfilled is threatened more than ever. The conductor becomes a disappointing object rather than a helpful one.

Group analysis offers an alternative option: while, in individual therapy, the good object (under positive transference) is mainly the therapist, in group analysis the good object is mainly the entire group (this can also apply to the bad object). The group offers a sense of belonging, which calms the anxieties of the participant and gives him time and space. The changing identifications with others enable the participant to expand his self-experience. The resonance of the emotions within the group and the discourse about them deepens the participant's understanding of himself. The group invites the participant to take part in giving–receiving relations in which he becomes a partner in his own and others' therapy. He can rediscover himself.

But what about the conductor? In the epigraph to this chapter, the conductor is not mentioned at all. Why? Because, in group analysis, despite his therapeutic experience, his professional understanding, his availability to his patients, his most important role is to help the group members to develop and recognise their own resources. The conductor's recognition of the participants' contributions and their mutual empowerment should be prioritised. In contrast, in the opening example, the therapists tried to give their best to each of the participants personally. Prioritising a patient–therapist relationship disturbs the founding of the group. The participants were trying to establish a preferred dyad with the conductor and invested in it at the expense of creating group discourse. As much as the participants' distress increases, this investment will inevitably fail. The participant who manages to speak with the conductor cannot be satisfied because he will eventually be interrupted (in order to mange to respond to at least one other participant), and because his turn will not be revived during the next meeting. A participant who does not manage to speak to the conductor might feel frustration, rejection, and jealousy. In a therapeutic group, in the sense that I offer here, patients might feel more self-fulfilled, helped, and could develop the ability to help others. (Paradoxically, the dedicated and compassionate conductor might increase hunger and frustration as he tries to be more faithful to dyadic therapy.) Analytic group therapy is not individual therapy in the presence of others.

The group entity according to group analysis

First of all, the group in group analysis is an open and continuous system of interaction between all the participants of the group, including the conductor. As the group develops, the participants share and respond to one another through being attentive to what arises within themselves and, as a result, share again. Schlapobersky (1993) suggests the term "discourse" for describing the transpersonal, chain-like associations that characterise communication in the group.

The system of interactions enables belonging and participation: ". . . Being a respected and effective member of the group, being accepted, being able to share, to participate, belong to the basic constructive experience in human life" (Foulkes & Anthony, 2003, p. 27).

Another aspect of the interaction in the group is "exchange" (Zinkin, 1994). When group members talk to each other and are exposed to one another's way of life and reactions, they give and receive aspects of experience that were missing for each of them. In the group, participants are exposed to different feelings and attitudes about each other. Some of those feelings and attitudes are not congru-ent with their own perceptions of themselves. Participants' self-percep-tion is continuously challenged in the group. As a result, one's ability to contain different feelings and opinions grows. In other words, one's ability to contain "otherness" in a therapeutic group is improving and bears a benevolent effect on one's close relationships. Participants also discover that whatever one says about someone else reveals some aspects of oneself. With the assistance of the conductor, the common belief in objectivity is transformed to the experience of intersubjectiv-ity (Benjamin, 1988; Mitchell, 2000), and the risk of judging people is gradually replaced by self-reflection and empathy. Together, partici-pants discover the meaning of reciprocity. Following the exchange in the group, participants feel that they become partners in building its therapeutic value. Their identification with other members helps them to internalise ways of dealing with life situations in different ways. The participant dares to try to experience new behaviour, he receives recognition (excited at times) of aspects within himself that he was unaware of, and he receives gratitude for his contribution to the other participants.

The participant learns to decipher his projections and gradually reattributes them to himself. It is important to mention Foulkes' concept of mirroring and "mirror reactions" (Foulkes, 1964). Unlike Kohut (1971), Foulkes refers to the Other in the group as a mirror to one's rejected self-aspects. Looking in this kind of mirror means know-ing oneself better.

The more abstract aspects of the group, in group analysis, concern the matrix. As a metaphor, we can say that cars drive on roads. As they each drive, all of them have relations between them. The whole system is called traffic (Foulkes & Anthony, 2003). This is also the meaning of the concept "the matrix" as describing the system of group interaction as transpersonal.

> The matrix is the hypothetical web of communication and relationship in a given group. It is the 'common shared ground which ultimately determines the meaning and significance of all events and upon which all communications verbal and non-verbal rest. (Foulkes, 1964, pp. 33–34).

Today, after the discovery of mirror neurons, it is clear that Foulkes was ahead of his time when describing the transpersonal interaction as equivalent to any intrapersonal occurrence. His concept of reso-nance accurately describes what is explained today by the operation of mirror neurons (Foulkes, 1990; Berman, 2012). Mitchell, when speaking about emotions, writes about the human interaction in simi-lar terms to the idea "matrix":

> Affect is contagious, and, on the deepest level, affective states are often transpersonal. Intense affects like anxiety, sexual excitement, rage, depression, and euphoria tend to generate corresponding affects in others. Early in life, on the deepest unconscious levels throughout life, affects are evoked interpersonally through dense resonance between people, without regards for who, is feeling what. (Mitchell, 2000, p. 61)

I suggest that the group and the personal are two concomitant modalities of human existence. However, the significance of the indi-vidual varies greatly following the concept of matrix and the recogni-tion of the group entity. Foulkes says,

> Personally I believe that the multipersonal hypothesis of mind is nearer the true nature of events . . . I found the old theory of perceiv-ing this in terms of individuals and their interaction as individual minds enclosed in each skull, interacting in the most complicated fash-ion with the others that this theory acted as a great barrier to my understanding (Foulkes, 1973).

The individual within the same matrix is like a nodal point of communication, as the neuron is a nodal point of nerve conduction. Since the individual in the group, as a nodal point of communication, affects and is affected all the time, he becomes an open system.

Hence, there arises the unique therapeutic benefit of group analy-sis: imagine that the personal difficulties that bring a man to therapy stem from the fact that he is imprisoned inside his skull. If he is lonely, or suspicious, or angry and attacking, or vulnerable and introverted, the cause for all of these could be personal aspects of seclusion. There-fore, the entry of a man to an open system can be the basis for change. The contribution of group analysis is the patient's transformation from a state of intrapersonal introversion into a state of integration within interpersonal communication and affiliation.

In addition to all of this, the participant receives, in his turn, a unique time investment from the participants and the conductor. This time investment reaches its efficiency peak only after establishing the group. Yet, the main difference between this focusing and individual therapy is that after every kind of this focusing, and sometimes even during it, the group returns (with the conductor's aid), to the group meanings through resonance and mirroring. All of what was said during the personal work with one participant enhances the work of other participants.

Moreover, group analysis encourages the conductor to recognise typical forms of group anxieties, and mechanisms of defence such as Bion's basic assumptions (1961), and Hopper's basic assumption of Incohesion: aggregation/massification) (2009): ". . .bi-polar intrapsychic constellations are associated with two types of personal organization: one, the 'contact shunning' or 'crustacean' and two, the 'merger-hungry' or 'amoeboid'" (Hopper, 2012, p. XXXVI). Another perspective is the categories of interpersonal pathology, like the deficiency relation disorder, rejection relation disorder, relation disorders of the self, or exclusion relation disorder (Friedman, 2013). "Using the complementary optic of multi-personal dysfunctions will not only improve indications for psychotherapy but also facilitate optimal contribution of the different therapeutic spaces" (p. 166).

The contribution of Bion (1988), although not a group analyst, could be relevant here: according to Bion, each participant may make and act upon a basic assumption. Therefore, I suggest that we should decipher the words of a participant as representing the group unconscious. We can elaborate the meaning of Bion's words and argue that when any participant becomes aware that his words also represent the inner world of others, his experience of affiliation and partnership increases.

The forming of the group entity is a process and is a professional challenge for conductors. In this chapter I focus on the conducting challenge, which is, in my opinion, the greatest of all: the difficulty in giving up the therapeutic dyad and replacing it with group conducting.

The challenge of giving up the therapeutic dyad

Some of the most prominent psychoanalytic theorists oppose any deviation from dyadic relations in psychotherapy. Although Freud himself (1921c) saw the importance of social and group psychology, he was sceptical about the therapeutic benefit of group therapy (Freud, 1926, Letter to Trigant Burrow, 14 November 1926, quoted in Campos (1992)). Winnicott (Rodman, 1987) also expressed his concerns about groups in general. He believed that the group might foster uniformity of thought, become a "grouping of supporters" (p. 45), impose and, thus, cause the participant to use more of his false self at the expense of his true self. I think that he was wrong. Group therapy, in my opinion, encourages just the opposite: it helps the participant to dare to express his true self in front of others. Kohut (1984) believed that empathy is indivisible, in that any shifting of the empathic attention of the therapist towards someone else might result in an empathic failure.

Let us recall the example I gave at the beginning of the chapter: one of the participants does not speak at all. She expresses her distress by staring at the therapist–conductor. What does the therapist feel in these moments? She feels great distress. She fears that any shifting of her gaze from the participant's gaze might be interpreted by the participant as abandonment. On the other hand, she knows that in due course she might cause the same feeling in other participants, who are waiting for her attention. In her countertransference, she shifts from feelings of compassion to feelings of guilt. As a result, she might experience disappointment in her professional contribution as a group therapist. Indeed, even experienced group therapists who feel that their contribution is not successful are hesitant in using it again.

The group therapist who establishes the dyad of individual therapy in the group might deny his narcissistic need that might lead him to an omnipotent intention of satisfying the participant's narcissistic wish. An individual therapist, experienced as he might be, cannot satisfy the emotional and developmental needs of all participants at a weekly meeting. He cannot do it alone. Only with the combined therapeutic help of all participants in the group, only with the "group as a therapist", might a meaningful psychotherapy be possible. Omnipotent input of the conductor could bring the group to a narcissistic regression: the participant's narcissistic needs lead to an over-dependence, incapability, and over-neediness.

The success of group therapy depends on a certain overcoming of the narcissistic wish and regression of conductor and patient alike. A conductor who knows his limitations can more easily recognise the ability of the group members to participate in creating the group's therapeutic value. This is no different to a mother's ability to see her child as more capable of coping, as not so lost, and as a partner in his own growth, and even as someone who helps her in fulfilling her role as a mother (Winnicott, 1963).

In Bion's (1988) view, every dyad in the group is a function of an unconscious group cohesion around the basic assumption of pairing. According to the basic assumption of pairing, the group as a whole unconsciously produces within it a pair of members that engage in tight discourse. In these moments there is an active and self-centred pair, while the other members are silent and passive. The content of the discourse does not count; pairing, as a structure, does. According to Bion, the unconscious wish of the group is that this pairing will give birth to an imaginary alternative to the group therapist. The illusion of the participant that salvation can come from any source other than himself may result in a developmental arrest, which might prevent personal transformation. In Bion's view, only by turning to internal resources, while renouncing wishes for dependency and overcoming difficulties and fears, can patients benefit from psychotherapy.

The conductor is also subjected to unconscious group process. Therefore, even a dyad of which the conductor is a partner is also under the influence of the basic assumption of pairing.

In this sense, Bion and Foulkes talk in a similar language. Bion deals with building a working group through giving up any dependent illusion and replacing it by turning to internal resources. According to Foulkes, the conductor is transformed from a focused, idealised central figure to a partner in the group. The conductor deals with the active role of the participants, and in their partnership of creating the group, he is included.

It is most likely that the conductor's avoidance of participating in the therapeutic dyad could be challenging, since it might evoke, at the beginning, hard feelings in the group. It could stimulate insults and introversion. It might provoke anger and protest. The conductor must be able to endure it and contain these possible group reactions for the sake of the profound therapeutic benefit that might be achieved later. If the therapist prefers the creation of the group entity rather than investment in dyads, he can be empathetic with the difficulty that he imposes on the participants' by frustrating their wishes for dependency and exclusivity. He can understand their anger at his refusal to participate in their wish that salvation comes from the outside. After all, people who come to us for treatment might feel that their own attempts to change have failed in the past. They fear to fail again and hurt their self-esteem further. They might also fear that other participants have failed, like them, and can hardly be trusted as partners. The empathy of the conductor to the inner world of the participants and his understanding of their personal and collective transferences is very important at this point (Hopper, 2007).

Comments on technique

The avoidance of participation in the dyad does not require the conductor to remain silent in the face of a participant's request to share his distress. The conductor can refer to the participant briefly and with empathy. Yet, it is important that the conductor immediately appeals to other participants and avoids remaining in tight discourse with the particular participant. Appealing to other participants is intended to encourage them to share whatever arises in their mind in the light of the words of the participant who talked first.

The invitation of sharing all that is said in the group is categorical, and is always in its place. Many therapists fear that turning to other members, especially when a participant is presenting his distress, might be experienced by him as a rejection. Moreover, other participants in the group might protest if they feel the conductor has abandoned one of their friends. But, in my experience, it is not the case. Sharing feelings and thoughts helps the patient feel included and supported. Often, he inspires their wish to share. He also hears about their similar and different feelings and attitudes. And, finally, the conductor can always go back to the patient to check if he really felt abandoned, and add a contribution.

As mentioned, the only possible dyads in the group are ever-changing dyads. One of the members of Foulkes' mythological therapeutic groups said that while she spoke, Foulkes' gaze was wandering over all the participants in the room. He was always attentive to their resonance responses. Indeed, this is the recommendation for the conductor: always see all the others.

Additionally, there is Bion's contribution about the participant as spokesperson of the group's unconscious mentality. According to Bion, each participant speaks of a theme common to all. Therefore, the conductor can offer to the group the fact that the words of each participant in the room reflects the inner world of the rest of them. He is a spokesperson for the group as a whole.

Also important is the way in which any contribution from a participant in a group reflects aspects of the contextual society in which the group is embedded (Hopper & Weinberg, 2011).

Consider this very brief clinical vignette which illustrates these points.

Ann says in the group, "I cannot say it here, because I'm sure I'll be criticised for this, but the truth is that I do not want kids."

The conductor suggests, "Let us check what feeling it arouses between us. Maybe this feeling is also familiar to others."

Jonathan: "I totally agree with you. I think people give birth to children without asking them if they want to be born. It seems to me like an injustice in advance. I doubt if I will ever have children."

Gale: "I'm glad you say that. I gave birth when I was twenty. I do not know why. I never heard my own voice. I did not know how to hear it. After a few years, I realised that it was too early. I missed the good years when I could have been living my life. I love my kids. I cannot see myself without them today. Maybe I'll have time to live when they are grown up."

Silence. The atmosphere in the group is pensive and perhaps even sad.

Dana: "It's not just children. I want to have the freedom to think about what I want and what I do not want. It's about work. It's about marriage. I do not want to live like an automaton or according to what my parents were expecting."

David: "It's not just the parents. These are social conventions. I killed people in the army and I was almost killed myself. My friends were killed. For me, social pressure is like a prison. I was never released from this prison."

Near the end of the session, the conductor said, "It seems that what Ann said aroused a lot of similar experiences about what society may impose on each of us and how difficult it might become to choose one's own way. And to you, Ann, I want to say that I think you could experience here the possibility of acceptance from people in the process that you are going through."

Following the conductor's invitation, each of the participants expresses something very personal, a clue to an important aspect of their inner world. Over time, each of the speakers would be able to continue their personal work. In the absence of the conductor's invitation to share, this important matter might not arise.

The Israeli point of view

Besides individualism (and also narcissism), it seems that something in the mutual neediness, the importance of exchange, and the necessity of the investment in the group is clearer to we Israelis at the beginning of our lives. To be precise: from the moment when each of us begins to be exposed to our social and political situation as Israelis. Moreover, "mutual responsibility" is a value in Judaism. Group analysis can add a professional contribution to this social and moral value.

We came from the ruins of the Holocaust, from diasporas, and physical and emotional dangers. Israelis, Jews and non-Jews, are familiar with the experience of minority and the threat of exclusion and oppression. Even today, we live in a reality in which there is a danger of attack and extinction from real enemies.

It seems to me that, in this situation, we have developed an understanding of the importance of the group entity. We realise, probably, that belonging to a group gives security no less than belonging to a family or a relationship. We need the group and the group needs us. I believe that there are two types of group affiliation. The first—based on the division of "Us and them" (Berman et al., 2000), strengthens us and comforts us in threatening situations. Yet, in this sense, we belong to a polarising society, which easily splits between groups and sub-cultures.

The second type of group affiliation is based on our wish for mutual and open universal affiliation. We understand relatively easily that the foreigner can become a relative and not necessarily an enemy. We tend to believe in the existence of a common language and contribute together to its constant creation. We use the group to learn to communicate more effectively and even to believe that a trans-society affiliation can, eventually, rescue us from the siege that threatens us from time to time.

Yet, in addition to the very real contribution of Israeli cohesion, it is advisable that we belong to an open society. Group analysis is based on the recognition of the personal, social, and professional value of the inclusion of others. I believe we should be inspired by it.

Note

1.   Entitativity is the degree to which members of a social group are perceived as a coherent unit (Campbell, 1958, p. 14).

References

Benjamin, J. (1988). *The Bonds of Love*. New York: Pantheon.

Berman, A. (2012). Resonance among members and its therapeutic value in group psychotherapy. In: J. L. Kleinberg (Ed.), *The Wiley-Blackwell Handbook of Group Psychotherapy* (pp. 187–197). Sussex: Wiley-Blackwell.

Berman, A., Berger, M., & Gutmann, D. (2000). The division into us and them as a universal social structure. *Mind and Human Interaction, 11*(1): 53–72.

Bion, W. R. (1988). A theory of thinking. In: E. Bott Spillius (Ed.), *Melanie Klein Today, Volume 1: Mainly Theory* (pp. 178–186). London: Routledge.

Campbell, D. T. (1958). Common fate, similarity, and other indices of the status of aggregates of persons as social entities. *Behavioral Science, 3*: 14-25.

Campos, J. (1992). Burrow, Foulkes and Freud: an historical perspective. *Lifwynn Correspondence, 2*(2–9): 8.

Foulkes, S. H. (1964). *Therapeutic Group Analysis*. London: Karnac.

Foulkes, S. H. (1973). The group as matrix of the individual's mental life. In: L. R. Wolberg & E. K. Schwartz (Eds.), *Group Therapy* (pp. 211–220). New York: Intercontinental Medical Book Corporation.

Foulkes, S. H. (1990). Notes on the concept of resonance. In: *Selected Papers of S. H. Foulkes* (pp. 297–305). London: Karnac.

Foulkes, S. H., & Anthony, E. J. (2003). *Group Psychotherapy: The Psychoanalytical Approach*. London: Karnac.

Freud, S. (1921c). *Group Psychology and the Analysis of the Ego*. S. E., *18*: 67–134. London: Hogarth Press.

Friedman, R. (2013). Individual or group therapy? Indications for optimal therapy. *Group Analysis, 46*: 164–170.

Hopper, E. (2007). Theoretical and conceptual notes concerning transference and countertransference processes in groups and by groups, and the social unconscious: Part II. *Group Analysis, 40*: 29–42.

Hopper, E. (2009). The theory of the basic assumption of incohesion: agregation/massification (ba) I:A/M. *British Journal of Psychotherapy, 25*(2): 214–229.

Hopper, E. (2012). *Trauma and Organizations*. London: Karnac.

Hopper, E., & Weinberg, H. (Eds.) (2011). *The Social Unconscious in Persons, Groups, and Societies. Volume 1: Mainly Theory*. London: Karnac.

Kohut, H. (1971). *The Analysis of the Self*. New York: International Universities Press.

Kohut, H. (1984). *How Does Analysis Cure?* Chicago, IL: University of Chicago Press.

Mitchell, S. A. (2000). *Relationally: From Attachment to Intersubjectivity*. Hillsdale, NJ: Analytic Press.

Rodman, F. R. (Ed.) (1987). *The Spontaneous Gesture: Selected Letters of D. W. Winnicott*. Cambridge, MA: Harvard University Press.

Schlapobersky, J. (1993). The language of the group: monologue, dialogue and discourse in group analysis. In: D. Brown and L. Zinkin (Eds.), *The Psyche and the Social World: Developments in Group-Analytic Theory* (pp. 211–231). London: Routledge.

Winnicott, D. W. (1963). The development of the capacity for concern. In: *The International Psycho-Analytical Library* (*Volume 64*, pp. 1–276, 1965). London: Hogarth Press.

Zinkin, L. (1994). Exchange as a therapeutic factor in group analysis. In: L. Zinkin & D. Brown (Eds.), *The Psyche and the Social World* (pp. 99–117). London: Jessica Kingsley.

CHAPTER THREE

Leader, society, sacrifice

Hanni Biran

The point of departure for this chapter is the myth of Oedipus, as it is portrayed in Sophocles' *Oedipus Rex*. The established notions regarding this myth were overturned by Bion (1967, p. 86), who marginalised the theme of incest and focused on the desire to know, investigate, and reveal the truth. Following Bion, I attempt to describe different kinds of knowing, offering my conjectures regarding the type of knowing that a leader must practise in order to be able to handle a traumatic social situation, which demands endless sacrifice. "Knowing" and "knowledge" have multiple unconscious meanings, especially associated with eating from the tree of knowledge.

I also draw on some of the work of Foulkes (1984) regarding the concept of the "foundation matrix", which refers to relationships, values and norms, and patterns of communication. The foundation matrix establishes the conditions for the development of particular styles of leadership (Hopper, 2003). Group analysis helps us to find several pathways into unconscious processes within groups and persons. In the analytic group, members tend to re-enact their Oedipal drama in the here and now. Through the dynamic matrix of the group, the members come face to face with what has been their manner of being within their respective families and, subsequently, other groups throughout their lives. They discover how they were born into each family and what kind of welcome they received. The analytic group provides a space wherein one can experience the tension between siblings and members of the same and opposite sexes, and, through relationships with the group conductor, their previous relationships with their parents. In other words, the group facilitates the recreation of the Oedipal drama and how it has been played out throughout their lives.

The figure of Oedipus represents a pattern that is endemic to every human life. Every child is destined to live out the oedipal drama within their own family. Every adult bears the unconscious traces carved in them by this childhood drama. The myth of Oedipus conveys that all human beings are born with a certain blindness, that each of us are actors within our own drama, often oblivious as to what drives our life-story forward. Our psychic blindness is also a tragic one, in the sense that we must acknowledge the fact that we are not the masters, rulers, or owners of our lives and deaths. The position from which one chooses to embark on a journey of self-discovery and seek psychoanalytic therapy is like that of a man driving against traffic. That is, while living his life from beginning to end, he studies them from their end, back to their beginning. This voyage is far from linear and is laden with vicissitudes, confusion, and disorientation. The journey of King Oedipus cannot be completed without suffering and angst, which must take its toll.

Another way in which the figure of Oedipus is metaphoric lies in his decision to enquire from his position as a leader, heading an afflicted society which offers daily sacrifices. Oedipus senses that he is about to uncover unbearable things, yet he does not relinquish his quest. The terrifying truth slips through by means of rumours, which say that King Laius has been murdered by a band of brigands, but Oedipus perseveres and continues his enquiry. As great anxiety shrouds his journey of discovery, he does not spare himself. This depicts a style of leadership that is unafraid to enquire wherein lies the sickness, what mistakes were made. It is a leadership that assumes responsibility, acknowledges social pain, and stops to ask questions. It is a containing leadership, which is willing to relinquish power and authority in order to save its society from the plague. This layer of leadership is linked to many aspects of the foundation matrix of a society of which its citizens are largely unconscious.

In this chapter, I discuss the interaction between the "human being" and the "leader". Great leaders are, first and foremost, in touch with the human being inside themselves. They find ways to maintain contact with the human and subjective aspects of their being. The human leader gazes into himself and liberates himself from dogmatic, stereotypical, and predetermined patterns of thinking. This kind of leader can depend upon himself and perform the unpredictable. A society that suffers chronic traumatisation requires containing leadership. In times of social distress, there is a need for a leader who can wait, who can withhold his militant reactions in favour of observation and the study of repetitive processes. This kind of leader is a hero, whose courage lies not in winning wars, but in his ability to experience human suffering and contain social trauma in order to heal it. This type of courage also relates to the ability to swim against the current.

I now present three types of knowing and address the question of which of them is most pertinent and appropriate for a leader in times of distress and accumulative traumatisation.

Omniscient knowing

This is the arrogant knowing of one who believes himself to be omniscient, who, confident that he possesses all knowledge, rests easy on his laurels. This kind of knowing is most dangerous for a leader, as it entails being drunk on his own power and the joy of victory. Before the plague overtook Thebes, Oedipus was entangled in his sinful hubris, assured that he had defeated the fate decreed by the gods. He thought he had it all: a queen, a kingdom, and a family. In fact, he was living on the brink of catastrophe, utterly unaware of the impending disaster. He oscillated between complete ignorance regarding the forces steering his life, and omnisciently disputing divine wisdom. These two ends are surprisingly close to each other: one who pretends to know everything often turns out to be altogether blind.

The leader is tasked with deciphering the riddle of society. The monstrous Sphinx, who devastates Thebes, killing all those who fail to solve her riddle, is a metaphor for a society that is in distress, lacks a beneficent leader, and is controlled by cruel and perverse instincts. In the myth, the Sphinx is strategically positioned at the heart of the social sphere, where she can perform atrocious acts against a helpless city whose king is dead. The Sphinx, thus, represents the unconscious processes of society at large: when a society is overwhelmed by disaster, this implies that something is amiss in the capacities of its leadership, that the riddle of the Sphinx awaits its solution. The abomination of the Sphinx, part woman and part beast, is a non-integrated and emotionless being, patched together in a horrifying manner. Born of the womb of Echidna, another monster oblivious to human emotion, the Sphinx lives in a world of totality, where no compromise is possible. She has an insatiable appetite for more and more victims, which she strangles and devours (the literal meaning of the name "Sphinx" is derived from the Greek for "to clutch" or "grasp tightly"). She only knows two extreme alternatives: knowing the answer or perishing. One cannot converse with the Sphinx; she speaks the language of violence, which knows only glorious victory or irrevocable doom. As soon as she is vanquished, she kills herself.

Extreme states of social violence are essentially inhuman, indicating that society has come under the influence of the monstrous Sphinx. This state draws forth an omnipotent leadership. Terrified, society becomes obsessed with fantasies of redemption; it then chooses the leader who can offer an illusion of strength and security and who promises to restore peace and quiet. Thebes, thus, seduces Oedipus to mount an omnipotent throne. Oedipus has solved the riddle of the Sphinx: "what creature has four legs, then two, then three?" The answer is man, who crawls on all fours as an infant, walks erect as an adult, and uses a cane in old age. In contrast to the agonising quest for truth in Sophocles' play, solving the riddle of the Sphinx suggests an instantaneous "Eureka", a miracle, the uncanny workings of a saviour: where everyone else has failed, Oedipus steps forward and nonchalantly claims, as it were, "I came, I saw, I conquered".

Oedipus's victory over the Sphinx is a euphoric one, accompanied by the grandiose gestures of inheriting both queen and kingdom. Oedipus has brought peace and prosperity to Thebes, but the peace is false, and prosperity barely lasts a generation. What seemed at first as redemption and victory soon turned out to be the most dreaded calamity. The Oedipus who solved the riddle without any significant effort or pain, was a young man lacking the true maturity required of a leader. His leadership, conducted in utter blindness to his own predicament, brought about a sequence of terrible disasters upon himself, his family, and society at large, which was tormented with the plague on his account. This demonstrates how near the pole of omniscience is to that of perfect blindness. In the first act of the play, we witness both poles in close proximity, with the abyss of failure lying right next to the peaks of success.

The riddle of the inhuman Sphinx is misleadingly centred on the human. Whereas it seems to tackle the meaning of life, it does so from a cynical, shallow, and linear perspective, implying that the essence of being human lies only in our limbs. Its solution, equally trivial, ignores the human spirit. The leader who offers ready and easy answers might occasionally find intelligent short-term solutions, but these deny the complexity of the situation and might bring about catastrophe in the long run, lacking any kind of vision of the coming future.

In Israel, we have had our share of quick and easily obtained solutions, especially the euphoric triumph of the Six-Day war, which was an arrogant solution to a profound social question. What, back then, seemed to be the pinnacle of glory has become our present disaster, for which society keeps paying with endless sacrifices.

Professed knowing

A second kind of knowing is professed knowing, manifest in the use of hollow words, clichés, and socially accepted jargon. This kind of knowing says the right things, but is detached from the accumulated experiences and events of social reality. Professed knowing distracts from, and even disguises, the pains that are difficult to face. It serves to maintain the prevailing social order, problematic or corrupt as it might be. Professed knowing grows even stronger in a society that has been traumatised.

In *King Oedipus* (Sophocles, 1947), Queen Jocasta, Oedipus's mother, and the shepherd both cling tightly to the existing social order. Jocasta tries to convince Oedipus to forego his investigation: "think no more of it", she tells him (p. 52); she would like to believe that their life, as it is, is perfectly fine. She even tells him that many men have dreamed of sleeping with their mothers, so why insist on the facts and make things harder on themselves? Jocasta's solution is to go on living, pretending that everything is normal.

Through the prism of professed knowing, I shall attempt to discuss our present social reality. As in the play, our present life in Israel is far from being "OK": our acts towards our neighbouring people are ones of force, domination, and occupation. For example, Palestinian farmers are instructed to harvest their olive plantations within a three-day time window—a technically impossible feat. The demolition of houses is referred to by the lovely sounding word "clearing", a euphemism that conceals the destruction of homes. Not to mention that a military operation, incurring many child casualties, was named "days of repentance", or the habit of giving military operations names suggestive of strength, without even a hint as to their disastrous implications, such as "Cast Lead" or "Protective Edge" (whose Hebrew title literally means "steadfast cliff").

Members of my generation, who grew up in the Israel of the 1950s, would rather gaze at the pretty headlines than acknowledge these facts. How can one brought up to uphold the ideals of humanism look at a photo depicting the practice of "dead-checking" or "kill confirmation" performed on a terrified thirteen-year-old Palestinian girl? We, the Sabras of Israel's first years, cannot stomach such images. It is only natural for us to protect ourselves by means of emotional dissociation, denial, and repression. Difficult material is filtered out, undigested, as it is too intolerable to constitute actual internalised knowing. These Sabras, therefore, are the victims of professed knowing: they want to believe in "the beautiful Israel"; they cannot abandon the ideals they were educated with. The members of my generation fought several wars, safe in the knowledge that Israel was ever striving for peace, and that every war is a defensive war, a last resort. Their willingness to make sacrifices was an integral part of their lives.

Meanwhile, the Intifadas broke out and war grew into occupation. Despite this difference, Israel kept declaring that it wanted peace, that the use of force is only a last resort. Such declarations, detached from the events and emotional experiences of this new reality turn into clichés and stay lodged in the heart of the consensus as slogans. The trap that my generation is caught in involves the tremendous difficulty of giving up our clichés. This is a generation that grew up on inspiring patriotic songs, praising the work of the soil, and dreaming of warships that would carry oranges for export instead of bombs and missiles; our yearning to become the heroic Sabra, ever loyal and devoted to his country, has not abated. When the day finally arrived when people of this generation began to send their own children off to the military, they encountered feelings of resistance, anxiety, and distress, but they yielded to the endless reign of the "last resort".

These generations, who grew up here and fought here, are caught in the trap of sacrifice, created through the continuous seeping of the notion that an individual's self-worth is measured by his willingness to make sacrifices. Caring for oneself and refusing to make sacrifices for one's country are the acts of a traitor, a deserter. This way of thinking has established a social–cultural narcissism, which towers above the personal one. Such narcissistic experiences are created through mantras such as "we have no other land". Social narcissism provides the individual with a sense of worth, through his or her merging with ideas that seem just and moral. The individual enjoys the feeling of cohesion, of being at one with a broad society which thinks just like him. In addition, these mantras possess a heroic quality that is both seductive and deceptive: their victims are tempted to burn themselves at the stake of the collective bonfire, like moths drawn to the flame.

Such mantras, appearing regularly in our social space, encourage parents to sacrifice what they hold most dear. From the protectors of their children, they become protectors of their land, which itself becomes the most powerful mantra. The land is not merely a place to live in and belong to, it is the Homeland, to be taken and conquered by force. The parent who sends his or her child off to the army learns to place society's demands well above his own self-love and his adherence to the value of human life. Society, thus, assumes the same sublime position that God took on in ordering Abraham to offer up Isaac. Hopper (2003) offers the notion of "massification" to denote a state in which a society unites itself through adherence to a single, often grandiose, idea. Such massification then lends additional power to the charismatic leader who fosters the particular idea heralded by society.

A social space that is filled with clichés invites people to cling to these in order to protect themselves from seeing the harsh reality surrounding them. This means that there is no room left for entertaining doubts, for scrutinising declarations, asking questions, moving towards change and re-examining the immutable professed knowing that lies at the heart of this space. Under such circumstances, one has no other options but to go with the flow or to refuse; freedom is not dynamic enough to allow a more varied social discourse. I contend that revitalising and reviewing these mantras would be worthwhile, but only if such processes begin through the creative thinking of a leader brave enough to undermine and unsettle professed knowing.

Emotional knowing

In 1959, Bion coined the term "link" to denote a space joining different elements in a lively and creative manner. One of the most vital links is the one between the capacity for conceptual thinking and that for emotional and intuitive thinking, which is grounded in utilising the senses and learning from experience. In times of distress, the leader is required to be able to feel and to contain the suffering of his society, while heading the search for new concepts. Bion mentions "reverie" as the capacity to contain present suffering while having faith in a better future. The leader capable of reverie, of envisioning a better possible future, affords a certain sense of security, even in trying times. He places his trust in the slow maturation of developmental processes. This approach is diametrically opposed to that of the omniscient, all-solving leader, who often hinders these gradual changes by performing restless, often violent acts, which bar the path to growth and maturation.

The story of Oedipus highlights the trying transformations one must undergo in order to discover one's humanity. In order to heal his society of its ailments, Oedipus sensed that he must gaze inside himself. His contact with pain and agony paved his way to becoming empathic to the suffering of others. Through his arduous journey of agonising enquiry, Oedipus departs from his false omniscience and becomes increasingly human. As soon as he uncovers his true identity, he is liberated from the perverse act of sleeping with his own mother and, by acknowledging that he murdered his own father, he frees society of its affliction. As king, blinded by triumphs and temptations, he was unable to see social suffering. In order to start seeing, he gouges out his eyes and gazes inwards. This human capacity to acknowledge one's own limitations is the force that healed a tormented society. While solving the riddle of the Sphinx endowed him with power and authority, solving the riddle of his own life gave him the strength to face his tragic truth. His journey into himself is his greatest conquest. Only by containing the terrible pain could he set the people of Thebes free.

The leader, as a representative of society, should be able to respond empathically to social pain, to achieve an intimate, emotional knowing of human suffering. This requires a transition from performing acts of violence to a process of emotional thinking and a willingness to enter into dialogue with one's enemies. While violence only offers one path, which is both extreme and repetitive, dialogue entails the discovery of new, creative options. When the leader is in touch with suffering and works through it by mourning, the sacrifice of human lives may gradually diminish.

Leaders capable of the transformative work of mourning are the ones better able to heal an agonised society. Leaders such as Anwar Sadat and Yitzhak Rabin underwent such transformations throughout their time in office. They exhibited a humane sensibility, a profound recognition of social suffering and a weariness of war alongside the determination to bring about change. The fact that both were assassinated attests to their vision and to the fact that both were ahead of their times, having left behind extreme social pockets that were not yet able to transform.

Muslim terrorist organisations are an extreme example of how violence can be taken up as a way of life. Their leadership practises the perverse and brutal exploitation of human beings as mechanical objects, as ticking bombs. This leadership has presented the world with unprecedented dehumanisation, ruthlessly utilising the younger generation for the arbitrary killing of civilians. Facing this repetitive and violent reality, the drama of Oedipus offers a different solution.

*   *   *

I will now exchange the prism of leadership for that of society itself. I will restrict myself to providing examples, in order to briefly demonstrate the various manifestations, in social space, of the three kinds of knowing that I have outlined.

Omniscient knowing blurs the differences between what is possible and what is impossible, creating the illusion that anything could be obtained immediately. This gradually leads to the formation of a perverse culture, which fails to acknowledge boundaries and limitations. Voyeurism takes over and becomes ubiquitous; one can even watch live breast augmentation surgery on television. Israel has taken to imitating American television series, which show people undergoing endless plastic surgery in order to copy the faces of their favourite film stars. As human ideals keep declining, exteriority becomes the only thing that matters. This is but one of the postmodern variations of solving the riddle of the Sphinx: a false, external solution, which ignores the internal journey one must undergo to achieve self-knowledge. The growing momentum of today's anti-aging trend has to do with the human pretension of triumphing over destiny. The desire to remain forever young is reminiscent of sinful hubris, of the will to become godlike and defeat the natural course of life. Through these examples, I have tried to demonstrate how human beings have been sacrificing their humanity to the totalitarian regime of beauty ideals.

Professed knowing, serving as a protective shield against true knowledge of reality, has helped my generation to survive. Subsequent generations saw the further debilitation of the capacity to maintain a position of knowing *vis-à-vis* their difficult political reality. New clichés have, thus, been coalescing into a new kind of all-embracing pretence, which keeps young people from profound observation of the particularities of reality. This detachment bars them from having any influence and they become the victims of their own dissociation. While they are trapped in this unaccountable pretence, other factions of society—such as the settlers—who are willing to take risks and get their hands dirty, end up dictating the national agenda. Unlike the settlers, considerable parts of the contemporary Israeli left tend to place their personal narcissism as a higher priority than social narcissism. However, the comfort of their personal little bubble weakens the urge to burst out of it and undermine the existing social order on which it, too, relies.

Finally, *emotional knowing* is that which does not fear coming into contact with pain. Some of its manifestations in Israel are NGOs and movements founded by women, such as "Four Mothers" and "Women Wage Peace", as well as more "masculine" organisations such as "Combatants for Peace" and "Breaking the Silence". While these organisations might be inconsequential in terms of their size, they have done much to unsettle professed knowing and to try to affect the social order. Such movements remind us that the biblical binding of Isaac was eventually rescinded and that we may yet save those still alive.

Following in the footsteps of these women's groups, the young members of "Breaking the Silence" began uncovering what was going on in the occupied territories and at the checkpoints. This inquisitive position engenders an emotional knowing that need not resort to immediate solutions. Simply by bringing difficult truths to light and acknowledging them, a healing process may be set in motion. The soldier who breaks his or her silence recounts the circumstances that have triggered his violence and rises against them. Having taken off his uniform, he is exposed as both vulnerable and human. This position is similar to that of Oedipus when he removes his royal garb, exposing intolerable anguish and, through his torment, acknowledging his errors and his disgrace.

*   *   *

Group analysis allows us to observe both the individual and society through several simultaneous prisms. I believe it is in order to focus especially on the "foundation matrix" and unconscious social processes. According to Foulkes, the foundation matrix portrays the social sphere and the myriad forces influencing people unconsciously—whether biological, cultural, or economic in nature. These forces are simultaneously and continuously at work, making up the fabric of our lives.

As both a method for studying the unconscious and an ethical standpoint, group analysis believes in the wisdom emerging from the group process. Hence, we might say that a leader who works as part of a team and who has faith in teamwork can make the transition from an arrogant position, breeding illusions, to a realistic position, which acknowledges limitations. A leader who is attentive and trusting in his relation to teamwork can acknowledge the group as a source of knowing, thus attaining more moderate and well-balanced views. Group analysis entails the ethical decision to trust the group, based on the assumption that the group contains implicit knowledge created through communication between its members. Paying heed to this knowledge could tone down extreme views. In contrast, in regressive states triggered by social distress or traumatisation, society needs a brave leader who would draw on his own inner wisdom, rather than the group.

The foundation matrix of Israeli society is composed, first and foremost, of the traumatic history of the Jewish people. The Holocaust has created so deep a wound and so dark an abyss in our history that its collective memories still dictate current events and prescribe the ideals in the light of which every new generation is educated. The foundation matrix is made up of collective memories, stored within the social sphere and transmitted through various means of communication (Scholz, 2011). I would add that these memories also unconsciously affect the material passed on through intergenerational transmission, including thoughts, feelings, and unconscious fantasies. This is how the emblematic figure of the Sabra was created to serve as the antithesis to the Jew in the Diaspora, who went "like a lamb to the slaughter". All the heroic myths that have been inculcating generation after generation in Israel create the impression that we are fighting for our very survival and that our enemies are demons, rather than human beings.

Aggregation and massification, the two polar states of the basic assumption of incohesion (Hopper, 2003), provide a profoundly apt portrayal of Israeli society, founded as it is on the fragments left by the Holocaust and the intolerable traumatic experiences that keep invading the social sphere. The more right wing a certain part of society is, the more massification becomes a prominent phenomenon: a passionate zeal for power and conquest, for one-dimensional ideas stemming from traumatic past persecution. The settlers believe that they are saving the people of Israel and they have fervour and faith that increase their social cohesion. In contrast, the more left wing a certain part of society is, the more we find evidence of aggregation—withdrawal into smaller family units, a loss of interest in society at large, and a narrowing of one's focus to include little more than one's own career and social status. Indeed, the Israeli left often seems to have disintegrated into tiny cells, lacking any unifying force.

Undoubtedly, a society that underwent such atrocious traumatisation is also laden with mechanisms of repression and especially of denial and disavowal. For the Palestinians, who are an indigenous people, such defences have been working impeccably since the establishment of Israel. Generations of Israelis were brought up without any conscious knowledge of the Nakba or the suffering of the Palestinian people; these hardships only entered public awareness with the outbreak of the Intifadas.

An anxious society tends to create the kind of arrogant leadership that could alleviate its fear of annihilation. Massification wins the day wherever social trauma is registered. One need only watch Hitler's speeches in Nuremberg to get a notion of how an arrogant, charismatic leadership can dazzle an entire society, whose anxieties are peaking after the traumatic events of the First World War. Further examples of contemporary massification can be seen in the rabid mass gatherings of movements such as Hezbollah and Hamas.

By observing broad social processes through the prism of psychoanalysis and group analysis, we may better understand the deeply unconscious connection between social processes and the emerging figure of the leader. As we witness these processes, we can only hope that our society, traumatised as it is, will succeed in fostering a moderate leadership that could hold emotional knowing and doubts instead of an arrogant knowing which strives for a single, exclusive truth.

References

Bion, W. R. (1959). Attacks on linking. *International Journal of Psychoanalysis*, *40*: 308–315.

Bion, W. R. (1967). *Second Thoughts*. London: Maresfield Reprints.

Foulkes, S. H. (1984). *Therapeutic Group Analysis*. London: Karnac.

Hopper, E. (2003). *Traumatic Experience in the Unconscious Life of Groups*. London: Jessica Kingsley.

Scholz, R. (2011). The foundation matrix and the social unconscious. In: E. Hopper & H. Weinberg (Eds.), *The Social Unconscious in Persons, Groups and Societies* (pp. 265–285). London: Karnac.

Sophocles (1947). *King Oedipus*. In: *The Theban Plays*, E. F. Watling (Trans.) (pp. 24–68). Baltimore, MD: Penguin.

CHAPTER FOUR

Beyond Oedipus in group analysis: the sacrifice of boys in the social unconscious of the Israeli people

Joshua Lavie

What do our children want? How do we know how to respond to their needs and desires? How can we distinguish between their need for our love, and their competition with us? How can we know if our sons begin to develop a special and exclusive relationship—a romance—with their mothers, and to distance themselves from their fathers? How can we know when our daughters distance themselves from their mothers—the "queen" of the family—and become their fathers' "one and only princess"? Are they jealous of us? And finally, *the* question: are these social psychological situations the result of fate? Are they hereditary and rooted in our DNA? Or—and a "big OR"—are we dealing with a completely different story?

What if the same questions could be reversed? What does it mean that our perspective *only* focuses on the children? Much has been written about Oedipus, but what if we look at him through the lens of his parents' feelings, their urges and anxieties? Is his blindness a punishment for murdering his father, for incest with his mother and for fathering her children? Is there not another kind of blindness here? Is it not the blindness of the parents, who, like Laius and Jocasta, abandoned Oedipus the baby, and mutilated him at the beginning of the play? Is this blindness related to the sacrifice of boys[1] on the altar of power struggles, and fights for control between various nationalities and religions, and between contradicting beliefs?

Does Oedipus's blindness actually represent the common blindness of us all? Does this blindness prevent us from studying the oedipal myth to its full extent and depth? Does this include the fathers, the mothers, and even the entire community across generations? Why do we usually seek only to enquire into the unconscious psyche of the little children who were just born, and not into the unconscious zones of fathers, of mothers, and of societies and their cultures in general? Or, in other words, might we explore the foundation matrix which is transmitted through "cultural inheritance", and not via "biogenetic heredity", as is often thought?

These are the true riddles that for thousands of years the monster from Thebes—the Sphinx—has attempted to conceal from us. What, then, are those conundrums?

Some psychoanalysts have attempted to provide answers to those conundrums. Initially, they did so with hesitation, in light of the "heresy" concerning Sigmund Freud, the founding father. However, thereafter they invested much more effort and courage into the search for the truth. These were psychoanalysts with a developed social awareness, who strongly emphasised the role of society and culture in shaping the human psyche throughout the life cycle. This perception strengthened their alternative stand to Freud's unique perception concerning the oedipal myth, in seeing its absurdity and the impasse to which it leads.

In this chapter, I emphasise the alternative, critical conception of the Oedipus myth, as developed, for example, by S. H. Foulkes, the founder of group analysis. His conception was strongly implicit in his *Introduction to Group Analytic Psychotherapy* (1948). Foulkes died in 1976, but had he lived for a few more years, he would have almost certainly completed writing his promised "Theory Book" in which his alternative conception of the Oedipus complex would have had an important place, which is clearly seen in his archived materials.

Alternative perspectives to the Freudian Oedipus: the transgenerational oedipal matrix

The "Oedipus complex" was defined by Laplanche and Pontalis (1967, p. 67) in *The Language of Psychoanalysis*: "an organized ensemble of love and hostility wishes the child has towards his parents". Psycho-analytic anthropology argues that the universal character of the Oedipus complex strives to locate the triangular oedipal structure in an array of cultures, including those in which the couple-based familial structure does not exist. This formula became the ruling paradigm in psychoanalysis.

In a letter dated 15 October 1897, on the anniversary of his father's death, Freud, who was forty-one years old at the time, wrote to his good friend, Wilhelm Fliess,

> I found love for the mother and jealousy towards the father in my case as well, and now I believe this is a *general phenomenon of early childhood* ... The Greek myth protrudes a necessity known by all, stemming from identifying from within the traces of his existence. Each spectator of the show was once a bud of Oedipus in his own fantasy. (Masson, 1985, p. 115, my italics)

Thus, whether it is the oedipal stage or the pre-oedipal stage, this perspective focuses only on children. Despite significant developments in psychoanalytic theory, for example, such as found in the work of Klein, Winnicott, Kohut, and others, the paradigm of the Oedipus complex remained unchanged. If we return to the wording of Laplanche and Pontalis, the questions related to the wishes of the parents: the desires of the mother and the cravings of the father were not addressed at all. Furthermore, children were positioned again and again at the margins of the primal scene, and the parents were left in the dark. This was a kind of a mechanism of social control that castrates curiosity and denies the parental contribution to this.

However, what is this trauma? Is it the revelation of the "awful secret"—the fact that their parents are involved in sexual relations? Or is it the revelation that parents have an oedipal history stemming from their own childhood, and that of their parents (the grandparents) as well? In other words, do parents have "oedipal feelings" toward their children? Such feelings are also connected to the elements that have coloured the atmosphere since the dawn of mental therapy; an era in which the study of the patient and his mind was located at the centre of the therapeutic discourse, an era in which interest in what takes place, simultaneously, in the mind of the analyst (countertransference) had not yet evolved.[2]

The effects of the familial–social matrix rolling from generation to generation can be seen in the myth that the early life of Laius is similar to the early life of Oedipus. Laius was also in danger. He underwent abusive abandonment in his childhood, once he was exiled from the Thebes kingdom, since he was the heir of his father, Labdacus, who passed away when Laius was one year old. King Pelops, who ruled Pisa in Peloponnesus, welcomed Laius and granted him a home, but Laius fell desperately in love with Pelops's son, the handsome young man, Chrysippus. Instead of wooing him and freeing him from his virginity, as was the custom in those days in Greece, he mercilessly raped him. In *Sexual Life in Ancient Greece* (Licht, 1932), based on *The Oedipodea*, Aeschylus's and Euripides' plays, as well as additional pragmatic Greeks, it is argued that Laius was one of the first individuals who committed violent sodomies against young men. The oracle from Delphi informs Laius of Zeus and Hera's spell, according to which, as punishment for the rape he committed, he will be murdered by his son (in time, Oedipus). Jocasta's crimes are also discussed in this anthology. The fact that Jocasta meets her death through suicide, while Oedipus remains alive, raises evidence on the extent of her harsh crimes, according to the society prevailing at that time, compared with those crimes committed by Oedipus; Jocasta did not fulfil her duty as a mother and was aware of the crimes she committed against her baby boy in her co-operation with Laius.

An article by the socially orientated psychoanalyst Erich Fromm[3] (1957) contains findings that indicate that the Oedipus complex, in its various layers—mainly the complete perspective on the three tragedies of Sophocles, *Oedipus the King*, *Oedipus at Colonus*, and *Antigone* (and not only Freud's perspective that focused exclusively on the *Oedipus the King* tragedy)—demonstrate the complex and entangled transition from the matriarchal culture (such as the Minoan culture in Crete) to the patriarchal culture (the Hellenistic in Athens). It is not the place here to discuss the historical, political, and social complexity stemming from the myths and written history, but it is clear that the interpretation provided by Freud based on the Oedipus myth is highly partial and fundamentally represents the spirit of the era in which Freud lived, at the end of the nineteenth century, and the patriarchal–paternalistic discourse that dominated this period. It is not coincidental that a psychoanalyst with a deep social awareness, such as Erich Fromm, was directed to relate to the social, political, and cultural aspects included in the context of the oedipal myth.

Fromm relied on the studies of matriarchal cultures of the renowned cultural historian Johann Jacob Bachofen (1973[1861]), who claimed that it was not men who created the deeds of community creativity in ancient days, but, rather, the women. This conception correlates with more communal and societal orientations, which are characterised by network figurations, and not by hierarchal patriarchal structures, in which a single leader rules from above one homogenous, collective human mass. Freud's perception of society (1921c) was based on such a hierarchal social structure, encompassing collective identification with a single leader (usually a male), who becomes a charismatic "ideal self" to the members of that society.

Disregarding Laius's and Jocasta's complexes also resulted in the evolvement of the dubious and discredited theories of phylogenetic (biological heredity) concerning children's fantasy life, not perceiving that fantasy life emerges unconsciously from the culture of the society, passing from generation to generation, from parents to their children, becoming, in turn, parents who bequeath to their children, and so on down the generations. The implementation of the hereditary–biological perception in relation to mental contents led to the belief that the oedipal impulses, in Freud's opinion, pass through genes in a phylogenetic process such as the transition of physical traits, and it develops in each child in an ontogenetic process such as the creation of the physical traits.

The alternative outlook of Foulkes was not based on a system of metaphors and analogies from the "biological heredity", but rather based on a completely alternative conception of "cultural inheritance", passing from generation to generation through language, education, and unconscious communications between parents and their children, who are actually co-constructing their shared social unconscious (Hopper & Weinberg, 2011, 2016). The oedipal struggles of parents with their children and *vice versa*, the anxiety of fathers that their sons will replace them, the jealousy stemming from it, the competition between sons and fathers for the mother's love, the mother's jealousy of her daughter and *vice versa*, and the entire complexity of the love–hate relations—all these are passed unconsciously from generation to generation through cultural heredity.

From this multi-dimensional point of view, we can detect a paradigmatic change, perceiving the oedipal relations as established within network configurations and reciprocal relations between all family members, in the synchronic dimension at present as well as in the historic diachronic dimension along the generations.

Oedipus in group analysis: theory, practice and case study

This paradigmatic change in perceiving the Oedipus complex is part of a wider paradigmatic revolution in group analysis—viewing individuals and their groups, individuals and the societies in which they intertwine, a multi-dimensional human web, deviating far beyond the common dichotomies prevalent in the discourses in human sciences: individual *vs.* society, heredity *vs.* environment, internal world *vs.* external world, subject *vs.* object, etc. The conception that human beings are intertwined in social–cultural networks expanding in the diachronic dimension (from generation to generation along history) as well as in the synchronic dimension (in a certain generation at a certain era), and that these two dimensions are also woven together, constructed by, and constructing, each other, stands at the basis of the developmental theory of group analysis as developed by Foulkes and the other co-founders of the Group Analytic Society.[4]

Returning to the subject matter of this chapter, a central and significant part in the group analytic theory—directly corresponding with the psychoanalytic theory—is related to an alternative theoretical and practical conception concerning the Oedipus complex. In an article published by Foulkes four years prior to his death, the oedipal conception underwent a radical transformation. According to Foulkes, simultaneously with the arrival of a new baby in the family, the entire family—all the subjects compounding it—"undergoes regression to infantile-like/child-like states": the mother, the father, as well as other children if they exist, and, of course, the baby himself, who is infantile/childish in his nature and essence.

Foulkes (1972) summarises the following points/highlights in this article:[5]

1.   The oedipal situation is a familial complex,[6] perhaps, earlier still, a tribal problem.

2.   The classical oedipal situation is the final result of pregenital development and conflict. The parents are its real instigators as much as the infant.

3.   Infantile sexuality on the part of *both* parents and children is key. There is, therefore, "cultural transmission" rather than direct "biological heredity".

4.   The prominent and most important contribution of group analysis is the study of human beings in a part of a common mental network: the group matrix.

5.   We are talking, therefore, about an oedipal network in which mother, father, children, grandparents, their parents, intertwine; in this web, regressive and progressive processes take place.

Case study

The following is a clinical example that demonstrates what has been discussed and claimed so far. It is taken from a group analytic group that I conducted. From this example, one can learn the extent to which the common Freudian conception of the oedipal complex dominates not only the consciousness of psychotherapists, but also that of patients and, actually, the consciousness of women and men and wide strata of modern western culture. The following is a description of the chain of events.

A member of an analytic group (consisting of eight participants), very talented and successful in his professional life, shares with great pain his sense of emasculation and his low self-esteem, being a person who seeks immediate gratification and one with a low level of morality, exploiting women in a concealed manner, demonstrated in a loyal and trustworthy appearance which is actually a false appearance. His phenomenal professional successes are negligible compared to his small and low valued personality. Out of habit, he always returns to comparing himself to his father, a person characterised by him as a saint, an honest man, a trustworthy man, and, compared to his father, he is merely a "worthless, useless creature". Most of the group members attempt to help him by encouraging him, emphasising his good qualities and traits, but also strengthening his spirit to overcome his sense of competition and jealousy towards his father. Here, we witness

the fact that the common oedipal perception dominates the consciousness of group members, and, actually, the consciousness of everyone
who was nurtured on the popularity of the Oedipus complex, as
constructed by Freud and the ruling psychoanalytic thinking. The
patient continues to further emphasise how difficult it is for him to
have thoughts on his unfaithfulness and disloyalty to his wife, which
show him again, and more strongly, how immoral he is. Here, he adds
admiringly that his father has a warm and fond connection with his
wife. In this moment, I, as the conductor of the group, ask him to elaborate on the relations between his father and his ex-daughter-in-law,
the patient's wife (and his ex-wife today). He talks about a relationship
of enthusiasm from his father towards his wife and *vice versa*. There
were numerous ongoing telephone conversations between them, and
warm hugs when they met. At this stage, two female patients in the
group raise their brows and say with anger, each in her own language,
that it seems that this is a really intimate connection between the
father-in-law and the daughter-in-law, and that the father, apparently
a great saint, is actually "stealing" his wife from him. To this, the
patient smiles with embarrassment, but also slyly, and responds, "Of
course, in the light of the emotional and sexual emptiness that lasted
for many years between my father and my mother . . . it is no wonder
that my father became so close to my wife . . . and sometimes . . . now
that you say this . . . I think he even wooed her . . ."

In this example, we learn how deeply the Freudian perception had
rooted itself in the domineering cultural discourse regarding the oedipal triangular relations. But, the power, the wisdom, the creativity of
groups was evident in allowing a wide range of reflective critical thinking concerning the triangular relations between the son (the patient),
his father, and his wife. The patient eventually divorced his wife, since
her attitude towards him was critical, tough, and without warmth, con-
solation, and forgiveness. Her love towards him was only expressed on
a few occasions, when he was perfect in her eyes (like his father).

Beyond Oedipus and the sacrifice of boys
in the Israeli social unconscious

In the last part of this chapter, I refer to the Jewish/Israeli aspects of the
oedipal network. In the biblical story of the binding of Isaac, God's

angel stops Abraham from slaughtering his son. We see here, in analogy to the oedipal myth, how Abraham, the father, leads his son to his death, while the mother, Sarah, silently connives and collaborates.[7] The connection between the Oedipus myth and the binding of Isaac can be seen in the light of the victory of the Hellenistic/paternal culture over the Minoan/maternal culture and the victory of the Israelite/paternal God (Yahweh) over the Canaanite/maternal Goddess Asherah. In both stories/myths, the law of the male/father is constituted by his victory over the son, and the female/mother becomes a secondary figure.

It is plausible to perceive the "solution" or the sublimation of the binding of Isaac—which represents the bare loyalty and devotion of the people of Israel to God (Yahweh)[8]—in the act of circumcision conducted on them from time immemorial, an act that symbolises the alliance of the people of Israel to their father/God.

If one perceives the act of circumcision as a sublimation of the binding narrative, it is also plausible to see it as an indication and clue to the social unconscious of the Israeli people, which sanctifies the sacrifice of boys in Israel's wars, for the sanctity of the country and its holy land. The act of circumcision is irreversible; therefore, it is used as an intergenerational and multi-generational materialisation of the father's dominant rule and law in the patriarchal culture. God, the male, is the big and absolute father ruler, ruling and guiding Abraham, the father of the nation, which dominates and guides the male Israelites from time immemorial. This is the web of relations between God the Father, the human father, and the sons, while the mother, Sarah, fulfils a secondary role. Jocasta, too, in the Freudian interpretation of the oedipal myth, is a secondary figure.

However, these narratives in both cultures are not the whole story. In the complete oedipal trilogy, *Oedipus Rex*, *Oedipus in Colonus*, and *Antigone*, we see that Oedipus reaches tranquillity and finds rest, comfort, and compassion among the ancient motherly goddesses (in *Oedipus in Colonus*), thanks to his daughter Antigone's loyalty, and in favour of her humanity and rebelliousness against the patriarchal order (compared and contrasted to her sister, Ismene, who was obedient to the patriarchal order). An equivalent and alternative additional story, referring to the wide context of the binding of Isaac, was written in Judaism as well. Just as Oedipus distanced himself from the paternalistic world that hurt him, so Isaac distanced himself from his father, Abraham, finding comfort elsewhere.

Consider the alternative story, in which Isaac is the protagonist: to the unstable state of Abraham's family and the traumatic mental state of Isaac following the binding, Elbaum (2000) dedicated an essay titled "Isaac—the father we have forgotten". Elbaum details a discussion on the term "Isaac's fear", a term taken from an ancient Jewish prayer: *"Answer us, Abraham's God, answer us: Answer us, and Isaac's fear, answer us: Answer us, hero Yaacov, answer us: Answer us, star of David, answer us: Answer us, fortress of the mothers, answer us . . ."* Elbaum writes, "a great fear had stricken me, Isaac's figure returned and captured me, battered and beaten, frightened, flowing in the wind demanding repair . . ." (p. 131).

Elbaum depicted and characterised Isaac as a man who underwent severe trauma as a child during the binding, and more than likely had developed a post-traumatic personality. He brings the traditional exegesis to the biblical text from the sages of the Talmud, interpreting that Isaac's eyes became blind due to the angels' tears, who cried out of grief during the binding. But Elbaum was not satisfied with this traditional interpretation, and brings the commentary of the Kabbalah tradition,[9] which describes what Isaac saw in the open skies above Mount Moriya's peak when he was bound, waiting to be slaughtered by his father. There and then heaven's skies had been torn apart, and the "black holes" of the divine cosmos revealed to Isaac; he glanced into the dark pockets of God, not the God of the Bible whom his father loved, but the other side of this love, the evil root of God himself. Perhaps his eyes, which momentarily crashed into the depths of the divine, discovered a peculiar dichotomy: an absolute love and absolute evil concentrated and expressed simultaneously at the moment of the binding. This would justify the attribute he was given in the holy prayer concerning his relationship with God: *"Isaac's fear"*. Unlike Abraham the "slaughterer", Isaac the "slaughtered" does not want any connection with such a God. He takes the risk that his character will be presented as meagre in the biblical tradition, in which God is always the main hero navigating the plot as he desires; but Isaac knows that he owns his own life without the assistance of, or dialogue with, God.

The fact that the Kabbalah tradition relates to Isaac's feelings, tears, fears, and weaknesses with understanding, empathy, and compassion, indicates a less masculine and paternalistic attitude. Isaac distances himself from the tradition of the paternalistic, masculine God. He criticises God and rehabilitates himself. He tries to cure his trauma by forming a new family based on his great love for Rebekah and the enormous love of Rebekah for him. The Kabbalah is a tradition that places the feminine/maternal world at its centre. This is, essentially, a horizontal network of relationships between angels and people feeling empathy for each other. Being a maternal/feminine network, this horizontal web differs completely from the vertical paternal/masculine structure of the Jewish tradition, with God on top, Abraham the chosen father below him, and the Israelite people at the bottom.

The group analytic reading of the whole Oedipus story also reveals a horizontal network of a womb-like matrix, a form of society in which people intertwine in horizontal networks rather than forming in hierarchal structures. If we look at Israel's society as it has developed since the 1967 Six-Day War, it seems that the belligerent, hierarchal side of Judaism unconsciously prevails in our culture. We educate our children to fight, binding them on the altar of wars together with the hero Joseph Trumpeldor, who is supposed to have said, just few minutes before his death, "It's good to die for our country", becoming a symbol for genuine patriotism. Generally speaking, we have put aside the Israeli prophets who preached for human compassion and social justice, who dared to dream: *"and they shall beat their swords into ploughshares, and their spears into pruning-hooks"* (Isaiah 2: 2–4). In the light of the present situation in Israel, I myself have a wish—maybe a naïve one—that the group analytic tradition, with its affinity to the spirit of the Israeli prophets, should prevail and influence the Israeli society and the Israeli/Jewish culture, and overcome the present nationalistic militaristic tendencies.

Notes

1. It is worth noting here that, in every army, the soldiers are recruited at exactly the same age—the end of childhood—as though there is a silent consent even between the worse enemies; or should we say that this consent is largely unconscious in all patriarchies, during millennia of army battles. See also, in this context, Friedman's (2015) article titled "A soldier's matrix".

2. Consider a controversial article titled "Why Oedipus killed Laius: a note on the complementary Oedipus complex in Greek drama", written in 1953 by George Devereux:

It is striking to note that psychoanalytic theory pays exceedingly little attention to certain complexes which, in a very genuine sense complement the Oedipus Complex. In particular, even though occasionally reference is made to the tender and even to the erotic components of what may be called the Laius and the Jocasta complex . . . the sadistic (and homosexual) components of these complexes are, generally speaking, ignored by psychoanalytic writers. (p.132)

3.   Erich Fromm was a psychoanalyst working with the Frankfurt School for social research at the end of the 1920s and the beginning of the 1930s. Fromm was acquainted with Foulkes, who was part of the Frankfurt Psychoanalytic Institute at exactly the same period. Both institutions shared the same building and collaborated. Foulkes and Fromm fled Germany in 1933 after Hitler came to power.

4.   Foulkes, Elias, de Maré, and other co-founders, developed a group analytic theory and practice, with its own language and a unique therapeutic technique (Lavie, 2005).

5.   It should be indicated and emphasised that this summary was omitted from Foulkes' (1990) volume of collected papers, edited by Elizabeth Foulkes and with a prologue by Malcolm Pines. This omitting, reduction, and deduction, or even distortion, of Foulkes' papers following his death does not appear only in this article in the book. I refer the readers to the paper written by Nitzgen (2010), in which he demonstrates how Foulkes' original paper on Kurt Goldstein's legacy and its influence on group analysis was also reduced and distorted. This act disrupted the understanding of what Foulkes wished to endow to us concerning the ideological and scientific origins of group analysis. The carelessness in handling Foulkes' scripts after his death deserves a deep analysis of the omitted contents as well as of the possible reasons for this anomaly in relation to the founding father of group analysis.

6.   This was, in fact, a return to Freud's original conceptualisation of what he first called the "family complex". This was reflected in the famous debate between Bronislaw Malinowski, the famous anthropologist, and Ernest Jones the psychoanalyst (I thank Earl Hopper for this important remark).

7.   See Frosh (2013, p. 130), who gives a group analytic interpretation to the story of the Akedah corresponding with the Laius complex: "In a savage reversal of Freud that is also psychically accurate, the classical commentators understood a father's murderous envy of his sons".

8.   See also Frosh (2013, p. 126): "For Jews specifically, the Akedah is an example of a template for intergenerational transmission of trauma and identity. Religiously, it is crucial in marking the confirmation of God's covenant with Abraham".

9.   Elbaum characterises the Kabbalah sages as "the psychoanalysts of the Jewish culture, who analyse the deep symbols of the bible, who tend to expose the unconscious abysses, and to say out loud what the Jewish culture fears to expose . . ." (2000, p. 134).

References

Bachofen, J. J. (1973)[1861]. *Myths, Religion, and Mother-right: Selected Writings of J. J. Bachofen.* Princeton, NJ: Princeton University Press.

Devereux, G. (1953). Why Oedipus killed Laius: a note on the complementary Oedipus complex in Greek drama. *International Journal of Psychoanalysis, 34*: 132–141.

Elbaum, D. (2000). Isaac—the father we have forgotten. *Akdamot, 9.* www.bmj.org.il/files/891294581423.pdf.

Foulkes, E. (Ed.) (1990). *Selected Papers of S. H. Foulkes.* London: Karnac.

Foulkes, S. H. (1948). *Introduction to Group Analytic Psychotherapy.* London: Karnac.

Foulkes, S. H. (1972). Oedipus conflict and regression. *International Journal of Group Psychotherapy, 22*: 3–15 [shortened and edited version was printed in E. Foulkes (Ed.) (1990), *Selected Papers of S. H. Foulkes.* London: Karnac].

Freud, S. (1921c). *Group Psychology and the Analysis of the Ego. S. E., 18*: 57–143. London: Hogarth.

Friedman, R. (2015). A soldier's matrix: a group analytic view of societies in war. *Group Analysis, 48*(3) 239–257.

Fromm, E. (1957). Symbolic language in myth, fairy tale, ritual, and novel. In: *The Forgotten Language: An Introduction to the Understanding of Dreams, Fairy Tales and Myth* (pp. 195–231). New York: Holt, Reinehart and Winston.

Frosh, S. (2013). *Hauntings: Psychoanalysis and Ghostly Transmissions.* London: Palgrave Macmillan.

Hopper, E., & Weinberg, H. (Eds.) (2011). *The Social Unconscious in Persons, Groups, and Societies: Volume I: Mainly Theory.* London: Karnac.

Hopper, E., & Weinberg, H. (Eds.) (2016). *The Social Unconscious in Persons, Groups, and Societies: Volume 2: Mainly Matrices.* London: Karnac.

Laplanche, J., & Pontalis, J.-B. (1967). *The Language of Psychoanalysis*. London: Karnac.

Lavie, J. (2005). The lost roots of the theory of group analysis: 'Taking interrelational individuals seriously!' *Group Analysis*, 38: 519–535.

Licht, H. (1932). *Sexual Life in Ancient Greece*. London: Routledge.

Masson, J. M. (Ed.) (1985). *The Complete Letters of Sigmund Freud to Wilhelm Fliess, 1887–1904*. Cambridge, MA: Harvard University Press.

Nitzgen, D. (2010). Hidden legacies, S. H. Foulkes, Kurt Goldstein and Ernst Cassirer. *Group Analysis*, 43: 354–371.

CHAPTER FIVE

The group analysis of the Akeda: the worst and the best feelings in the matrix

Robi Friedman

Introduction

Trying to identify and describe the worst and best social processes and feelings that a group can elicit has implications for group analytic therapy. A well-known story from the Bible, which has troubled the minds and hearts of every generation, is used as an example of the worst. Isaac's binding, the Akeda, viewed from a group analytic perspective, provides a further step in understanding the complex dynamics of scapegoating. The best feelings that can be generated from within a group are also discussed.

The worst

According to Genesis, at a location not too far from where I am writing, a small group started a secret and lethal mission.[1] Abraham was bringing his son Isaac to Mount Moriah, with the intention of sacrificing him to God. Certainly a great man, Abraham was as close to God as anyone has ever been. God had said to him, "Take your son, your only son that you love, and sacrifice him . . ."

Isaac's binding is an example of the worst outcome of interpersonal relations, when they are characterised by a specific mixture of aggression, extreme faith, and unconscious human connectedness of a certain kind. I have characterised these dynamics as the "scapegoating position", which describes a relationship between a group and a member who is going to be expelled from it, ousted, and sent to some kind of extermination. The "scapegoating position" goes beyond classic definitions of scapegoats, who are supposedly subjects and objects of projections and envy (Garland et al., 1973). Sometimes, the destructive tendencies of scapegoating result from group members' hate towards the scapegoat. Yet, they are often based on a mixture of the anxiety of becoming a scapegoat and of selection processes in the group, which are thought to "improve" the group's standards, almost as a kind of breeding process. Scapegoating is based on unconscious relations between a rejecting group and the scapegoat, who is unable to separate from the wish to belong to his perpetrator's group. Violence-inhibiting emotions, such as empathy, shame, and guilt, become progressively absent.

Isaac's binding as an example of a scapegoating position can be understood in the context of two spheres of relations: the social and the personal, which can never entirely separate and which are, in fact, completely interpenetrating. The social aspect of the story describes the end-phase of the establishment of a covenant between Abraham and God, and the personal aspect describes Abraham as a father. Abraham was obliged to prove time and again that his covenant with God was stronger than any doubt or conflict that stems from personal relationship. The final test was that no matter how much he loved his son, he must bring him to the mountain and sacrifice him in a most powerful "act of faith". It was necessary to show that he had subordinated the "personal" in favour of the "social".

The Akeda is a troublesome notion that stops 'normal' life and calls for second thoughts, understanding and interpretation, and also for leadership. The angel's intervention is a beautiful example of the complexity of a clinical intervention. Could it be used as a guideline for the group conductor's interpretations in the case of a "scapegoat position"? Foulkes, the founder of group analysis, thought that "interpretation comes in where analysis fails" (1975, p. 117). Interpretations are only a small part of the therapeutic project—even if they are sometimes absolutely necessary to it. Far from being a solution, interpretations might be only an emergency handbrake.

In passing this test, Abraham would finally be included in the highly valued group of the truly faithful to God. Inclusion rituals, such as certain kinds of tests in school, challenges in adolescent groups, military initiative tests, and even acceptance into analytic institutes are all part of social life. Longing to belong to "unique" groups arouses strong anxieties of exclusion and rejection. Individuals need to prove their integrity and loyalty to the group and its leaders, especially with respect to potential members. The emotional burdens that humans are willing to take on in order to join and belong (Schlapobersky, 2016) are surprising. The conscious and unconscious fear of rejection is one of the most painful aspects of human existence (Friedman, 2013). Rejection and fear of rejection are a central, chronic element of rejection relation disorders,[2] in which relations and individuals are threatened with annihilation by expulsion from the groups (Hopper, 2003a).[3] Thus, the scapegoating position results from many possible motivations, such as hate and projected negative qualities, the desperate need to belong, separation problems associated with fears of exclusion and rejection, etc. Also, in the absence of a drastic intervention, a member who threatens the group's view of itself as the "best", or a member who threatens the group's leadership needs, can be ejected. The efficiency principle of groups concerning the group's basic need to be "the best" tends to ignite rejective processes (Friedman, 2015).

It is worth considering how old Isaac was when he was brought up the mountain by his father. Whereas some interpreters of the Bible believe Isaac was still a child, others think that he was at least thirty years of age, judging from the age of his mother. I prefer to think of Isaac as being approximately eighteen years of age, which is when we in Israel send our sons and daughters off to military service. For most families, this is a moment of special awareness, which might be denied or repressed.

In the Bible, Sarah, Abraham's wife and Isaac's mother, misses the Mount Moriah "session". However, as we know, the existence of unconscious transpersonal communication among close persons suggests that Sarah must have had some knowledge of the impending event. Her "absent presence" raises questions about women's roles in such dreadful group processes, in which commitment, idealisation, identification, and inclusion are tested. How do women function in wars, sacrifice, and social events connected with them? What kind of partners are they to the fighting men?[4] Perhaps the absent presence of Sarah is a reminder of a former "binding": Ishmael's double sacrifice by his father in which it was not God but Abraham's wife, Sarah, who demanded the expulsion of his child, together with his mother, Hagar, to die in the desert.

Personal and social aspects of Isaac's binding

While the naïve Bible reader wishes to believe that the Akeda has a happy ending, the Bible itself, which usually exposes the bad and the good sides of humanity, points to a triumphant social glory, and, at the same time, hints at the personal tragedy of Isaac's binding. While the covenant between God and mankind, on the one hand, and between God and Abraham's offspring, on the other, appear to be fulfilled, a deeper reading of the text suggests that, as a consequence of these tests, Abraham and his family experienced the worst and most cruel relational processes. After the Akeda, the wonderful communication between Abraham and God breaks down, Sarah dies immediately after the events on Mount Moriah, and not a single word was uttered again between Abraham and his son Isaac.

The conflict between socio-political and individual processes seems to have the power to destroy even a healthy family matrix. The personal is always secondary to public, social, or national obligations (Berman, 2011). Needs of belonging to the larger community and threats of rejection from it seem to induce selfless modes of relating (Friedman, 2013), which might even be a ubiquitous source of the annihilation anxieties which are at the root of aggregation and massification processes (Hopper, 2003a).

Participating in the scapegoating process: the unconscious relations between victims and perpetrators

The Akeda includes all the ingredients of scapegoating as an interpersonal process: Abraham's conscious willingness to sacrifice his own child for a "higher cause" is a human tragedy; Abraham destroys and rejects someone from his group without empathy, without shame and guilt, while the scapegoat stays submissively and masochistically faithful to the group, as led and represented by his father; by threatening everyone's existence, scapegoating also strengthens the group's influence. It unconsciously terrorises its members towards being included. These dangers subdue individualisation. A group characterised by massification unites through its shared wishes to eliminate the scapegoat, who is increasingly perceived as deviant, thus "earning" his fate. However, the scapegoat himself usually does everything possible to avoid being rejected from the group. The meeting between two movements ignites a destructive tragic cycle of loathing and craving. The scapegoat's craving for inclusion seems to further influence his being perceived as superfluous, as narcissistically childish, and, together with the scapegoater's wish to reject it, might become fatal to the group. In the final stage, the scapegoat is rejected or eliminated without remorse or shame, and the scapegoating group hopes for a more "efficient" group.

Is the moment of rejection also the moment where the deep unconscious connection between the worlds of all those involved in the scapegoating position are cut off from each other? Do the complementary fantasies that tie both sides—selfless delivery and shameless rejection and hurt—continue even after the scapegoating position is enacted? Rejection anxieties seem to be a fundamental, collective, unconscious human emotion, which threaten even the most privileged and central members of groups and societies. It is likely that the scapegoats' "inclusion miracles", such as planning some heroic action in which they "save the group" by selfless sacrifice, goodness, and usefulness are a fundamental defence against their fear of rejection. While the scapegoat's selfless acts do not usually serve their aim of ensuring his inclusion in his group, the selfless hero is highly appreciated and even venerated.

Why are the scapegoat's "inclusion fantasies" reciprocated by rejection instead of a positive transformation of the relationship? One of the scapegoat's main flaws seems to be his excessive dependency, his difficulty in separating, and his need to belong, all of which are interpreted as weakness by the group. The aggression and even sadistic aspects of this seem to originate in a fundamental rejection of this part of ourselves. This poisons the matrix. History is full of examples of this process.

Abraham's fatherhood: the worst in a family matrix

Isaac's binding was the climax of Abraham's problematic role as a father. Climbing Mount Moriah, Isaac must have been aware of his father's failure as a "father". He had enough evidence not to trust Abraham. The Bible pictures Abraham, whose name is connected to "fatherhood", as failing twice with Ishmael, his first-born son. Before his birth, Abraham agreed to send Ishmael's pregnant mother, Hagar, to the desert. Many years later, Sarah's recurring wish for Ishmael's social and physical destruction was again accepted by Abraham (Genesis 21, 9–21). Ishmael was to be scapegoated and annihilated. Instead of having the security that arises from the conviction that his father would fight for his wellbeing, Isaac must have doubted his father's ability to be faithful. Indeed, Abraham betrayed both his sons.

One of the principal aspects of a father's role is his unquestioned endless devotion to the physical protection of his son. This selfless devotion position might be called "primary paternal preoccupation", which can be seen as the equivalent of "primary maternal preoccupation" (Doron, 2014; Winnicott, 1958). This primary "paternal preoccupation" is a fundamental element in the relationship between fathers and their children, and can deeply influence the development of self-confidence (Friedman, 2015).

The lack of faith that Isaac must have felt in his father, who had already proved twice his absolute lack of primary "paternal preoccupation" towards his brother Ishmael, gives this story of the Akeda an even more poignant quality. Pointing to the child's personal and emotional difficulty, and the basic insecurity of growing up with such a father, it directs us to both Abraham's and Isaac's anxious victimhood. Both identify with the aggressor.

Isaac also "understands" his father's aggression not only as Abraham's deep identificatory loop with God's aggression, but also as syntonic with the culture of the time. The story of the Akeda represents "the cultural inheritance of paternal violence" (Frosh, 2016, p. 5), a seemingly eternal subject. Abraham treats his sons as God, his "father", treats him. We continue to adhere to the tradition of haunting the next generation as the former generations haunted us (Frosh, 2016).

The victim's compliance

Isaac seems to have started the journey with a strong desire to please his father by playing the naïve child's role and subserviently going along with the plan. Again, knowing his father had given up his concern, not only because of God, but also because of his wife's anger and envy, must have eroded Isaac's self-confidence and pushed him to identify with paternal aggression. Climbing Mount Moriah, he questions his father by asking naïvely: "Where is the lamb?" Abraham tries to disguise the imminent violence and denies the cruel reality. Isaac then naïvely colludes with the "game" and plays his role of victim. As discussed previously, Isaac's position represents the typical collusion of the scapegoat's appeasing position with the scapegoater's rejecting attitude. Scapegoats often seem unconsciously to deny their group, particularly their "father's" failure, and continue to delegate power to him. Isaac's binding illustrates the dynamic of sacrificing sons, or children in general, when the individual is wasted in favour of a "cause" or another "group obligation" (Friedman, 2015). Such situations often happen in group analytic therapy. This can be understood as a test for the group and of their conductor's "fatherhood".

Many painters, sculptors, and poets of the Akeda have dealt with the feelings between father and son, between perpetrator and victim, between scapegoater and scapegoat. Most of them do not question Abraham's love of his son, even if he loves his God more. Reciprocally, Isaac is not driven by the same unconscious revenge against his vindictive father, as is sometimes evident in transgenerational conflicts. If Abraham hated his son, it stays unconscious; we can only imagine, as we experience in groups, that something pushes someone in the group to transform a "subject" into an "object". In the absence of any evidence of shame, guilt, and empathy in Abraham, in the Akeda it is up to us to draw from our personal and social experience, and project our feelings in this situation, or use the story in order to understand group situations. This is how Wilfred Owen (1920), a soldier poet who was killed in action just a few days before the end of the First World War, describes scapegoating dynamics in "The Parable of the Old Man and the Young":

> "... Abram bound the youth with belts and straps
> and built parapets and trenches there,
> And stretched forth the knife to slay his son.
> When lo! an angel called him out of heaven,
> Saying, Lay not thy hand upon the lad,
> Neither do anything to him, thy son.

. . . But the old man would not so, but slew his son,
And half the seed of Europe, one by one."

Scapegoating, shame and guilt

The absence of shame and guilt is a unique feature of this interaction between Abraham and Isaac. Although guilt is a fundamental feeling in everyday family and group dynamics, it is denied in the rejection relation disorder. In the "sacrifice" situation, scapegoating is stronger than guilt or empathy, together with a dismissal of the pain inflicted on the inclusion-needy individual or sub-group. If dissociated, or perceived only superficially, there will often be more than a dismal degree of satisfaction in the face of the scapegoat's suffering.

The total denial of guilt displayed during a (long) violent process will not always be transformed. Only a few scapegoating societies allow aggression-inhibiting emotions such as shame and guilt to re-enter their matrix (Friedman, 2015; Rustomjee, 2009). Shame can be considered as one of the earliest social emotions. Like signal anxiety, it senses and warns, consciously and unconsciously, of the danger of immediate social rejection. Socially unacceptable acts may result in rejection and expulsion from society. Shame will be non-existent when the matrix legitimises scapegoating. However, in a humane society, one can fantasise about mature individuals and groups continuing their development until ambivalent and guilt positions are reached, even in soldiers. This would make it more difficult for fathers to sacrifice their "children" for the sake of the cause.

Scapegoating, hate, and the group
analytic conductor's leadership

Understanding the scapegoating position has significant implications for group analysis. Can we "trust the group" (Foulkes, 1948) or is scapegoating one of these relation crises which demands a conductor's intervention before it becomes a relation disorder (Friedman, 2013). Like the angel who stays Abraham's knife, the conductor can provide some preventative leadership. Group conductors should be aware of inclusion and rejection anxieties, as well as tensions arising from annihilation anxieties. Hate, rejection, and the sacrifice of one, or a whole subgroup of "deviant" group members has to be controlled, limited, interpreted, and transformed by practising tolerance in the group, modelled by the leadership. All societies know the dynamics of scapegoating only too well, and they evince an unconscious tendency either to fragment and attack each and every individual, or to coalesce under one umbrella and attack those who do not find protection beneath it. Hopper (2003b) describes these processes in terms of the basic assumption of Incohesion: Aggregation/Massification.

Liberman and colleagues' (1973) investigations into encounter groups found that the highest probability of scapegoating exists in groups led by charismatic, unprofessional leaders. Foulkes' (1948) invigoration of the group, together with the decentralisation of the conductor, which is the fundamental group-analytical position, leans on the group's innate abilities to relate (Behr & Hearst, 2005). In my view, however, the group-analytic conductor has to read the dialogue between these mainly constructive elements of the group dynamic with the opposite elements of annihilation and rejection anxieties and the group's efficiency principle. The conductor's activity, generally responsible for the setting and the group's boundaries, helps to establish a "free resonance" or free associative attitude in the therapy group,[5] where the two sides of a dialogue increasingly reach the group's awareness and are subject to some reflection and control. Promoting growth by mutual containment and healing, which includes the conductor, makes a scapegoat situation less likely to develop. Equality in the group, including even the most charismatic conductor, supports the courage to exert interpersonal reciprocal influence. This enables more tolerance for differences and deviances in dialogue and discourse (Schlapobersky, 1993), and is one of main group analytic instruments. The group analytic approach cannot blindly and naïvely be immune to the possibility of creating scapegoating positions, but it may offer a matrix which enables the detection and prevention of enactments of this kind.

A few words about the best in groups

Group conductors who describe optimal group situations emphasise closeness and cohesiveness, mixing feelings of inclusion together with some measure of personal recognition. This mixture can be a harmonious one. For example, in one of my groups, a patient's shocking announcement of leaving the group was responded to with a generally warm and concerned response. It elicited in her a most powerful resonance: she felt that they were together, and as if they were making love. What transpired is that the best in groups is the momentary elimination of the fear of rejection, which might be the worst one could expect in a group.

Lars von Trier's film, *Dogville* (2003), illustrates both rejection and inclusion processes in the same group: the best is represented by the successful process of inclusion by providing a beautiful and graceful fugitive with a refuge. The group seems gracefully to dedicate itself to saving her, filling the matrix with generosity and growth. Sadly, destructive emotional moments of inclusion and benevolent reciprocation take over later, and transform into the classic scapegoating position of this refugee.

The dialogue between the constructive and destructive aspect of the group collapses, and is transformed into dreadful behaviours characterised by annihilation and rejection anxieties. Finally, as in the Akeda, the dialogue and the group are destroyed. The authority, too weak to intervene, cannot prevent the group from scapegoating. For the best in a group to happen, fears of annihilation or rejection cannot take over and must not be allowed to do so. Maybe only a "father", meaning an authority (it can be a female: Sarah, Abraham's wife, leads and even dominates the family's emotional life) can provide a basic degree of security, and can meet the standards of the efficiency principle for the group as a whole.

In Israel, we are close to Mount Moriah. Annihilation and rejection anxieties are ubiquitous. As a society and nation state, we need to be as efficient as possible, and we seem to tend to a discourse concerning growing rejection tendencies. In order to face annihilation anxieties and the possibility that a father figure is failing to hold the group, as he is expected to, basic needs have to be met. Conducting a group analytic group may be about a social unconscious dialogue between the representatives of the foundation matrix and the representative of the dynamic matrices of our constituent groups. This means understanding intergenerational conflicts, on the one hand, and holding and containing huge measures of aggression, mostly of paternal violence characteristics, on the other.

Notes

1.

(Genesis 22: 1–18) And it came to pass after these things that God did tempt Abraham, and said unto him, Abraham: and he said, Behold, here I am. 2 And he said, Take now thy son, thine only son Isaac, whom thou lovest, and get thee into the land of Moriah; and offer him there for a burnt offering upon one of the mountains which I will tell thee of. 3 And Abraham rose up early in the morning, and saddled his ass, and took two of his young men with him, and Isaac his son, and clave the wood for the burnt offering, and rose up, and went unto the place of which God had told him. 4 Then on the third day Abraham lifted up his eyes, and saw the place afar off. 5 And Abraham said unto his young men, Abide ye here with the ass; and I and the lad will go yonder and worship, and come again to you. 6 And Abraham took the wood of the burnt offering, and laid it upon Isaac his son; and he took the fire in his hand, and a knife; and they went both of them together. 7 And Isaac spoke unto Abraham his father, and said, My father: and he said, Here am I, my son. And he said, Behold the fire and the wood: but where is the lamb for a burnt offering? 8 And Abraham said, My son, God will provide himself a lamb for a burnt offering: so they went both of them together. And they came to the place which God had told him of; and Abraham built an altar there, and laid the wood in order, and bound Isaac his son, and laid him on the altar upon the wood. 10 And Abraham stretched forth his hand, and took the knife to slay his son. 11 And the angel of the LORD called unto him out of heaven, and said, Abraham, Abraham: and he said, Here am I. 12 And he said, Lay not thine hand upon the lad, neither do thou any thing unto him: for now I know that thou fearest God, seeing thou hast not withheld thy son, thine only son from me. 13 And Abraham lifted up his eyes, and looked, and behold behind him a ram caught in a thicket by his horns: and Abraham went and took the ram, and offered him up for a burnt offering in the stead of his son.

2.   The four relation disorders are: deficiency relation disorder, rejection relation disorder, self relation disorder, exclusion relation disorder. They were described as interpersonal pathologies, which help obtain a social perspective and clearer indications of who should be optimally treated in groups (Friedman, 2013).

3.   The escalation of hostile feelings and motivations to reject a group member who is perceived to be an obstacle for the group's ambitions is a process worthy of investigation in itself (Hopper, 2003b).

4.   I have included mothers as well as other members of war communities in what I call a "soldier's matrix", in which everyone is enlisted, becomes identified with a military ideal, and marches together (Friedman, 2013, 2015).

5.   I do not mean the army, or organisations in which decision-making is a sharp, clear, and speedy process and the participation has group-as-a-whole purposes.

References

Behr, H., & Hearst, L. (2005). *Group Analytic Psychotherapy*. London: Whurr.

Berman, A. (2011). The Jewish groom and the broken glass: men's transformation of passion. In: L. Navarro, R. Friedman, & S. L. Schwartzberg (Eds.), *Desire, Passion and Gender. Clinical Implications* (pp. 5–18). New York: Nova.

Doron, Y. (2014). Primary maternal preoccupation in the group analytic group. *Group Analysis, 47*(1): 17–29.

Foulkes, S. H. (1948). *Introduction to Group Analytic Psychotherapy*. London: Heinemann [reprinted London: Karnac, 1991].

Foulkes, S. H. (1975). *Group Analytic Psychotherapy: Method and Principles*. London: Gordon and Breach [reprinted London: Karnac, 1986 & 1991].

Friedman, R. (2013). Individual or group therapy? Indications for optimal therapy. *Group Analysis, 46*: 164–170.

Friedman, R. (2015). Using the transpersonal in dreamtelling and conflicts. *Group Analysis, 48*(1): 45–60.

Frosh, S. (2016). Born with a knife in their hearts: transmission, trauma, identity, and the social unconscious. In: E. Hopper & H. Weinberg (Eds.), *The Social Unconscious in Persons, Groups, and Societies: Volume 2: Mainly Foundation Matrices* (pp. 3–20). London: Karnac.

Garland, J., Jones, H., & Kolodny, R. (1973). A model for stages of development in social work groups. In: S. Bernstein (Ed.), *Exploration in Group Work* (pp. 17–71). Boston, MA: Milford House.

Hopper, E. (2003a). The fourth basic assumption: Incohesion: Aggregation/Massification or (ba) I:A/M. In: *Traumatic Experience in the Unconscious Life of Groups* (pp. 66–90). London: Jessica Kingsley.

Hopper, E. (2003b). Aspects of aggression in large groups characterized by (ba) I:A/M. In: S. Schneider & H. Weinberg (Eds.), *The Large Group Re-Visited: The Herd, Primal Horde, Crowds and Masses* (pp. 58–73). London: Jessica Kingsley.

Liberman, M. A., Yalom, I. D., & Miles, M. (1973). *Encounter Groups: First Facts*. New York: Basic Books.

Owen, W. (1920). *The Parable of the Old Man and the Young*. London: Sassoon.

Rustomjee, S. (2009). The solitude and agony of unbearable shame. *Group Analysis, 42*(2): 143–155.

Schlapobersky, J. (1993). The reclamation of space and time: political applications of psychotherapy. Conference—The Political Psyche, Institute of Contemporary Arts, London. Medical Foundation Proceedings, 27 November.

Schlapobersky, J. R. (2016). *From The Couch To The Circle: Group Analytic Psychotherapy in Practice*. London: Routledge.

Von Trier, L. (2003). *Dogville*. Lions Gate Films.

Winnicott, D. W. (1958). Primary maternal preoccupation. In: *Through Paediatrics to Psycho-Analysis* (pp. 300–305). London: Tavistock.

CHAPTER SIX

The black hole in the social unconscious: a collective defence against shared fears of annihilation

Yael Doron

I n this chapter, I discuss the concept of the social unconscious in group analysis. I focus on the "black hole" as a collective or social defence against extremely painful shared anxieties. I illustrate the use of the collective black hole with data from a group analytic group.

The social unconscious

The concept of the "unconscious" constitutes one of the cornerstones of psychoanalytic theory. According to the *Language of Psychoanalysis* (Laplanche & Pontalis, 1967, p. 381), "If one wished to summarize the Freudian discovery in one word, it would undoubtedly be that of the *unconscious*". Although Foulkes (1948), the founder of group analysis, was a Freudian psychoanalyst, he introduced the concept of the social unconscious in order to stress the importance of sociality and socialisation in the life of persons and groups. In the context of field theory (Lewin, 1951), the social unconscious came to include notions of relationality, transpersonality, transgenerationality, and collectivity (Hopper & Weinberg, 2016). Moreover, as Foulkes shifted from the "collective mind" to the "foundation matrix" and the "dynamic matrix", the theory of group analysis began to function as a bridge between sociology and contemporary psychoanalysis (Hopper, 2009), and the conceptualisation of the social unconscious became central to the basic theory of group analysis (Hopper, 2011).

Historically, the theory and concept of the social unconscious can be traced to the work of Marx, Weber, and Durkheim, as well as to many other sociologists and social psychologists in Europe and the USA. The Foulkesian concept of the social unconscious is both similar to and different from Jung's concept of "collective unconscious", Pichon Rivière's "co-unconscious", and also to Moreno's "interpersonal unconscious" (Hopper & Weinberg, 2011). Foulkes used the concept of the social unconscious in reference both to the internalised social world of which people were unaware and to the properties of the external social world of which people were unaware. Unfortunately, he did not elaborate his conceptualisation of the social unconscious, define it systematically, or explain how he used the concept in clinical work (Doron, 2014a; Hopper & Weinberg, 2011).

As a sociologist and psychoanalyst as well as a group analyst, Hopper often discussed the concept in detail with Foulkes. On the basis of these discussions, Hopper (1996) eventually defined the concept of the social unconscious in terms of

> . . . the existence and constraints of social, cultural and communicational arrangements of which people are unaware; unaware, in so far as these arrangements are not perceived (not known), and if perceived not acknowledged (denied), and if acknowledged, not taken as problematic ("given"), and if taken as problematic, not considered with an optimal degree of detachment and objectivity. (Hopper, 2001, p. 10)

Based on Foulkes' writings, Dalal (1998) described two possible views regarding the social unconscious: according to the orthodox view, the social unconscious is not conscious, because it is automatic, just like walking or driving; a more radical view is that the social unconscious is part of our personal matrix, created when the social penetrates into the individual. According to this view, the social unconscious is the structure, the container, or the very "bones" of the psyche.

The concept of the social unconscious has been defined as a part of the individual unconscious, located inside it, but has also been defined as a property of society itself (Hopper, 2001). Weinberg offered an intersubjective definition that positions the social uncon-scious in a transitional space: "The Social Unconscious is the co-constructed shared unconscious of members of a particular social system such as community, society, nation or culture" (Weinberg, 2008, p. 150). Weinberg (2009) emphasises that when aiming to reveal the social unconscious of a particular social system it is especially important to consider the anxieties, fantasies, myths, and collective memories, as well as chosen traumas and chosen glories (Volkan, 2001) that are typical of it.

For various reasons, social trauma is of particular importance in the formation of the social unconscious of societies and other social systems such as organisations (Hopper, 2012). It is important to consider collective defences against shared anxieties that have been caused by social trauma, such as secrecy and normative taciturnity (Hopper, 2003a). I wish to consider another collective defence.

Black holes as a collective defence

In astronomy, a black hole is a region of space–time which exhibits such a strong gravitational pull that no particle or electromagnetic radiation can escape from it, not even light. Since they do not emit light, black holes cannot be observed, and their existence can only be deduced from phenomena that are caused *by* them. This resembles Freud's view of the unconscious as ". . . an unconscious conception . . . of which we are not aware, but the existence of which we are nevertheless ready to admit on account of other proofs or signs" (Freud, 1915e, p. 161). As the product of a denial, the "material" of a psychological black hole is neither available for narrative nor readily visible. This material can be apprehended only through indirect indi-cations of it, such as slips of the tongue and other parapraxes, the repetition of mal-patterns of relationship, etc., which can be regarded as symptoms of anxiety associated with matters that have been repressed and/or denied. Nevertheless, just like other phenomena that have been made unconscious, psychic black holes control our actions as well as our feelings and thoughts related to what has been made unconscious.

Psychoanalysis has utilised the image of the black hole several times in the past. Ullman (1975) argued that the processes that occur in the dream which transform implicit material into explicit material begin in the black hole of the psyche and end with words and meaning. Drawing on the theory of negative hallucinations, Bion (1970) used the term "black hole" to describe the "infantile catastrophe" of the psychotic patient. Glasser (1979) conceptualised the black hole as the characteristic defence of the "core complex" of perversions as a defence against psychosis. Grotstein (1990, p. 378) understood the black hole as "the ultimate traumatic state of disorganization, terror and chaos". Hopper conceptualised (2003b) a process of encapsulation as a form of protective disassociation with respect to the fear of annihilation, separation, and death, following the traumatic experience of catastrophic loss in the earliest stages of development. He argued that an encapsulation was associated with a psychic black hole, but that it was unclear whether the black hole existed within the self or within the other, or within both. Hopper (1995) also argued that the black hole was typical of the defensive structures of drug addicts of various kinds. Eshel (1997, p. 195) described the gaps between sessions in psychoanalytic treatment, especially the therapist's vacations, as "black holes of discontinuity in the containment and in the holding environment of the treatment". In summary, the concept of the black hole has been used to refer to the consequences of denial and/or disavowal as a defence against the fear of annihilation as a consequence of various kinds of traumatic experience, including strain and cumulative and catastrophic trauma. The black hole has also been used to refer to the defence itself.

I would hypothesise that black holes exist not only in the mind of an individual person, but also in the dynamic and foundation matrices of his groupings, ranging from small groups who meet for the purposes of psychotherapy to organisations and their contextual societies. These collective black holes are associated with material that the members of a particular social system deny and/or disavow, because the recognition of such material would give rise to guilt and shame, various distorted patterns of relationship, and even the fear of annihilation, separation, and death. Actually, the recognition of these feelings and the open discussion of the phenomena that cause them can also precipitate attempts to change the situation, which is likely to set up a further set of anxieties (Hopper, 2000).

How does this kind of collective defence develop? In her discussion of the relationship between a therapist and the patient, Eshel

(1997, p. 199, translated for this edition) asks, "how can the therapist experience the patient's emotions . . . when the experience is one of a 'black hole'—of being gripped, sucked into, distorted and annihilated by enormous forces of death and destruction?" Bollas (1987) discussed what he called the "un-thought known" in the context of the analytic situation in which the suffering of one person becomes the illness of two persons.

Similarly, in a therapeutic group, the mental pain of a person and, especially, the mental pain of two persons in a relationship can become the pain of a group as a whole, or, at least, of a sub-group of it (Friedman, 2007). If we wish to build a bridge between psychoanalysis and group analysis, we need to remember that "groups become the personal and collective transitional, mediating and self-objects of their members" (Hopper, 2009, p. 412). Hence, processes that exist in persons are enacted and recapitulated within the "here and now" of the group through projective and introjective identification and group specific processes, such as resonance, mirroring, condensed phenomena, and so on. Thus, we can see a collective black hole as a collective defence against shared anxieties of the people in the group, and it is especially relevant to clinical group work with traumatised patients, and especially within the context of organisations and societies that might themselves be traumatised, such as Israel (Nuttman-Shwartz & Weinberg, 2008).

Clearly, groups can and do co-create collective representations within their dynamic matrices of situations from the "there and now" and "there and then" that are characterised by feelings of helplessness and loss involving chosen traumas and chosen glories as elements of the foundation matrix. Hopper (2007) has discussed these processes in terms of equivalence, group microcosm, and traumatophilia. These collective black holes are highly likely to endanger the group as a whole as well as every individual member of it, because they are unconsciously re-lived and re-enacted in the "here and now", long before the material emerges consciously.

"Friendly fire" attack

I will now present a clinical vignette from a session of a clinical group that illustrates a collective black hole in its dynamic matrix in the context of the foundation matrix of the wider contextual society in which the group was embedded.

About a year ago, I introduced a new participant to my analytic group. My group was seven years old. It was composed of three men and two women, between twenty-five and fifty years of age. All of them had been members of this group for at least one year. Three of them were in combined therapy with me, one was in individual therapy with me before entering the group, and the last one was in individual therapy with another therapist before joining this group.

The new member, Barak, was severely wounded six years before during his military service, in a "friendly fire" incident. (The expression "friendly fire" describes a situation in which a military or police force opens fire on its own soldiers due to misidentifying the target as hostile. The expression is based on an oxymoron: a linguistic expression composed of two contradicting components that, when put together, create a new, paradoxical meaning.)

In the first months of Barak's participation, I felt how the "friendly fire" attack was re-enacted over and over again in the group sessions. With time, I began to realise that the term "friendly fire" is a fundamental element of the Israeli social unconscious, which controlled and affected us as a group.

The context of Barak's injury was the war in Gaza in 2009, in which approximately 1,300 Palestinians were killed. The Israeli forces had ten casualties. Four Israeli soldiers were killed in two "friendly fire" incidents. In addition to these, dozens of other soldiers were physically and psychologically injured during these incidents.

Barak was one of those severely injured soldiers. After a difficult and intensive day in battle, he and his comrades went to sleep in an empty building in a Gaza city neighbourhood. A communication failure led to their misidentification as a hostile force and the incident ended with an Israeli tank shelling them. Two soldiers died on the spot, whereas Barak was severely injured. He was unconscious for many weeks, and, after he regained consciousness, most of his body remained paralysed for a long time, during which he had numerous operations. His right arm was amputated below the elbow and, with time, replaced with a prosthetic arm. His capacity to move his left hand remained limited. He also suffered from a head injury, due to shrapnel pieces sprayed into his brain. In addition to all these injuries, there was also the psychological trauma.

Six years had passed since the injury, during which Barak under-went physical and psychological rehabilitation. I met him when he participated in a group of IDF disabled veterans, which I facilitated in the Ministry of Defence. A short while afterwards, he approached me seeking individual therapy, and, as a part of his rehabilitation process, I invited him to join "normal" group therapy.

Barak's joining of, and adaptation to, the group was not simple, to put it mildly. The significant difficulty that emerged made me think that the group was re-enacting in the "here and now" the intolerable experience of a "friendly fire" attack. I will demonstrate this point by using a vignette from the session in which Barak joined the group.

Usually, when a new member was about to join the group, I noti-fied the group a month in advance, sharing with them only one detail about the new member—his name. In Barak's case, I made an excep-tion and asked the group members how they would feel about the joining of a member who was an IDF disabled veteran, and, as a result, had a prosthetic hand and other injuries. In retrospect, I think that this unusual preparation constituted an unconscious reaction to the vague sense of danger I had felt prior to Barak's joining.

At first, the group members reacted with acquiescence. Later, they dedicated a prolonged period of time to discussing Barak's approach-ing introduction to the group. The reactions to the expected entrance varied from one week to the next: in the beginning it was charac-terised by indifference ("No problem, you can bring him in"), then some of them denied the problem ("I saw yesterday on TV a disabled man who had recovered wonderfully . . ."; "My neighbour is an IDF disabled veteran . . ."), but, at the same time, questions and doubts began to emerge ("Perhaps I will be scared to talk to him, what gives me the right to address him, me, who did nothing important in the military?"). Midway, the atmosphere had transformed to anger towards me, and they accused me of being discriminatory towards the disabled ("Actually, we are all disabled, each of us for his own inter-nal reason"; "Why do you even present this to us in this way, as if we have the right to choose or to decide not to accept him?"; "This is your prejudice against the disabled. You should have just brought him and that's that"). Eventually, everyone agreed to allow Barak to join the group.

The decision that was made was accompanied by optimistic comments ("Perhaps we have something to learn from him"; "Maybe we can help him fit into healthy society"), alongside heavy concerns ("Now the group progress will stop"; "Maybe in the future we will regret agreeing to this").

The process of preparing Barak for the group was also longer than usual and was probably influenced by my concerns. We dedicated a long time to exploring his expectations and wishes from the group. Together, we tried to picture possible scenarios of the group's reactions to him and *vice versa*.

Despite the prolonged arrangements, nothing prepared me for what actually occurred in the "joining session".

When I walked into the clinic, I found Barak sitting in one of the chairs in the waiting room, and in front of him, sat Yonatan—a long-time group member. I greeted them. Barak said that he arrived over an hour ago because he was afraid of being late. Later, it turned out that Yonatan was also there with him in the waiting room during that time. Yonatan knew very well who was sitting in the chair in front of him but did not dare to say a word to him. Only after I arrived and talked with them did Yonatan greet Barak and introduce himself. Soon after that, he returned to his tense silence.

In the meantime, Orit, the group's longstanding member, entered the clinic. She sat down next to Yonatan and started talking to him very loudly with uncharacteristic enthusiasm, turning her back towards Barak to avoid greeting him.

Immediately afterwards, Romi, another group member, entered. She went to the kitchen, poured herself a glass of water, and remained there "in hiding" until the beginning of the session.

The last to arrive was Gadi, a flight attendant who was very used to expressing politeness. He sat down beside Barak and introduced himself, and even shook his left hand (which was almost paralysed, but not a prosthetic).

The last group member—Alon—did not show up at all to that session and did not notify me of his absence. I could feel, through his absence, his great fear of meeting Barak. Later he explained that he had "forgotten" the group, for the first time, after two years of punctual arrivals to the sessions.

This unusual welcome that took place in the waiting room before the session foreshadowed what was about to occur later. The session itself strangely combined two opposing movements: on the one hand, the group members ignored Barak completely, talked only to each other and continued discussions and updates from the previous sessions. On the other hand, each of them demonstrated a kind of "presentation" of themselves, that supposedly was not addressed to Barak, and reported significant and uncharacteristic steps that they had taken in the preceding week: one of them signed up for a dating site after many months of hesitation, another participant went for a date after a long period of avoidance, a third participant signed up for school, and a fourth member had an extraordinarily open conversation with her mother. None of the participants made eye contact with Barak, introduced themselves, or asked Barak to introduce himself.

After some time, I decided to intervene and said, "I see that it's not easy for us to welcome Barak, even though we have prepared ourselves for a long time. Perhaps it is not so simple." After a short silence, the group members decided that they really should do "official" introductions, and suggested introducing themselves in turns. Yonatan was the first to begin, explaining thoroughly how difficult it was for him to get used to the idea of Barak's joining, and the process he went through, until he finally realised that his joining could be beneficial for him and for the group. He spoke very lengthily, with too much exposure for this early phase, without noticing how hurtful his words were. In his speech, he used the word "disqualified" three times, until finally, when he ended a certain sentence with the question, "does it make sense?", Barak replied sarcastically, "Yeah, I got it: I'm disqualified."

The other members' introductions were slow, bizarre, and estranged, in my experience. My attempts to make it easier for them or to normalise the situation repeatedly failed. At a certain point, I gave up. I realised that this was what needed to happen—the welcoming had to be weird and strange for all of us.

Barak, who I had known in an IDF veterans' health care group as a dominant, funny, and talkative young man, was almost completely silent throughout the session. In the last five minutes, the group members asked him to say something about himself and he replied with one laconic sentence: "I'm Barak, from a settlement in the south of Israel. I'm twenty-four years old." The questions he was asked following this sentence, and throughout the next sessions, were related to his rehabilitation only—did he work? Did he study? What would he like to do in the future? The question about the accident—what had actually happened to him—was not asked and was left hanging in the air for many weeks. It came up for the first time after ten more sessions, two and a half months after Barak had joined the group.

I left the first session with Barak feeling that it was the wrong deci-sion to introduce him into the group and that we were all going to pay for this mistake. I knew that I had already been shaken several times before by the introduction of new members to the group (Doron, 2014b), but this time it seemed more extreme. I was angry with myself; I thought that I had not prepared the group and Barak well enough and that I had damaged all people concerned. The expression "friendly fire" continued to buzz in my head.

In the next few weeks, the group space was filled with feelings of guilt, anxiety, and aggression and with mutual vulnerability of the group members. Long before the story of Barak's injury unfolded, the term "friendly fire" hovered in the air, "attacking" us. Using Foulkes' terms, we could say that the group was already "playing it out in the room" and the symptom was "mumbling to itself secretly, hoping to be overheard" (Foulkes & Anthony, 1957, p. 259).

One of the roles of the group conductor is to "translate" the symp-toms to the group in a way that offers them insight and understand-ing, which is considered by Foulkes (1990) as the first stage in the healing process. In contrast, the term "friendly fire" implies the blind-ness of the leader of the forces, that is, the group's therapist, and, indeed, part of the processes that took place in the group resulted from my blindness as a group conductor, beginning with how I prepared the group for Barak's joining, followed by the panic and guilt I was struck with when I felt that the group "was not all right" and did not welcome Barak sensitively and appropriately. I had a hard time being patient and allowing the process of Barak's entrance to the group to occur. As a result, not infrequently, it was also I who attacked the group and participated in the "friendly fire" process, which resulted in a state of deep insecurity for all participators.

"Friendly fire" as an example of a
black hole in the social unconscious

Ever since Barak had joined the group, the "friendly fire" motif was expressed in a variety of ways within the group. It had traces in the communications by the group members as well as in the relations that developed among them. Thus, for example, the repeated attempts of the group members to get closer and help each other resulted in reciprocal attacks. "Friendly fire" was present in the room, expressed in thoughts, but no less in the emotions: the aggression, anxiety, and mostly in the guilt that controlled us. We all attacked and suffered attacks, injured each other and were injured.

All the group members (including me) are Israelis who served in the army and we all have siblings or children serving in the IDF. We are all living in a "soldier's matrix" (Friedman, 2015), and, as such, were all raised on slogans connecting us directly to states of wars, survival, and glory, such as "It is good to die for our country", "You do not leave wounded on the battlefield", and the officer's command in the battle: "Follow me". We all occasionally hear of disasters occurring in the military service and are overwhelmed with anxiety. But, as opposed to the heroic stories, we have no myth, song, story, or national memory that deals with the "friendly fire" issue.

I believe that the very term "friendly fire" resides in the dark part of the foundation matrix, within its deep, hidden areas of collective black holes. Thus, the exposure of a collective black hole elicits anxiety, aggression, guilt, and shame, and exposes the feelings that have been blocked from perception. These feelings attack all the more forcefully those people who survived such events and stayed alive. The feeling of losing the "safe place" remains with them for the rest of their lives (Friedman, 2013). This was Barak's personal experience, but it resonated with the experiences shared by all of us as representatives of the people of Israel, sending their children to war time after time.

The therapeutic group can turn out to be the place in which the severe injury is re-enacted over and over in the "here and now", but it can also become the safe place that enables reparation and growth (Friedman, 2007), a positive psychic retreat (Mojovic, 2011). In the months that followed the events described in this chapter, we have learnt, and continue to learn, how to turn the group into a safer place. Mainly, we have tried to understand how to stop being caught in the hurtful dynamics of "black holes" that originate in the foundation matrix but which are recapitulated within the dynamic matrix of the group.

Epilogue

The term "friendly fire" in Hebrew—*Esh Kochotenu*—means, literally, "the fire of our forces". When I wrote this chapter, I checked the most popular Hebrew dictionaries, and was amazed that I could not find this term—not under the word "fire" and not under "force". The phenomenon of "friendly fire" is so common, and occurs, unfortunately, in every war and many military routines. So, why do the Hebrew dictionaries omit it? Is it an accident? A consequence of a lack of attention? I think not. In my opinion, ignoring "friendly fire" is not a matter of conscious, deliberate policy. Instead, it represents a social or collective denial and/or disavowal—a black hole within the social unconscious of the Israeli people—matters that we cannot allow ourselves to be aware of, at least not fully.

References

Bion, W. R. (1970). *Attention and Interpretation*. London: Tavistock.

Bollas, C. (1987). *The Shadow of the Object*. London: Free Association Books.

Dalal, F. (1998). *Taking the Group Seriously: Towards a Post-Foulkesian Group Analytic Theory*. London: Jessica Kingsley.

Doron, Y. (2014a). The Israeli social unconscious as revealed to me during the GASI International Summer School in Serbia. *Group Analysis, 47*: 128–141.

Doron, Y. (2014b). Primary maternal preoccupation in the group analytic group. *Group Analysis, 47*: 17–29.

Eshel, O. (1997). On "black holes", death and analytic existence. *Dialogues ('Sihot'), 11*: 195–205 [in Hebrew].

Foulkes, S. H. (1948). *Introduction to Group Analytic Psychotherapy*. London: Karnac.

Foulkes, S. H. (1990). *Selected Papers*. London: Karnac.

Foulkes, S. H., & Anthony, E. J. (1957). *Group Psychotherapy: The Psychoanalytic Approach*. London: Karnac.

Freud, S. (1915e). The unconscious. *S. E., 14*: 161–215. London: Hogarth.

Friedman, R. (2007). Where to look? Supervising group analysis—a relations disorder perspective. *Group Analysis, 40*: 251–268.

Friedman, R. (2013). Overcoming shame through dreamtelling. *International Journal of Counseling and Psychotherapy, 10–11*: 39–44.

Friedman, R. (2015). Soldier's matrix. *Group Analysis, 48*: 239–257.

Glasser, M. (1979). Some aspects of the role of aggression in the perversions. In: I. Rosen (Ed.), *Sexual Deviation* (pp. 278–305). Oxford: Oxford University Press.

Grotstein, J. S. (1990). Nothingness, meaninglessness, chaos and the 'black hole' II. *Contemporary Psychoanalysis, 26*: 377–407.

Hopper, E. (1995). A psychoanalytical theory of drug addiction: unconscious fantasies of homosexuality, compulsions and masturbation within the context of traumatogenic processes. *International Journal of Psychoanalysis, 76*(6): 1121–1143.

Hopper, E. (1996). The social unconscious in clinical work. *Group, 20*(1): 7–42.

Hopper, E. (2000). From objects and subjects to citizens: group analysis and the study of maturity. *Group Analysis, 33*: 29–34.

Hopper, E. (2001). The social unconscious: Theoretical considerations. *Group Analysis, 34*: 9–27.

Hopper, E. (2003a). *The Social Unconscious*. London: Jessica Kingsley.

Hopper, E. (2003b). Encapsulation as a defence against the fear of annihilation. Appendix II. In: *Traumatic Experience in the Unconscious Life of Groups: The Fourth Basic Assumption: Incohesion: Aggregation/ Massification or (ba) I:A/M* (pp. 199–211). London: Jessica Kingsley.

Hopper, E. (2007). Theoretical and conceptual notes concerning transference and countertransference processes in groups and by groups, and the social unconscious: Part II. *Group Analysis, 40*: 29–42.

Hopper, E. (2009). Building bridges between psychoanalysis and group analysis in theory and clinical practice. *Group Analysis, 42*: 406–425.

Hopper, E. (2011). Foreword. In: E. Hopper & H. Weinberg (Eds.), *The Social Unconscious in Persons, Groups, and Societies. Volume 1: Mainly Theory* (p. xvii). London: Karnac.

Hopper, E. (Ed.) (2012). *Trauma and Organizations*. London: Karnac

Hopper, E., & Weinberg, H. (Eds.) (2011). *The Social Unconscious in Persons, Groups, and Societies. Volume 1: Mainly Theory*. London: Karnac.

Hopper, E., & Weinberg, H. (Eds.) (2016). *The Social Unconscious in Persons, Groups, and Societies. Volume 2: Mainly Foundation Matrices*. London: Karnac.

Laplanche, J., & Pontalis, J.-B. (1967). *The Language of Psychoanalysis*. London: Karnac.

Lewin, K. (1951). *Field Theory in Social Science. Selected Theoretical Papers.* Washington, DC: American Psychological Association.

Mojovic, M. (2011). Manifestations of psychic retreats in social systems. In: E. Hopper & H. Weinberg (Eds.), *The Social Unconscious in Persons, Groups, and Societies. Volume 1: Mainly Theory* (pp. 209–232). London: Karnac.

Nuttman-Shwartz, O., & Weinberg, H. (2008). Organisations in traumatized societies: the Israeli case. *Organizational and Social Dynamics, 8*: 138–153.

Ullman, M. (1975). The transformation process in dreams. *American Academy of Psychoanalysis, 19*(2): 8–10.

Volkan, V. D. (2001). Transgenerational transmissions and chosen traumas: an aspect of large-group identity. *Group Analysis, 34*: 79–97.

Weinberg, H. (2008). The social unconscious. *Dialogues ('Sihot'), 22*: 149–159 [in Hebrew].

Weinberg, H. (2009). The Israeli social unconscious. *Collection ('Mikbatz'), 14*: 11–28 [in Hebrew].

CHAPTER SEVEN

The immune system and group analysis: communication between "self" and "non-self"

Nurit Goren

"Between the body of birth,
the body of present
and the haste of its wanderings,
the body of death is present"
(Lider, 2005, translated for this edition)

Introduction

This chapter compares certain aspects of the work of one of my analytic groups to the biological immune system that operates in our bodies. Concepts of mechanisms from immunology are used to examine the communication within the group and the ways of maintaining the dialectical destructive and creative forces in it. The tension between the group's "immunity" and its dealing with "foreign invaders" and "self-destruction" presents the group and its conductor with complex challenges to their clinical work.

About the immune system

We live in a world filled with bacteria, viruses, parasites, and mould, which are found in the air, water, soil, and in all the organisms that surround us. Most of the time we live in harmony with them, but sometimes some of them invade our tissues and cells. If they are not confronted, they are likely to generate serious injuries or even kill. None the less, given their large numbers, it is surprising that we are affected by only a small number of diseases which can be traced to these invaders. Most people are equipped with a sophisticated and effective system, which operates around the clock and ensures our good health: the immune system (Ackerman, 1986).

This immune system runs a sophisticated and complex "fight" on multiple fronts. Our health depends on the order and the match between the body's cells, tissues, and organs. The immune system maintains the balance in our bodies through the destruction of any "non-self" organism, including variable and proliferating cancer-causing cells, or foreign invaders, which can cause serious illness and infections. If the system detects a sign of belonging to the "self", it is likely that it will cherish the material. If the system discovers signs of "non-self", it usually attacks, aiming to destroy the invader (Cohen, 2000). By deciding which will be the hosted cells in our body, the immune system builds the human border. It defines its cellular individuality, creates, documents, and even protects it. One of the most important characteristics of this system is the immunological memory. Exposure to a foreign factor, which it has already faced in the past, evokes a memory response that allows it to act vigorously against the polluter, removing it effectively and preventing the development of disease.

Immunity, however, is not only a blessing. It can turn upon the body itself and damage vital organs, thereby causing a devastating set of so-called autoimmune diseases (such as multiple sclerosis, juvenile diabetes, lupus, etc.). Normally there are checks and balances mechanisms in the system that regulate and prevent it from attacking the body itself. But, for various reasons, such as heredity, environment, age, as well as those that are idiopathic, interference is created, and the immune system attacks the organs of the body as if they were foreign invaders. In fact, Shoenfeld (2001) uses a military term to describe autoimmune diseases, "Shooting on our forces", referring to the military failure in identifying its associates, sometimes due to a disconnection in communication, which carries the risk of creating victims. Cohen (2000) argues, metaphorically, that autoimmune diseases occur when our guardian becomes our antagonist.

Autoimmunity is essential to the healthy behaviour of the immune system, and, consequentially, our bodies and mental health. There is no absolute antigenic distinction between the self and the not self. The immune system can recognise and respond to either. The ability of our lymphocytes to recognise our own antigens is of critical importance to our health and survival. The danger of acting against components of self creates a well-controlled balance of immune cell forces between the "anti-self-cells" and other immune cells that directly control the anti-self potential of those cells and, thus, create a delicate balance. When the body mistakes parts of it as being foreign and attacks them, the immune system destroys the attack that threatens the body ("anti-self cells" network), "attacking the attacker" ("anti-anti-self cells" network), either by killing it or by causing the attacker to commit suicide, and, thus, returning the system to balance. Sometimes, destruction can be essential to creation (Cohen, 2000, pp. 191–192).

About group analysis and the dialectic approach

Once the participants enter the group space, a tension begins between opposing forces, alternating between harmony and disharmony, creativity and destruction, progression and regression. Psychoanalysis has, as always, dealt with the complex connections between life and death, construction and destruction, good and bad, love and hate. Forces that advance and hinder the development of the group are not isolated, but are in a complex, persistent relationship, similar to the relations between Eros and Thanatos: "Neither of these instincts is any less essential than the other; the phenomena of life arise from the concurrent or mutually opposing action of both" (Freud, 1933b, p. 208).

Winnicott believed that what really affects the infant's capacity to be integrated is the ability to differentiate between "me" and "not-me". For him, that is the way to be "a whole person, with an inside and an outside, and a person living in the body, and more or less bounded by the skin" (Winnicott, 1988, p. 90). Further elaborated, "in favorable circumstances the skin becomes the boundary between the me and the not-me. In other words, the psyche has come to live in the soma and an individual psycho-somatic life has been initiated" (Winnicott, 1988, p. 90).

Foulkes, the founder of group analysis, saw the group as a rich therapeutic resource. He conceptualised the foundation matrix as based not only on the biological properties of the species, but also on society and culture (Foulkes, 1975, p. 15). Foulkes believed in existence of the death instinct as a "universal biological phenomenon" (Foulkes, 1971, p. 246), and connected it to destruction and self-destruction. For him, "Nothing is more certain than the ubiquity of destruction—a fact difficult to accept" (Foulkes, 1964, pp. 138–139). He recognised the reciprocal relations between progressive and regressive forces, but that most of the time ". . . aggression could be canalized into constructive directions in the group" (Foulkes, 1964). Foulkes saw the disease as a result of "the society and inter-personal processes" (Foulkes & Stewart, 1969, p. 24), but also as a disruption in the free flow of communication. Hence, "when autistic meaning is converted into social meaning then communication flows again and health is restored" (Dalal, 2000, p. 58).

Nitsun (1996) thinks Foulkes failed to appreciate the oscillation between destructive and constructive forces that occur during the life of the group (Nitsun, 1996, pp. 8–11). Nitsun's concept of the anti-group refers to a system of references, attitudes, and impulses, conscious and unconscious, which represent the destructive forces. These forces, directed against the group itself, threaten its functioning and its cohesion, but are also important as a functional nucleic forming creative impulse. As long as there is a balanced dialectical motion between the poles, the flow and normal development of the group will be possible (Nitsun, 1996, pp. 42–45).

I examine the group's "immune system" by making a comparison between processes occurring in the group with terms from immunology.

Death shows

Seven people were meeting for the first time. The newness, the strangeness, the anxiety associated with beginning a new analytic group, as well as the excitement and curiosity, all came to a standstill in the face of Nira's bombshell twenty minutes after the first meeting began. Nira announced that she would not be able to attend the meeting scheduled for two weeks hence, because her twenty-eight-year-old sister should be undergoing surgery to remove a brain tumour. The group had yet to be born and it was already being forced to deal with the fear of death.

Death's appearance at the first meeting created a unique pattern of claiming a place in the group through dramatic stories. It seemed that the positioning depended on the intensity of the tragedy told. At one of the sessions, Ronnie described it: "Nira holds a trump card, death wins everything."

Death stories also serve as initiation rites conducted by the senior group members to the newcomers. This is how their ability to survive was tested. It was a kind of repetition compulsion of the "test" experienced by the senior members at their first meeting, but also an attempt to deny feelings involved in separation and in familiarity with the new. In immunological terms, it is possible to compare it to how the implant saves lives in the human body, while it is being attacked by the immune system, which considers it to be a "foreign invader". It is essential to identify the exact balance between the weakening of the strength of the group in order to integrate the new while maintaining the strength of the existing members.

Death appearances, which accompanied the group in the early stages of its existence, sowed seeds of destruction, but were an equally important part of its struggle for existence, serving its survival and its development.

During a meeting that took place one year after the start of the group, I was informed that Nira's sister had died. After the end of the meeting, six of the seven members of the group decided to visit Nira at her home. Consoling the bereaved custom in Shiva is important in the Jewish religion, but the group members knew that they had violated one of the group rules, which prohibited meetings outside of therapy sessions. In the next meeting, the group members looked at me with some subservience, along with a sense of victory.

It is possible to understand it as "acting out", breaking the group rules and boundaries. Breaking the therapeutic setting by patients, a subset, or group as a whole, is a critical issue in therapy. Hoffman points to the dialectic that exists between the official position of the therapist, and his personal inclination, that responds to the needs of the patient, to react from a personal place. Hoffman opposes the linear conception, which claims that maintaining the therapeutic setting allows security and violation of it creates a danger (Hoffman, 1994).

Inwardly, I thought that this was not the appropriate time and place for an interpretation about acting out. I realised that the "immunity" of the group had been tested a long time before the real death occurred, which penetrated and threatened its work and increased its anxiety, with its feelings of guilt and aggression.

In retrospect, I understood that what had occurred was enactment, which involves the members, the group-as-a-whole, and the conductor (Wright, 2005). Sometimes, "acting out may serve as proof that the body and drives are still alive" (Roth, 1979, p. 11). It was as if the group had forced me to take part in the breaking of boundaries, from within a shared, unconscious, omnipotent fantasy that this condolence visit would "save" the group from the both tangible and metaphoric dying that had invaded and taken up long-term residence within the work of the group. After a while, I said,

> "You chose to meet outside the group, to be with Nira in the Shiva. I believe it was your way of finishing the journey of death that accompanied us this year, thus trying to save the group and bring it back to the path of life. Maybe you also did it because you tried to save me, too."

The statement reassured the group, fear of blame and punishment was dissipated, and we were able to rebalance the group's "immune system". The transformation occurred in more advanced developmental stages, with the distressing recognition of the existence of destruction and aggression wishes, along with life wishes and thanks to the group's "immunological memory".

Bion refers to the double motion, which occurs in learning from experience, as the basis of the acquired experience during learning, but also as a waiver of past experience, in order to enable new learning (Bion, 1962). In the same way, the immune system organises itself through experience, "helping us adapt to life and so preserve us, and makes a record of what has happened" (Cohen, 2000, p. 5).

An attack on the attacker

Self-destruction

Aviv, journalist and author, was in individual therapy for many years. When he joined the group, he chose to present himself in a haughty and dismissive tone. He focused on his new relations with me as someone who had abandoned him. Thus, he re-enacted a traumatic experience related to his mother, who abandoned him after the birth of his sisters. His longing for an exclusively dyadic relationship encountered a reality in which I shared my attention with rest of the members—an unbearable situation for him—and he fought my statements and ignored the words of his "siblings" in the group. Aviv diminished the value of any assistance offered to him at the meetings. The interventions operated in front of him as a "malignant mirroring" (Zinkin, 1983), a reflection of a persecutory experience of a person standing before the truth that is revealed to others, but he is not ready for it. He experienced all communicative experience as dangerous and contaminated. Group members were afraid of his reactions, but, through their avoidance, they collaborated in the reduction of communication in the group by reducing self-disclosure and authenticity.

At one of the meetings, Aviv was attacked by some members of the group. They accused him of destroying the group and informed him that they were not ready to go on like this. In spite of my attempts to contain his anxieties and to recognise his longing for an exclusive connection with me, I could not calm his wishes or soothe his anxiety. Aviv could not remain in the group, and, after a year and a half, he left.

Aviv adopted an "autistic" self-defence and stubborn destructive attitudes, unable to turn them into words. In immunological terms, he represented the group "anti-self", which attacks the "organs of the group". Because of a "mistake in interpretation", his distorted behaviour affected his understanding the group's meanings. Aviv represented the yearning of group members for exclusiveness, but, because of his desire to take revenge, he was ready to destroy the others and even himself. The tendency towards intense hostility and towards self-destruction and the destruction of the others was the result of "malignant narcissism" (Kernberg, 2009, p. 1019).

The attack on Aviv was caused by the desperate wish of the participants to save the group. This was similar to the immune system's struggle against "self-destruction". Did Aviv's "suicide" save the group from annihilation? We will never know. In a way, his leaving stopped the development of "autoimmune disease".

Self-destruction

Yafa was single and thirty-five years old. Envy burned in her when two group members announced their pending weddings. Those weddings symbolised her failure with the opposite sex. In order to absolve herself from the painful condition of envy, she had to damage and hurt the group. She did this by tardiness, quiet but massive attacks on the work, and threats to leave the group. These threats became a pattern, taking over and creating damage in the group space by "silently" attacking the communication.

At one meeting, after she announced yet again her wish to leave the group, I said,

> "It seems that the only way you allow yourself to have a meaningful place here is through the threat of leaving."

Later, I connected this pattern to her complex relationship with her married partner. Yafa was excited in the context of this "insight" and announced that she would stay in the group.

In the next meeting, she announced that she had finally decided to quit the group. Yafa spoke in a quiet detached tone, with a kind of stoic, estranged calm. In her words, she made a split between her ideal individual therapist and the disappointing group that made "no contribution".

After this, I felt restless in the face of the solidarity of the group members and their attempts to please Yafa. The room was filled with countless empty words, attacking the group space and communication. Denial of the aggression in Yafa's behaviour created a "group-immunisation" against feelings of competition and envy, and, thus, the destructive power of envy was untouched (Nitsun, 1996).

The envy, the false communication, and the "anti-self" responses of the entire group, enraged me and made me anxious about the destruction of the group.

After unsuccessful attempts to expose the fantasies of destruction from their isolation and to translate them into words, I said, towards the end of the meeting,

> "Today, everything here is nonsense . . .",

but the group's members pretended they did not hear me at all.

After the meeting, disappointed and frustrated with myself, I wondered why I was not able to release the group, and also myself, from its angst. I recognised the difficulty that lay within me, coping with "elusive" aggression, one that destroys authentic communication, which could alert my instincts and activate my aggression. In retrospect, I realised that the group communicated in a transpersonal modality (Foulkes, 1971). Feelings of envy and fear of annihilation received a form of helplessness that penetrated the souls of the group's members in a transpersonal way and created a defensive matrix. The group almost destroyed itself, but my aggressive feelings, which were directed towards the group, revived it again. In the next meeting, the group members responded to my words in different ways. They were angry as well as sympathetic. Recognition of the failure and understanding of its group context calmed the anxiety and it was possible to transform this event into an open and emotional communication.

In immunological terms the "attack on the attacker", which could hurt the group even more, had eliminated the group's "anti-self" and allowed the healing forces to re-emerge. Was this a matter of luck, dicing with my own self-destructiveness and even destructiveness of the group, a kind of postnatal envy of them of what I was trying so hard to give them? After all, the wars of autoimmune sponsors begin in the womb.

An attack from the outside

"Foreign invaders"

A few years ago, a Palestinian suicide bomber blew herself up near Gaza. At the time, the media reported, with scathing criticism, on the brutal behaviour of the Israeli soldiers. The terrorist had reached the checkpoint, passed the inspection under false pretexts, and in one moment exploded. Three soldiers and a civilian were killed.

That evening, our group met. Only four members arrived and the meeting was characterised by long periods of silence and a sense of suffocation.

> Dina: I didn't feel like coming to the group today. Avi [her husband] can't find a job and is thinking of dropping out of his studies. I'm sick of being the only breadwinner in the family, I don't feel like taking care of Avi—if I talk to him there would be an explosion [silence].

> Meyer: I'm depressed, do not leave the house, do nothing. What's the point of having succeeded when my presentation is being bashed? The

Israeli society does not know how to protect its artists . . . [and I thought to myself that maybe he spoke about my inability to protect the group] [silence].

Ronnie: [academic, unemployed] It's a country that devours its inhabitants; I'm considering emigrating to the USA, perhaps there I would find myself [silence] . . . even at home I have no place . . . well, it's not interesting, never mind . . . [silence].

Nira: I've had a terrible explosion with my mother, but I do not have the desire to talk about it today [silence].

Four people struggled with the need to assert their existence in words in the face of their lack of ability to communicate. The inner reality, with its different representations, was paralysed with fear of the external reality. The communication was flat and emotional defence made the group members alienated. The room was flooded with the basic assumption of "'incohesion' through which group members oscillate between aggregation and massification, based on fission and fragmentation in oscillation with fusion and confusion in their doomed attempts to overcome the traumatic experience" (Hopper, 2001, p. 150). For a moment, I was captivated by the collective alienation of the group. However, I knew that this had to be transformed into more self-reflective clinical work. None the less, even I withdrew into myself, as I was frightened of the flood of intolerable feelings. I wondered if it was necessary to touch the pain, to fight the defences— but these very feelings made it clear to me that I should find words that would release the group from its chains. I knew I had to find a context for the group's alienation and a meaning for the anxieties, in order to restore the dialogue to the group space. After a while, I responded,

"What comes to my mind, regarding the atmosphere in this room, is connected to the explosion at the Erez checkpoint today. When the external situation is so outrageous and feelings of despair and hopelessness are rising, each group member builds a barrier around himself, to prevent 'blowing himself up', or 'detonating' the group."

The linking process is especially difficult and threatening during a period like this, because it requires meeting with unbearable feelings that threaten and endanger us, and sabotage the wish to deny and not to feel. The ability to verbalise feelings in view of the vulnerability outside, as well as the vulnerability and the attacks inside the group, enables a release.

The immune system, by determining which cells will be hosted in our bodies, builds the borders of each person.

A traumatised country, whose borders are not marked, which finds it difficult to distinguish between friends and foes, threatens its social immunity and the wellbeing of its citizens. In the face of a society that is stuck in polar behaviour patterns, the group was able to return to its "balanced dance".

The "immunity" of the conductor

At the initial stage of the baby's life, the mother lends her immune system to her helpless baby. While nursing, a two-way system operates and an intersubjective dyad is tuned; the baby's saliva secretes components to the mother's nipples that stimulate her immune system to produce antibodies which the baby needs to survive foreign invaders (Cohen, 2000, Hassiotou et al., 2013).

Could I, during the early stages of the group, lend my "immunity" to decode distress signals and to find them a precise reply? Did I learn to allow the group to wean itself from its needs of dependence and encourage it to flourish?

As any new "mother", I tried to create a good enough enabling environment, to hold, contain, and recognise the forces of destruction along with the creative forces, to accept the intensity of anxiety that accompanied the entire group and myself, to repair "shorts" in the group communication, and to invert destructive fantasies into words and dialogue.

I chose to contain the "group revolt" (arrival of the Shiva) and interpret it as a life-saving operation. I chose to bear a group that "puts to death" a valued patient because it cannot tolerate his/its claim to exclusiveness. In Yafa's case, the group was able to activate my aggression, but, in an interesting way, it was all for the best. Finally, when we were all exposed to a transgressed threat—a terror attack— I tried to collect the remnants of my immunity, to breathe, and to respond to the group and its "immunity" through objective evidence, from my intersubjective place.

Over time, our "immunological memory", along with the ability to survive and grow out of crises, made it possible to return the dialectical motion to the group space and transform a "suckling" group into a mature one, a group where the conductor was not an exclusive therapeutic factor and the group members mutually healed each other.

Discussion

Proper and accurate communication between the immune system cells is critical to our physical health. The system cells tend to talk to each other in a language composed of chemical signals. Each cell transmits and receives messages, designed to stimulate or inhibit other cells and regulate their activities. A breakdown of proper communication among the immune cells leaves the body defenceless (Ackerman, 1986).

The decisive impact of communication on our physical health is strikingly similar to the role of communication in the group's health. Through an awareness of the flow of communication in the group, the members develop higher capacities of participation in the interpersonal and the transpersonal space, to improve interactions. As in the immune system, the transpersonal processes create communication with a special quality, made possible by high permeability between participants' selves (Friedman, 2014). Sometimes, this communication creates "transpersonal cohesion" in the group, designed to protect it from intolerable anxieties, leading to a defensive group matrix. On the other hand, sometimes, this flow enables a fruitful dialogue that promotes recovery and creates a channel to mental change.

Foulkes argued that the psychopathological aspects, caused by an interference to the free flow of communication, decrease at the moment they become understandable and communicative to the participant and to the group. When communication is achieved, the energy that was invested in efforts to come out of the communicative isolation is released and is invested in creative activity and in growth. Thus, a movement is created from "autistic" communication to free communication, from the language of symptoms to the depths of meaning (Foulkes, 1948).

I suggested immunological mechanisms for those occurrences when the group's immunity fails to act in defence. I presented moments in which "death appearances" accompanied the group and worked as "multiplying cells" flowing through its body, and "social inflammation", as in the terrorist's attack, penetrated its mind's skin. The risk of destruction revived itself, restored in the group, and activated different "anti-group" mechanisms. The group's immunity was undermined and it became difficult to deal with the fragility of life in the light of the repeated forays of death. Usually, the recognition of the developmental and creative powers of destruction, and the ability to survive them and turn them into discourse, allowed an end to the threat of "illness".

In other meetings, however, the aggression and destruction threatened the group. At these moments. "autoimmune factors" attacked the group from the inside, which threatened to destroy it. As with the immune system, this occurred due to a failure in identification. Thus, Aviv and Yafa joined the group with narcissistic nourishment in mind. Because of their "helplessness and powerlessness, loss and separation, fear of damaging and being damaged" (Hopper, 2001, p. 142), they experienced the group as an "enemy" that was coming to destroy them, so they attacked the therapeutic space and blocked the communication. In view of this behaviour, the group and/or the conductor responded with an "attack on the attacker" in order to save them and the group. This terminology sounds dramatic and aggressive, but it is the key to our integrity and homeostasis, to the transformation of the forces of destruction into dialogue. As communication became freer, and it became possible to have a discourse around attacks, destruction fantasies, pains, losses, and damages, the group's immune system was strengthened, thus enabling creativity and development.

Acknowledgment

Dedicated to Professor Lider, Weizmann Institute of Science, who taught me much more than immunology.

References

Ackerman, G. J. (1986). The healer within. In: L. Thomas, S. Schiefelbein, G. J. Ackerman, & I. Anderson (Eds.), *The Incredible Machine* (pp. 217–219). Washington, DC: National Geographic Society.

Bion, W. R. (1962). *Learning from Experience*. London: Heinemann.

Cohen, I. R. (2000). *Tending Adam's Garden: Evolving the Cognitive Immune Self*. London: Academic Press.

Dalal, F. (2000). Some group-specific ideas. In: *Taking the Group Seriously. Towards a Post-Foulkesian Group Analytic Theory* (pp. 52–59). London: Jessica Kingsley.

Foulkes, S. H. (1948). *Introduction to Group Analytic Psychotherapy: Studies in the Social Integration of Individual and Groups*. London: Heinemann.

Foulkes, S. H. (1964). *Therapeutic Group Analysis*. London: Allen and Unwin [reprinted London: Karnac, 1986].

Foulkes, S. H. (1971). The group as matrix of the individual's mental life. In: E. Foulkes (Ed.), *Selected Papers of S. H. Foulkes* (pp. 223–234). London: Karnac.

Foulkes, S. H. (1975). *Group-Analytic Psychotherapy: Methods and Principles*. London: Gordon and Breach [reprinted London: Karnac, 1986].

Foulkes, S. H., & Stewart, P. G. F. (1969). *Psychiatry in a Changing Society*. London: Tavistock.

Freud, S. (1933b). Why war? *S. E., 22*: 197–215. London: Hogarth.

Friedman, R. (2014). Group analysis today: developments in intersubjectivity. *Group Analysis, 47*: 194–200.

Hassiotou, F., Hepworth, A. R., Metzger, F., Ching, T. L., Trengove, N., Hartmann, P. E., & Filgueira, L. (2013). Maternal and infant infections stimulate a rapid leukocyte response in breast milk. *Clinical & Translational Immunology, 2*. Accessed at: www.nature.com/cti/journal/v2/n4/pdf/cti20131a.pdf.

Hoffman, I. Z. (1994). Dialectical thinking and therapeutic action in the psychoanalytic process. *Psychoanalytic Quarterly, 63*: 187–218.

Hopper, E. (2001). Difficult patients in group analysis: the personification of I: A/M. *Group, 25*: 139–171.

Kernberg, O. (2009). The concept of the death drive: a clinical perspective. *International Journal of Psychoanalysis, 90*(5): 1009–1023.

Lider, O. (2005). *Between Time. Poems and Prose*. Tel Aviv: Hakibbutz Hameuchad [in Hebrew].

Nitsun, M. (1996). *The Anti-Group: Destructive Forces in the Group and Their Creative Potential*. London: Routledge.

Roth, B. E. (1979). Problems of early maintenance and entry into group psychotherapy with persons suffering from borderline and narcissistic states. *Group, 3*: 3–22.

Shoenfeld, Y. (2001). *Autoimmunity Diseases: "Shooting on our Forces"*. Jerusalem: Ministry of Defense [in Hebrew].

Winnicott, D. W. (1988). *The Maturational Processes and the Facilitating Environment*. New York: International Universities Press.

Wright, F. (2005). Valuing enactments in group therapy: discussion of three case studies. *Group, 29*: 399–406.

Zinkin, L. (1983). Malignant mirroring. *Group Analysis, 16*: 113–126.

CHAPTER EIGHT

The group "not-me"

Ilana Laor

Introduction

In the year 2003, I completed a four-year training programme in group analysis. As part of the programme, I conducted analytic group therapy with one group which consisted of seven participants over a period of three years. This period coincided with many serious terrorist attacks that took place on the streets and buses of Tel Aviv, often killing innocent civilians.

At the end of this programme, I wrote a final paper to fulfil the requirements for the diploma granted at the end. The paper dealt mainly with destruction and development in group analysis. It is only now—reflecting upon the experience in order to write the current chapter—that I realise that all the terrible events that occurred outside the therapy room at the time were not brought up by any of the participants. Neither did I refer to these events explicitly during the group sessions, although I do recall fleeting thoughts regarding the absence of this topic. Interestingly, I also did not refer to any of these events in my final paper. In retrospect, I believe that the participants and I did not bring up the events in the real world due to the unbearable emotions that they evoked and an unconscious fear of the group's disintegration.

In this chapter, I suggest using certain concepts in the intersubjective psychoanalytic literature for describing processes pertaining to members of a group. These concepts help the analyst identify various underlying currents in group analysis that might otherwise not be recognised, and to consider these currents. The specific concepts are: recognition and destruction (Benjamin, 1990), surrender (Ghent, 1999), multiple selves (Bromberg, 1998), and, especially, the concept of the not-me self (Bromberg, 1998; Stern, 2006). These concepts facilitate an understanding of processes of destruction and development in group analysis. I also demonstrate the relevance of each of these concepts to the group as a whole by means of a clinical vignette.

Development and destruction in therapy groups

The theory of groups is characterised by a type of polarity between a view of the group as facilitating the development of both the group itself and its individual members, and a view of the group as potentially impeding their development. Foulkes (1964) believed in the beneficial power of the group. Bion (1961) emphasised the tendency of the group to foster destructive processes. Roberts (1991) attempts to reconcile Foulkes' and Bion's respective ideas. He draws on two central concepts: malignant mirroring (Zinkin, 1983) and the anti-group (Nitsun, 1986). Regarding the notion of mirroring, Foulkes and Anthony (1957) compared participating in group therapy to being in a hall of mirrors, claiming that the effect of finding oneself in such a hall of mirrors is beneficial to the individual and to the group. In contrast, Zinkin argues that the view of oneself gained in the hall of mirrors can sometimes be experienced as intensely persecuting. Nitsun (1986) points out that the therapeutic group necessarily contains what he terms an anti-group, which refers to the destructive aspect of groups. According to Nitsun, the anti-group is not a static "thing" that occurs in all groups in the same way, but a set of conscious and unconscious attitudes and impulses that manifest themselves in different ways in different groups. Roberts (1991, p. 135) concludes his paper as follows:

> Foulkes' notion about destructiveness in the group was that the
> members of the group would apply their aggression to attacking one

another's neuroses, rather than one another . . . When a group enters a destructive phase this I believe no longer holds true. What one may then see is "destruction of the group, by the group, including the conductor".

In this chapter, I explain and extend the relationship between destruction and development regarding the individual and the group. From an intersubjective perspective, I suggest that destruction and development are actually two facets of a single process. Intersubjective concepts have been applied to group theory and practice (Billow, 2003; Brown & Zinkin, 1994; Friedman, 2014; Grossmark & Wright, 2015; Hopper, 2001; Pines, 1984; Rubenfeld, 2003; Yalom, 1995). I now elaborate on each of the relational concepts.

Basic relational concepts

Recognition and destruction

Destructive states or processes are existential states—we need the other to confirm our existence, but also protest against this need in both conscious and unconscious ways (Benjamin, 1990). This is the inherent tension between the destruction of the other by seeing him as a subjective object (Winnicott, 1969), that is, as the sum of my projections, and my need for the other to be external to me, to recognise me, and to confirm my existence, as well as arouse my curiosity. Destructive states or processes are neither specific phases in the development of the group, as suggested by Bion (1961), nor derivatives of destructive impulses or defence against them, as suggested by Roberts (1991). Moreover, they are not derivatives of the personal neurosis of the individuals in the group, as suggested by Foulkes (1964). Rather, the movement between destruction and development is part of a single process of expanding the individual and the group's respective emotional repertoires. At any given moment, recognition may occur, thus enabling the group as a whole, like each of the individuals in it, to attain a new stage of development.

What makes this movement between recognition and destruction possible? What impedes the fluctuation between these two states? I suggest that this movement is facilitated by the ability to surrender.

Surrender

Ghent (1999, p. 213) defined the difference between surrender and submission as follows: ". . . [Surrender] has nothing to do with hoisting a white flag . . . [The] term will convey a quality of liberation and expansion of the self as corollary to the letting down of defensive barriers".

Surrender facilitates movement within and between the partners of the interaction. According to Ghent (1999), the opposite of surrender is submission to the situation. That is, in terms of group processes, the individual becomes fixed in a group role. The individual is locked in his/her sole experience and submits to it, so to speak. In analysis, such situations are defined as enactments or impasses (for example, Benjamin, 1990; Davies, 2004; Jacobs, 2001). In these situations, each partner is unconsciously driven to an "I am right" position. Each of the partners in the interaction fears that her pain might increase if she changes her position. Mutual surrender becomes possible as both partners might feel that the possibility of surrendering is not dangerous.

Multiple selves

The ability to surrender is directly related to the individual's capacity to contain multiple and opposing versions of the self. Bromberg (1998) argues that the role of the analyst is to enable the restoration of self-states and the links between them in order to attain a state in which the individual might experience herself as capable of containing inner conflict. He argues that each person has a set of discrete, roughly overlapping schemata of whom she is, each of which is organised around a particular self–other configuration held together by a powerful affective state. He goes on to say the following: "It is when this illusion of unity is traumatically threatened with unavoidable . . . disruption that it becomes in itself a liability because it is in jeopardy of being overwhelmed by input it cannot process" (p. 98).

Not-me

According to Bromberg (1998) and Stern (2006), not-me[1] states are emotional states in which the individual does not recognise himself as the agent responsible for the situation at hand. In the case of patho-logical dissociation, or dissociation in the strong sense, "self-preser-vation is accomplished almost or entirely at the expense of growth, and the individual is removed from full involvement . . . in the here and now experience of life" (Roberts, 1991, p. 135). For certain people, here and now experience—the living present—cannot, in fact, be mentally experienced without the felt danger of traumatisation. The dissociation creates self-states that are not acknowledged as part of the self (not-me states) and, therefore, cannot be articulated. Analysts and patients alike may have their not-me states. Bromberg's and Stern's concept of the not-me resonates with Hopper's (1991) concept of encapsulation, which protects the individual from annihilation anxiety. The role of the not-me self is to protect the individual and the group from emotional experiences currently beyond their capacity.

I suggest that a group member's ability to acknowledge previously unrecognised self-states within himself might cause the group and the individuals within the group to progress from states of destruction to states of recognition, which results in the development of multiple self-states in both the individual members of the group and the group as a whole. The group leader participates in therapeutic processes just like the other members of the group. On the other hand, she is supposed to help them to progress from states of destruction to recog-nition in both intra- and interpersonal processes.

Clinical vignette

The purpose of this section is to describe an incident that occurred in one of my own groups in order to illustrate the interpersonal and intrapersonal processes mentioned above.

Description of the incident

From the moment Dana joined the group, she appropriated a special and singular place for herself. She usually arrived very late, making a lot of noise as she entered the room, putting down her bags, and removing her coat and scarves. Under her coat, she often wore a short miniskirt with a slit revealing one thigh and a very tight blouse emphasising her figure. Her hair was long and bouncy and her face was very pretty and appealing. After the typical dramatic entrance, which was often also accompanied by the ringing of her mobile phone, Dana would sink into her chair as if she were disappearing into it. It seemed that after all the fanfare and the struggle to make space for herself, the drama was over, and Dana seemed to have nothing more to contribute to the group. Sometimes, she would doze off. When she did speak, she did not try to relate to what had just been said. She seemed to be completely disconnected from herself and from the others in the group. The events described below occurred after approximately two years of group work.

Joel joined the group approximately one month before the incident described. All the members of the group, including Joel himself, had initially agreed to participate in the group for at least one year. However, Joel left the group only one month after joining it. He had evoked much hope and curiosity among the other participants and had formed a special relationship with Dana. He seemed to be particularly fond of her. He presented himself as a man who often felt rejected and did not dare to make contact with other people. None the less, the group regarded him as a man of great promise for the group. When he left, he said that he was going to India because of its festivals for vegetarian women, and he was going to look for a bride. The women in the group tried to tell him that there were vegetarian women in the group, too, but emotionally he was already on his way to India. To the outside observer, this description of events might sound bizarre and almost psychotic. However, it did not sound that way to the members of the group, which was made up of intelligent people (all of whom were university graduates) dealing with extreme emotional difficulties and distress.

At the meeting following Joel's departure, I rearranged the chairs, leaving out Joel's chair. The group had been meeting for over two years and the participants knew that it was standard practice after someone left the group to remove their chair. During this meeting, Dana arrived late as usual. Her high heels made tapping noises and her mobile phone rang as she entered the room. She added a chair to the circle, which she took from the pile of additional chairs in the back of the room. She placed her bag on this chair and, with a loud sigh, sat down on the chair next to it.

I commented that by adding another chair to the circle, Dana seemed to be making a statement. Dana gave me a puzzled look and said, "I needed a chair for my bag." I tried again, and said that introducing another chair into the group was meaningful, "Perhaps it is a statement regarding what is absent." Dana responded, "But the bag needed a chair." Or, in other words, a bag is a bag and a chair is a chair and beyond that, things have no meaning. I tried again, as I was not willing to go along with the group's destruction of its capacity for symbolisation. This therapeutic group had been meeting for two years and had engaged in symbolic interpretation in the past. I regarded this particular denial of the meaning of the bag and the chair to be regressive. Although there are additional reasons for my attempts to ascribe symbolic meaning to the events that took place in the group, in retrospect, it is now clear to me that my insistence on interpreting the meaning of the empty chair was an enactment. From this moment on, the entire group seemed to side with Dana against me, whereas I positioned myself against them. I commented that Dana's introduction of the chair was a message from the whole group to me, and that Dana was the spokesperson delivering this message. The group as a whole informed me that I was mistaken. Without giving it much thought, I then made a slightly ironic comment, "The Holy See." (In Hebrew, the phrase Holy See—that is, the Pope and Vatican City—is derived from the same root as the word for "chair".) The group members immediately understood my irony regarding the specific event concerning the chair. Dana laughed and repeated "the Holy See". The group seemed to be relieved and the enactment seemed to have been forgotten. For the remainder of the meeting, the members of the group spoke mainly about their emotional reactions to the way Joel had entered the group and then left it:

Tom said he was jealous of Joel's determination.

Gali spoke about Joel's behaviour, which was against the rules of the group. She felt I had erred in accepting him to the group.

Anna said that Joel had introduced new content and hope.

Dana said that she was anxious about the stability of the group.

Analysis of the incident

The group

The group's working through Joel's departure seemed to help the members of the group as well as myself. It allowed me to think that perhaps I, too, was anxious about the fate of the group and that this had led me to insist on interpreting the significance of the bag and the chair over and over again. In hindsight, I believe that this anxiety was due to a process of projective identification, that is, the group's fear that the group would disintegrate, as well as the personal history of certain group members (for example, broken homes in which the parents were divorced, or families where a parent had died and the children were sent to boarding school). As a child of parents who had lost their families in the Holocaust, I readily identified with their projections.

During the above event and also towards the end of the group process, I had difficulty identifying my own feelings and emotions. Dana, the other group members, and I were all trapped in a negative experience that none of us could understand or explain at the time. Any attempt at interpretation on my part only made things worse. It was only when I made the ironic comment regarding the "Holy See" that we could somehow begin to unravel and work through this enactment.

As noted earlier, the word *See* in Hebrew, in the phrase *Holy See*, which refers to the Pope and the Vatican, is derived from the same root as the word for "chair". In the Israeli or Jewish social conscious and unconscious, any reference to the Vatican is often associated with Pope Pius XII, who allegedly failed to save Jews from annihilation during the Second World War. My ironic remark seemed to resonate with the group's expectations and subsequent disappointment. They expected Joel to bring hope to the group and were disappointed when he suddenly left and their hopes were not realised. They were disappointed in me since I had failed to shelter the group from any experience of disintegration. My reference to the Holy See was, in effect, an unconscious interpretation of the events that occurred in the group. In making this remark, I surrendered to another self-state, which was not my formal role as group facilitator. In effect, this also allowed the group to surrender to a group self-state other than the previous one, in which the group resisted any interpretation. Getting out of this trap was made possible by the "Holy See", which made it possible for the group and I to regain our ability to think, which, until that moment, was under attack. One might say that the "Holy See" was an event where I did not insist on my interpretation, and did not retaliate against the group's rejection of it, and the group was able to acknowledge this. However, I am proposing that this event entailed a great deal more than this. The event of the "Holy See" was an act of mutual recognition. I understood that the group was not allowing me to take the route I had taken, and that the group was not accepting the interpretations I was offering, and so I stopped. I gave in, but only seemingly. In fact, this was a moment of surrender in the sense that Ghent (1999) intended:

With my statement "the Holy See", I relinquished a certain interpretative direction but I did not relinquish my asymmetrical role (of course, only one aspect of my role) of interpretative leader because, at the same time as I relinquished the interpretation which stemmed from conscious understanding, I actually produced from within myself an interpretation stemming from a place that I was not conscious of, from an other self inside me. This interpretation resonates within me to this day, giving rise to more and more memories and personal meanings that I had no contact with at the time of the event.

"The Holy See" was a statement from my unconscious that met the group unconscious, thus creating relief and unravelling the impasse. In retrospect, it seems to me that the meaning of my statement for the group was as follows: "We all seem to be saying something similar, the meaning of which is not yet known to us, because neither you nor I can understand what it is about right now". It seems to me that the statement "The Holy See" managed at that moment to preserve the mystery, the authority of the unknown, the unformulated experience, the unconscious, which somehow belongs to all of us and which, for each of us in a different way, remained unattainable. The term "The Holy See" connects the argument about the chair with its unattainable but potential meanings which was open potentially to all of us. This statement, as I say, was loaded with a lot of meaning for me: how do I feel as that group leader, on whose chair am I sitting theoretically and in my clinical practice, the place of humour in my life as a grown-up, as a therapist, and as a child growing up with parents who survived the Second World War, lost their families, knew a lot of sorrow in their lives, relinquished their religious faith, but had a special place for humour in their lives. Humour helped us as a family to step out from difficult situations. My father, who was the one to rely on emotionally and financially, also went through difficulties with his health (inflicted on him during the war). Humour was his special way to step out of difficulties and we as a family cherished it without really giving it special attention. Maybe, instead of looking for a great help from the outside world and from the "group analytic authority", I leaned emo-tionally on my inside group, my family, as a place for help and the group followed me.

Thus, paradoxically, the event of the "Holy See" can be regarded as an act of mutual recognition of our ability as a group to formulate a joint understanding of our experience. However, as I say, I only understood the significance of this particular moment in hindsight.

Dana and her multiple selves

What happened to Dana during this meeting? Which selves of hers were expressed? Dana was the eldest child of a family in which there had been many battles between the parents, who eventually divorced. Dana had been "chosen" by her father, who regarded her as a promis-ing athlete. When Dana went through puberty, her athletic perfor-mance weakened. Subsequent to this, she felt that her father aban-doned her, who, in her words, no longer loved her. She had become the disappointing child. When her parents separated, Dana's standing in the family deteriorated even further. She became the black sheep of the family because, as she put it, her mother sought revenge for the relationship Dana had had with her father.

As is characteristic of group meetings in general, different and varied selves emerged at the meeting described here, which the partic-ipants did not necessarily identify with, but which manifested them-selves in the group. The participants were exposed to these selves. As the group developed, these selves were gradually appropriated by their owners in processes which are beyond the scope of this chapter.

I shall now describe Dana's different selves as manifested in the group. Dana identified with the story of having been chosen and then abandoned by her father, and her mother's subsequent acts of revenge. However, additional selves, which are described below, were expressed in the group. For the sake of clarity, I have given each of these selves a name.

The chosen and abandoned self

The event of Joel's leaving the group was so traumatic for Dana that she was unable to express it in words. Her relationship with Joel had been a repetition of her experience of having been chosen and then abandoned by her father. When her father left, her mother took revenge on her and she became the black sheep of the family, whereas this negative experience did not reoccur within the group. The experiences of isolation and rejection were not repeated in the transference. The group joined Dana in standing up to me. My insistence on interpreting the meaning of the chair might have been experienced by Dana as my having put myself in the position of the retaliating mother, specifically when I commented that she was destructive. Dana realised that the present does not necessarily have to repeat the past and that repair was possible. Dana was now capable of being there for herself and for the group in roles that differed from those that she had internalised as a result of her personal history. After the event of "the Holy See", Dana found herself both supported by the group and also not abandoned by me. For the first time, Dana brought her sense of humour to the group meeting.

The humorous self

The self with a sense of humour was a side of Dana that was previously unknown to the group.

The leader self

Not only was Dana not a black sheep during this event, but she also became the group leader. When Dana surrendered and stopped confronting me, so did the rest of the group.

The group members, who were capable of verbally expressing what Joel represented for them, made it possible for Dana to be helped and to express her anxiety about the disintegration of the group.

Dana and the group's not-me

As described above, in the first session after Joel had left the group, a struggle developed involving Dana, other members of the group, and me regarding the additional chair that Dana had brought into the circle. In my opinion, this was an enactment; all of us were dissociating since we feared that the group would disintegrate. It was only after my sarcastic comment regarding the Holy See that Dana began to talk about her fear that the group might fall apart. It was then that the group really began to work and that I myself realised that I had also been afraid that the group would disintegrate. In other words, this fear constituted a not-me for Dana, the other group members, and myself.

I suggest that the group participants' fear of the disintegration of the group was so dominant that they could not process the dramatic events currently occurring in the real world outside. In my experience as a group facilitator, in most group processes, group participants do often refer to events in the real world. I believe that the anxieties experienced by the group participants and myself were not only due to our respective personal histories or processes occurring in the group, but were reactions to the frequent terror attacks in Tel Aviv.

Epilogue

Surprisingly, it had not previously occurred to me that therapeutic processes—whether they involve individuals or groups—should have characteristics unique to a specific place or environment. As noted earlier, it was the invitation to write a chapter for this volume that triggered a reflective process and led me to analyse the therapeutic processes I had previously encountered and am currently involved in. This last summer (July–August 2014) was also a traumatic period for most Israelis due to the war in Gaza and the south of Israel. It is interesting to note, in both individual and group therapy that I have been conducting since this last summer, I encountered the same phenomenon described above. That is, patients and group participants rarely mentioned traumatic events concurrently occurring in the outside world. The context matters. Yet, sometimes it cannot be acknowledged, since the members of the group are strongly dissociatiated from the recognition of it (Hopper, 1982). Patients and analysts alike need to live their not-me states together.

Note

1.   Bromberg's and Stern's concept of the not-me is very different from Winnicott's concept of the not me, which referred to the characteristics of a developmental stage (Winnicott, 1992).

References

Benjamin, J. (1990). Recognition and destruction: An outline of intersubjectivity. In: S. A. Mitchell & L. Aron (Eds.), *Relational Psychoanalysis: The Emergence of a Tradition* (pp. 183–200). Hillsdale, NJ: Analytic Press.

Billow, R. M. (2003). *Relational Group Psychotherapy: From Basic Assumptions to Passion*. London: Jessica Kingsley.

Bion, W. R. (1961). *Experiences in Groups*. London: Tavistock.

Bromberg, P. M. (1998). *Standing in the Spaces: Essays on Clinical Process, Trauma, and Dissociation*. Hillsdale, NJ: Analytic Press.

Brown, D., & Zinkin, L. (1994). *The Psyche and the Social World: Developments in Group-Analytic Theory*. London: Routledge.

Davies, J. M. (2004). Whose bad objects are we anyway? *Psychoanalytic Dialogues, 14*: 711–732.

Foulkes, S. H. (1964). *Therapeutic Group Analysis*. London: Allen and Unwin.

Foulkes, S. H., & Anthony, E. J. (1957). *Group Psychotherapy, the Psychoanalytic Approach*. Harmondsworth: Penguin.

Friedman, R. (2014). Group analysis today—developments in intersubjectivity. *Group Analysis, 47*(3): 194–201.

Ghent, E. (1999). Masochism, submission, surrender: masochism as a perversion of surrender. In: S. A. Mitchell & L. Aron (Eds.), *Relational Psychoanalysis: The Emergence of a Tradition* (pp. 211–243). Hillsdale, NJ: Analytic Press.

Grossmark, R., & Wright, F. (2015). *The One and the Many: Relational Approaches to Group Psychotherapy*. New York: Routledge.

Hopper, E. (1982). Group analysis: the problem of context. *Group Analysis, 15*(2): 136–157.

Hopper, E. (1991). Encapsulation as a defence against the fear of annihilation. *International Journal of Psychoanalysis, 72*(4): 607–624.

Hopper, E. (2001). The social unconscious: theoretical considerations. *Group Analysis, 34*(1): 9–27.

Jacobs, T. (2001). On misunderstanding and misleading patients: some reflections on communications, miscommunications, and countertransference enactment. *Relational Psychoanalysis, 2*: 175–205.

Nitsun, M. (1986). *The Anti-Group: Destructive Forces in the Group and their Creative Potential*. London: Routledge.

Pines, M. (1984). Reflection on mirroring. *International Review of Psychoanalysis, 11*: 27–42.

Roberts, J. (1991). Destructive phases in groups. In: J. Roberts & M. Pines (Eds.), *The Practice of Group Analysis* (pp. 135–145). London: Routledge.

Rubenfeld, S. (2003). Encouraging personal agency in analytic group therapy. *Group Analysis*, 36(3): 391–406.

Stern, D. B. (2006). Opening what has been closed, relaxing what has been clenched: dissociation and enactment over time in committed relationships. *Psychoanalytic Dialogs*, 16: 747–761.

Winnicott, D. W. (1969). The use of an object. *International Journal of Psychoanalysis*, 50: 711–716.

Winnicott, D. W. (1992). Aggression in relation to emotional development. In: *Through Paediatrics to Psychoanalysis: Collected Papers* (pp. 179–193). London, Karnac.

Yalom, I. D. (1995). *The Theory and Practice of Group Psychotherapy* (4th edn). New York: Basic Books.

Zinkin, L. (1983). Malignant mirroring. *Group Analysis*, 16: 113–126.

PART II
PRACTICE

CHAPTER NINE

On arrivals and departures in slow-open group analytic groups

Marit Joffe Milstein

I n this chapter, I focus on the joining and leaving of participants in a group analytic group during the course of their therapy, and on the challenges that these processes present to the group and the group analyst. Slow-open groups are not time limited and allow individuals to join and leave the group during the process according to their needs. Arrivals and departures are terms that can be understood in the context of the Foulkesian concept of "traffic" (Foulkes, 1975, p. 253).

Foulkes argues that the timing of a new member's arrival is crucial, since it can be experienced as a catastrophic interference if the group is in crisis, or as a reviving action when the group is at a point of lack of relatedness and movement. "In certain families, difficulties are sometimes resolved by 'getting a new child' . . . It is important before such events are contemplated that the group motivation is fully explored" (Foulkes & Anthony, 1964, p. 137).

When a patient arrives and/or departs, she has an experience that is at once both new and familiar. The opportunity to understand her arrival in the group over and over again through the hall of mirrors effect in connection with the arrivals of new members of the group, as well as the possibility of preparing herself for her own departure by watching others leave the group before her, is unique to the slow-open group, and simulates a situation that is similar to everyday life. In every arrival and departure, patients have the opportunity to experience themselves anew and from different angles, and to get to know their various reactions. A slow-open group does justice to the patient's needs by allowing her to finish her work in the group, and depart from it when she believes that she has completed her work in the group.

Foulkes and Anthony (1964) conceptualise the situations in which new members join the group while others leave it as a process that reflects a cyclical movement of life. It is a difficult, challenging movement that can interfere with the course of the group process, and lead to regression in individuals and/or in the group as a whole, but this movement can be productive, and can promote the development of the group and its members.

Foulkes (1975) argues that "if well handled the slow open group is nearer a closed group than is generally realized, and has great advantages over it. After all", he argues, "it is very much like life, that is to say, people are not together for ever and ever, but they come and go. There is a constant slow move to which to adjust" (p .69). However, Foulkes (1975) also notes that the main difficulty in slow-open groups lies in all that is involved in the arrival of a new member—that is, her selection, the timing of her arrival, the timing of the departure of another patient, and the ending of her treatment and her separation from other members, etc.

Behr and Hearst (2010) believe that "both arrivals and departures offer group members rich opportunities for working through psychic events such as loss and trauma. The group has to deal with losing established group members" (p. 31, translated for this edition). They say that the slow-open group simulates the member's original groups: the multi-generational family, school, and work groups, and it allows a dynamic working through of associated themes. Of course, whereas the patient and the therapist need to decide on the timing of arrival and departure from the group, the therapist also has to take into account the feelings of the other group members. However, Behr and Hearst also argue that a slow-open group that has no end-point in sight "sometimes provokes concern in would-be group members and referrers" (p. 31, translated for this edition). Nitsun (1996) writes that the slow-open group is prone to greater vicissitudes than more structured, time limited groups, and the ensuing uncertainties and ambivalence can feed the anti-group process.

In this chapter I would like to draw our attention to the therapist's experience of the arrivals and departures of patients in slow-open groups. The therapist can lose her capacity to reflect on her internal experience of these processes, and on what is unfolding in the treatment. This capacity can disappear when the immediate experience captivates the therapist, interfering with her capacity to think analytically. She can experience herself as shaking the secure environment in which the group acts, and, at the same time, participants lose their confidence in her and in the group as a whole. A conductor whose group members feel this way is likely to become even more anxious. From an intersubjective viewpoint, this can become a process of aggregation (Hopper, 2003). Special effort is required of the therapist and patients to define and make sense of the experience (Grossmark, 2007). However, it is possible that, as Ben Zur (2011) suggests, by the end of the therapeutic hour, a new space will have been opened, one that allows the revival of the fear of breakdown, but this time in safe conditions. It is likely that more than one therapeutic hour will be required to elaborate this process.

During these times of transition, there is often an increase in hostility and tension, directed variously at the therapist, participants, or the group as a whole; an increase in neurotic anxiety, a temporary loss of trust in the therapeutic process—cynicism, scepticism, absences, a weakening of group relationships and chaotic attempts to turn the clock back. For a while, it seems that the group is out of control and that there is a halt in the development of the group; a kind of paralysis of process occurs. Yet, after a period of time, these panic-related responses are likely to pass, and the benefits of group analysis are revealed once again. Feelings of togetherness, belonging, support, and mutual protection resurface. The recurring experiences of departure and arrival in the group provide a vehicle for reflecting on the growth and change in the conductor and participants. They promote an exploration of the intra- and interpersonal impact of the process of role reversal on the reactions of participants and conductor to these changes. At the same time, this allows members to learn more about the dynamic matrix of the group and the contextual foundation matrix of it.

In group supervision, I started to identify in my colleagues and in myself various complex and intense reactions to the arrival and departure of participants. Despite my own long experience as a patient in a slow-open group analytic group, the transition to the chair of the group analyst proved to be a complex and unexpected challenge. The example presented below is derived from an analytic group I conduct. Three men and two women participated in the group originally. In the sixth month of the group's life, one woman left; one year later, another woman left, and a man and a woman arrived.

First vignette: arrival and departure

Dor, one of the first participants in the group, who arrived along with Amnon, Roni, and Anna, announces that he has decided to begin the termination process. Amnon and Roni have strong reactions: Roni is angry about my quiet acceptance of the announcement and compares my reaction to Anna's case; Anna joined the group together with the three of them and left after six months. It seems to Roni that, at that time, I did not accept Anna's explanations and invited her to stay and explore her decision to leave. Amnon also reacts angrily and incredulously, saying, "Under what circumstance did Dor decide to leave now? I think that he should have consulted with the group first!" It seems that Amnon, who protests against being excluded from an important group decision and claims his right to influence it, implicitly raises a new theme, one of sibling competitiveness. Having started together, when Dor suddenly quits the race, it is as if he is telling the others: "I won! I finished before you!" Amnon shares his feelings of betrayal and anger at the loss of the balance established between them.

During the two months between his announcement and leaving the group, I asked myself why I accepted his decision to leave. I allowed myself to experience the great sorrow I felt, and the sense of loss, since Dor contributed to the group in a unique manner, sharing his coping mechanisms as a doctor with difficult, terminal patients. Amnon and Roni's intense reactions mirrored my own difficulty to separate from Dor, and my fear that the group would be poorer without him. During these two months, I received a new referral of a possible participant in the group, and decided to meet her to prepare her for the group, but I chose to delay her arrival in order to allow a proper separation.

In the first session after Dor's departure, I forgot to remove his chair from the circle. Embarrassed, I invited the group to understand the mistake together, and to see how it resonated with the participants in view of Dor's departure and the expected arrival of the new participant. It seemed that I was having a difficult time experiencing the narrowing of the circle, the absence, even for a few sessions. The patients, too, had a difficult time processing the event and filled the room with comments such as, "With all due respect, we had two months to deal with him leaving!" and preferred to talk about the expected addition to the group. I felt that the group chose to ignore my error, as if they were telling me, "It is your need to keep him in our memory, not ours!"

Amnon expressed his concern about the change in the balance between the genders and worry about the expected "cat fight". He looked mostly at me, while directly expressing his fears for the group's security and stability. I, too, wondered whether, and to what extent, we would be able to hold on to what we had built so far, whether what we had together was strong enough to shake it up with this new member.

Later, Yigal, the last man to join the group, became angry with the discussion in general and said, "Forgive me for being blunt, but it's like a form of masturbation and it doesn't work this way for me. When she comes—she'll come!" After which he softened, explaining that it is his way of coping with his lack of control over intolerable feelings elicited in him by arrivals and departures. I suggested that Yigal's words expressed his helplessness and anger towards me, who supposedly decides the timing: who dies and who is born. I felt stuck between group members' expecting me to be in control and my lack of it. I shared my reflection that masturbation questions the potency of both participants and conductor.

The entrance of the new participant evoked memories of the way Yigal's older sisters had persistently treated him only as their spoiled youngest male sibling.

About a month after Dor's departure, Orna joined the group. Rather soon, tension emerged between the women and the feeling was that, despite Rina's wish to have another woman join the group, the change bothered her. This experience resonated with a traumatic transition between educational settings she had experienced in the past, which devalued her position within her peer group in high school.

However, as the process went on, greater closeness between the women was achieved through the introduction and elaboration of feminine themes. Sibling competition and romantic relationships became part of the open dialogue in the group.

Second vignette: "together in life and death"

Four months later, Amnon announces that he intends to begin the termination process. The group is very surprised, since, in the past few weeks, it seems that Amnon has started to communicate his emotions more effectively, and begun to change the "analytic engineer" image he had in the group. Roni says he thinks Amnon should stay because his progress process has only started. Silence falls, after which Roni adds, "And besides, you beat me!", as he also intends to announce his leaving. The group and I cannot believe our ears. When the participants try to explore the reason for his decision, Roni replies, "I feel that even though there is always a lot more to do, I've had enough of therapy . . . two years is a long time . . . I want some air . . . I need a break from all this analysing!" The women react: Rina says that she feels strange; Roni is actually telling Amnon, "I can leave, but you, you should stay." Orna says that if they leave, she will feel as if she missed the whole relation, since she has not had time to get to know them. Yigal relates to the departures with supposed indifference saying, "What can you do, people come and go." This expression elicits a world war in the group, especially through the attack of the two women. They seemed furious with him, doubting their capacity to trust him, after the two other men will depart. Astounded, I observe the way in which the two abandoned women are furious with the man who is actually staying with them. Yigal is upset: "And if I tell them that I need them to stay for two more years, will that change anything? My real friends in life are always there for me!" The working through of this conflict demands that the group and I take a deep breath and contain what is experienced as an uncontained rampage.

In the next sessions, Roni becomes aware of the terror he begins to experience once he realises that he will be the last of the original trio to remain in the group, as if it has transformed him into the loser of the race. Realising the influence of this sibling rivalry on his former decisions, he announces to the group that he has decided not to leave.

The process helped him to attune himself to his own personal needs.

Catching me by surprise, Amnon reacts to Roni's announcement by expressing envy of Roni's strength of mind but sticking to his own decision to leave. I reflect to him that he is acknowledging both of their unique journeys, but may be unable to learn from Roni because of the competition and envy.

A few years later

The group is four and a half years old, and, once again, we are in the midst of a separation process from one of the participants. The group associates to overly strong bonds between mothers and children, which makes separation difficult. I join by sharing that it came to my mind that the sentence "people come and go" belongs to the group history. Orna laughs and says, "I was there, and you, Irit and Amir, only heard stories about it . . . it was so annoying and we made a fuss here!"

I let myself be carried by the past and present through the group history. Somehow, this dream-like state enables me to process and contain the recurring changes in the group's emotional movements.

From interference to mutual fruitfulness

The interruptions to the regular analytic rhythm caused by joining and leaving means the group has to move from the elaboration of the material the participants are preoccupied with to coping with separation and discontinuity of relations. Thus, various powerful themes emerge instead, mainly anxieties about rejection, exclusion, loss of stability, fragmentation, and death. The participants are confronted with defences against these anxieties—for example, wishes to escape from anxiety-provoking interactions in the group—and they find themselves examining reactions of denial and disengagement, fears of being taken over, and especially the implications of a change in gender composition. The group therapist's treatment of different people is scrutinised, and the participants wonder if her treatment and help in these critical situations reflects the importance of each participant in his eyes and in the group's hierarchy. "How much will she fight for me?", they ask.

Brown (1998) describes the sibling search for equality and fairness in their relationship with authority and argues that "a well-functioning group can replace rigid equality with flexible fairness" (p. 320). By starting to differentiate between the different treatments of participants as an expression of responding to their unique needs, our group grew more mature and able to separate from early attachments in the family.

Ben-Naftali (2000) offers another angle from which one can observe the occurrences between the men in the group, when she argues that this friendship always involves the knowledge that there will come a day when one will eulogise the other. The wish to co-operate through existential threats is expressed in the biblical verse "they were together in life and in death" (2 Samuel, 1:23). Aharoni writes in this context about the "impressive caesura of birth", "perhaps from pregnancy and birth we 'know' deep inside that there will come a day when one will eulogise the other, and this 'knowledge' is always resonated in the consulting room" (Aharoni, 2012, p. 142, translated for this edition). The continuous structure of the analytic group contains these registers: the conflicted desire to live and die together, and the re-enacted violations of "being". In the good, strong relationship between Amnon and Roni, they preferred not having to "eulogise" each other. The contagion (expressed by the joint wish to leave) can be understood not only in terms of competition, but also as being related to their deep friendship, closeness, partnership, and unwillingness to separate. The movement of the group member (Amnon, in this case) between different positions—that of the newcomer, that of the abandoned, and, finally, the "abandoner"—allows a broadening of the point of view and capacity to recognise and admire Roni's separateness. In the separation from Amnon, the participants meet his capacity to admire and encourage otherness and to recognise the group as a valuable place for him, which expresses his gratitude for the process—even if complicated and difficult—that the group undergoes as a whole. In the beginning, this was experienced as a catastrophic interference, but it was transformed into a fruitful process for both group and therapist.

Balance was created between the mirroring effect that acknowledges the participants' similarity, and exchange, which recognises and accepts differences and the unique value of each participant (Zinkin, 1994). Amnon, who felt valued due to his position as the group's elder, learnt to appreciate Roni, while Roni gained from his sibling recognition and permission to be different from him, and to act according to his own rhythm. The group seems to have grown and developed a greater capacity for tolerating differences and changes. The solution created by the group process, that is, the leaver's blessing of the remaining participants, allowed an appreciation and recognition of both positions, as well as of the group and conductor.

Reflection on the process experienced by the therapist

Throughout the process of working through the departures, I felt, at times, that I was infected with panic and general fragmentation anxiety that challenged my capacity to think. I was shaken, together with the group, from the position of the one that accepts to the position of the one left behind. At certain times, I experienced the group situation as a mirroring of my failure and as an attack on my sense of professional competence. Thankfully, the supervisory group served as a container for my difficult emotions and helped me to recognise both the anger that I felt towards the leavers and the appreciation. I also understood that my anger resonated the group's anger, which was not allowed to be expressed by the group members.

My countertransference has been significantly influenced by difficulties in my own early family history and, later, being a mother who gives birth. Only when I became a mother could I appreciate my own mother's difficulties in the first year of my life. In my own analysis, I became aware of the impact that "departures and arrivals" in my first year of life had on my ability to contain these changes as a conductor.

The first year of my life was shaped by the death of my maternal grandmother when I was three months old, as well as by my mother's pregnancy with my brother and his premature birth. Being then less than one year old, I seem to have been deeply influenced by this excessively intensive sequence of "arrivals and departures" which had unfolded since my own entrance to this world.

During the pregnancy, the child will try in his or her way to understand the mother's experience, and will become aware that the relationship with mother is changing. Changes in the mother foster changes in the child. Abarbanel (1983) found that the mother's own feelings of intensive and unresolved sibling rivalry could be amplified during the pregnancy, and seem to adversely affect her first child's preparation for arrival and his or her relationship with the new baby.

My experience as a new mother, giving birth to a premature baby, and the death of my mother-in-law just when my youngest daughter was born, contributed to my attitude towards those themes in the groups. It seems that, in my own motherhood, some of my early infancy's turmoil was repeated. All those experiences might unconsciously be revived in the group analyst before and during the arrivals of new participants. A supervisory group with group analysts who are willing to explore their countertransference during those times is necessary to provide a containing and elaborative space for the group conductor's growth (Doron, 2014).

Every time the group was forced to survive separation from a participant and, later, every time I introduced a new participant, I was blamed and attacked for undermining the group's feeling of security. I also experienced myself as a therapist guilty for not being able to protect her "children", doubting my decisions to accept new participants. I became suspicious of my own thinking, supposed to be influenced by my fears of the group falling apart, as well as by my financial needs. I longed for a stable working space for a while, without the turmoil that resulted from arrivals and departures.

In times of transition, the group therapist stands on the boundary on which arrivals or departures of group participants occur. Our responsibility for the departures and arrivals seems to become the main dilemma group analysts' face.

In the example presented above, I decided to dedicate all the time necessary to Dor's leaving process, and even to wait a few weeks before introducing the new member. This time was important to allow for a repeated exploration and assessment of the processes of arrival and departure from the group, both in my own mind and between the group and me. As a woman and mother of three, I learnt that every child enters the world in his own way: even though I always wanted to give birth naturally, my first was born prematurely and required special attention, my second was a natural birth, and my third required a C-section. There seem to be strong similarities to the birth of new group members in the group analytic group.

The next seven years as a group conductor immensely enhanced my experiences with the arrival of new participants. I had to accept the limitations of my capacity to control separation and inclusion processes and the limitations of my ability to control the transition resembled woman's capacity to control the timing or method of giving birth. In spite of the wish to control the process, it was actually the capacity to accept my negative capability that allowed me new degrees of freedom and helped me and my patients to grow.

The change I underwent is demonstrated in the following brief example: two weeks before Yigal left the group, Rina also announced that she started incubating the idea of finishing her participation in the group. During the subsequent transitory period, a potential participant had been waiting for a long time to join the group. It was during the "pregnancy" with him that Yigal, who had introduced to the group the ground-shaking expression, "people come and go", announced his leaving. The things that were being discussed in the group made me think that both the group and Yigal could benefit from the encounter between the men who are arriving and the men who are leaving. This was mainly because Yigal's departure highlighted and cherished the process that he had experienced in the group.

Yigal, the youngest child in his family, who, therefore, never had a little brother, now had the opportunity to function as a big brother. It could have been possible for him to receive the "admiring" gaze of the new member, to greet him, guide him, and enjoy a role exchange opposite to his experience in the group's start, when he looked at the old-timer Dor "with the wondering eyes of a recruit looking at a veteran", as he said. These roles and role reversals prove the therapeutic effect of the re-enactment of sibling relationships (Ashuach, 2012). I found that this role reversal and the opportunities that it offered for group analytic work to be a unique contribution of the long-term open group model for the individual development and cure.

In this phase of the group life, the group has become a partner which co-contains the transition with me. In this case, I saw the encounter between the newcomer and the participant who left as similar and parallel to the passing of the baton in a relay race, an encounter that contributes to individuals and the group, including its history, its memory, and the continuity of participation in the group.

Summary

The resulting void following the loss created by the change rests on the group history and culture and the ways in which it coped with previous changes. Something from the group's old matrix continues to roll forward. As in a relay race, the old, experienced siblings pass on to the newcomers the hope and faith that they can overcome this difficult phase, and even outgrow it and overcome it. Group conducting in this setting calls for exceptional devotion on the conductor's part, without which it might be sometimes difficult to "survive" departures and arrivals. This devotion seems to function for the conductor as a support in the tolerance of a lot of tensions involved in arrivals and, especially, departures. The participants need to handle the complicated task of digesting the changes that occur in the group. My experience with conducting this slow-open group taught me that it is possible to negotiate the arrival of new members and the departure of existing members in the group, to be conducted by the therapist in a sensitive, flexible, and open way which seeks understanding, recognition, and consensus.

I believe that the conducting of, as well as participation in, a continuous long-term group in Israel can be an important and challenging developmental experience for both conductor and participants. The Israeli society can be described as post traumatic, especially regarding separation anxieties. Large parts of our society went through the Holocaust, in addition to a history full of pogroms, being refugees, and suffering from difficult separations and departures in the transition between countries, languages, and peoples. The society itself feels on the verge of catastrophe and disaster. Many societal processes, such as the difficulties in accepting similarly fated immigrants to our country, seem to be influenced by anxieties fuelled by deep existential insecurity. Being a conquering society not only failed to provide the promised security, but it intensified insecurity and existential anxiety. Israeli society seems constantly preoccupied with security issues (infiltrators, street terrorism of various kinds) and concerned with the protection of its actually non-accepted borders. The resonance to such polyphony can often be an anxious acting out, caused by mistrust, disbelief, and fears of future terrors. In groups, we hear how difficult it is to hold to a feeling of security that might provide a belief that the future can be planned and that continuity can be dreamt about. In this context, participation in a slow-open group could provide a secure and continuous space for the participants' growth and development, especially if the conductor is aware of the connections between group processes and social contexts and allows a process of mutual growth.

References

Abarbanel, J. (1983). The revival of the sibling experience during the mother's second pregnancy. *Psychoanalytical Study of the Child, 38*: 353–379.

Aharoni, H. (2012). The Covenant. In: *Caesura* (pp. 99–145). Tel Aviv: Bookworm [in Hebrew].

Ashuach, S. (2012). Am I my brother's keeper? *Group Analyis, 45*(2): 155–167.

Behr, H., & Hearst, L. (2010). *Group-analytic Psychotherapy: A Meeting of Minds*. Kiryat Bialyk: Ach [in Hebrew].

Ben-Naftali, M. (2000). *On the Unrequited Love of Deconstruction*. Tel Aviv: Resling [in Hebrew].

Ben Zur, M. (2011). A lecture at Winnicott Center. On the endings of the analytic hour [in Hebrew].

Brown, D. (1998). Fair shares and mutual concern: the role of sibling relationships. *Group Analysis, 31*: 315–326.

Doron, Y. (2014). Primary maternal preoccupation in the group analytic group. *Group Analysis, 47*(1): 17–29.

Foulkes, S. H. (1975). *Group Analytic Psychotherapy: Method and Principles*. London: Gordon and Breach.

Foulkes, S. H., & Anthony, E. J. (1964). *Group Psychotherapy—The Psychoanalytic Approach* (2nd edn). London: Maresfield Reprints.

Grossmark, R. (2007). From familiar chaos to coherence: unformulated experience and enactment in group psychotherapy. In: M. Suchet, A. Harris, & L. Aron (Eds.), *Relational Psychoanalysis, Volume 3: New Voices* (pp. 193–208). New York: Analytic Press.

Hopper, E. (2003). *Traumatic Experience in the Unconscious Life of Groups*. London: Jessica Kingsley.

Nitsun, M. (1996). *The Anti-Group: Destructive Forces in the Group and their Creative Potential*. London: Routledge.

Zinkin, L. (1994). Exchange as a therapeutic factor in group analysis. In: D. Brown & L. Zinkin (Eds.), *The Psyche and the Social World* (pp. 99–117). London: Routledge.

CHAPTER TEN

The group, the boundaries, and between

Hagit Zohn

"Almost all the non-Jews live in boxes called England, France and Russia. These boxes protect them. Jews do not have a box, and if they do it is a fluid box, which might collapse on them in times of crisis: the Jew lives in space, it makes him proud, sensitive and cautious. It makes him not take anything for granted, he knows that the disaster is just around the corner"

(Warburg, 1936, in Handelsalz, 2004).

Introduction

For us, Jews of Israel, it seems as if many things have changed since these comments were made, yet our mentality has not changed at all. We live in a unique and distinctive "box", a well-fortified stronghold on the outside, filled with internal disputes and a strong sense of existential anxiety on the inside.

Yehoshua (2002) wrote, "If I had to define Zionism in only one word, I would choose the word boundaries". Awareness of boundaries, the reality of boundaries, is the basis of our existence. It appears that the boundary is an object of desire for we Israelis. It represents and defines sovereignty, independence, and security, on the one hand, and prohibition, restriction, and the urge to cross it, on the other.

The group, whose first two years of existence I describe here, existed in a complex Israeli context. Through this group, right from the start, I was confronted with the complexity of boundaries. The group tested both my and its members' boundaries of containment and holding, and has contributed greatly to my dealing with the issue.

The concept of boundaries in psychoanalytic theory

The boundary regulates human efforts to combine and to separate. Through it, what is inside of me and what is outside of me, what is me and what is the other, what is real and what is imaginary, is determined.

Boundaries have two functions: one function is identification, which distinguishes the boundary and indicates its essence. The other function is regulation, which protects, restrains inwardly, and wears armour outwardly. Both functions involve the two most basic human needs that exist side by side: the need for security and the need for belonging. By managing his "boundary policy", the individual aims to adjust, and is in a constant process of learning and expanding his repertoire of behaviour. This process takes place in light of the other (Rosenwasser & Nathan, 1997).

Hartman (1991) speaks of "boundaries in the mind". These are boundaries perceived as a dimension of personality, qualities, or characteristics of the mind. He distinguishes between four dimensions of boundary: an external boundary (interpersonal) and an internal boundary (intrapsychically), a thin boundary (penetrable), and a thick boundary (opaque). Hartman suggests looking at the concept as a wide modality for observing variation between individuals, and as an aspect of organising the personality as a whole. According to him, a certain amount of thickness in the inner boundary is required for normal psychological functioning, and a certain amount of thinness in the external boundary expands social interactions by enabling sensitivity to the other's psychic reality. In extreme situations, thin internal boundaries might indicate fluidity and lack of internal cohesion, when the boundary between the self and the other are fused. Thick external boundaries might indicate a rough, protective, and even persecutory attitude toward the other, when a boundary becomes a barrier (Urlic, 1999). Failure to create an integrated structure of the self leads to endless effort to maintain the boundary. On the basis of Tustin's work, Hopper (2001) suggests that following the encapsulation of traumatic experiences, individuals may protect themselves by "amoeboid" or "crustacean" character structures. Whereas the amoeboid hardly distinguishes between self and non-self, the crustacean is covered by a thick protective shield.

Winnicott (1971) speaks of "boundary experience" as a position with which the Other comes to meet the subject. A boundary is not a fixed and static structure, but a dynamic experience that exists between man and his environment. This encounter experience creates a potential space where man creatively rebuilds his world and realises his creative potential. The boundary is a product of interaction and differentiation processes. According to Winnicott, the boundary is dynamic, constantly re-forming, creating and enabling a sense of life, permeability, and openness.

The concept of boundaries in the context of the group

"The line drawn around a group, creating a boundary, makes creativity possible" (Barnes et al., 1999, pp. 29–30). The group is defined by a singular boundary, which encircles it and draws what is inside and what is outside of it, included or excluded. The boundary which surrounds the group from its beginning creates a space in which meetings that constitute the matrix take place. The processes of interaction between the participants are "the mind" of the group (Foulkes, 1990). These are the communication channels within the boundaries by which differentiation becomes possible. The matrix consists (phenomenologically) of space, its boundaries, and a constellation of object relations that occur within them (Ashbach & Schermer, 1994).

The relatively permanent structure of the analytic group holds people together in two ways: one way is the predictable external structure of the holding (setting). This is an array of time and space, which leads to an inner feeling of being held in a safe place and "holding environment" (Winnicott, 1971). The other way is related to a good enough holding external environment, which becomes an internalised holding environment. The external environment is conscious and refers to the shape and structure of the group. The internalised environment is mostly unconscious and refers to the movement of projections and internalisation relating to the holding external environment. When the group feels it is held safely, it creates the possibility of developing a space for thinking in which the participants feel contained (Bion, 1962). Like the mother, the group therapist is in contact with the mental state of the group and, by using the "reverie function", his attention and support enables its psychological development.

Foulkes wrote,

> Anything that comes to our knowledge belongs to the therapeutic situation whether the event takes place in the consulting room or elsewhere . . . I do not see them . . . as belonging to an inside–outside polarity. . . . To me, they are inside. The therapist is clear how far he extends the boundaries of the T situation on his part, how far he himself goes in his contact with the patient . . . (Foulkes, 1975, p. 134)

It seems that the boundary Foulkes writes about is borderless. That is, whatever is said happens and continues in the lives of the patients, and the group belongs to the group. Boundaries are relative to the position the therapist adopts, consciously or unconsciously. Foulkes adds that the boundary of inside or outside is in constant shift, and the experience that these changes create is of particular importance (Foulkes, 1990).

The therapist aims to increase and expand his boundaries so that they can hold and contain the needs of the group and its members. The group and the participants strive towards a movement which expands and increases their boundaries of containment, understanding, and mutual recognition. The group aims to expand its common ground as a whole, and, at the same time, aims to recognise the unique diversity of each of its participants. Each time those who are outside the zone of communication are accepted by the group, they leave their position of alienation and loneliness while expanding the group's ability to contain. Whenever a participant or any content is thrown outside the boundaries (of communication) of the group, the loss is double: the group loses because of the reduction in its free communication zone, and the individual loses because he preserves his psychopathology.

The "tragedy" which is structured in group therapy is rooted in the fact that the individual comes to the group in order to build a protected mental space within more flexible boundaries. He aims to achieve an intrapsychic, balanced adaptation to the group situation (parallel to the social or existential situation) and to obtain the best compromise between the need to belong and the anxiety of being swallowed. However, the mere fact of belonging to the group raises anxiety in each of these areas. The concern about boundaries is cyclic and volatile in the attention required—both inward and outward.

Therapist–group relations are similar to container–contained relations. Their best modality offers mutual changing and adaptation towards one another, so that they shape and are shaped by one another. These container–contained relations are flexible relations, which develop and constantly grow in a continuous process of mutual influence and operative survival (Bion, 1970).

The "boundaries in the mind" of the group

During the first meeting, there are five participants and two empty chairs. Immediately after introductions, the participants define their identities. Two of the participants have an immediate salience: Keren for being a twin sister, and Bosmat for being an Arab. The group members linger on Keren's twin experience, and through it they begin to indicate the issue of the boundaries—fusion and separateness.

Bosmat tells the group that she is an Israeli Arab. By joining the group, she is breaking her familial and social boundaries and is anxious that she will pay a heavy price for this within and outside the group.

The reference to boundaries is visible and clear at once, and will be central. In the final minutes of the first meeting, Bosmat asks to move the day and time of the next meeting. In fact, she wants the group to change for her. She tests me and the group: can we recognise her uniqueness and singular needs? How and will we maintain our boundaries?

It turns out that the group's boundaries were breached after the first meeting. Anat accepts a lift with Keren. The boundaries in Anat's mind are thin and fluid. She seeks immediate rapport, to shorten processes, and to reduce the boundary area to a thin line.

Several months pass and Uri leaves. Bosmat leaves shortly after him. Bosmat's leaving is highly charged, as it takes place in light of the outbreak of the second intifada in Israel. During this period, the existential threat is most tangible. The sense of danger pervades the atmosphere. The internal and external boundaries "collapse" and fail to provide any protection, and sabotage the group's ability to fulfil its duty of curing. Anat dreams about leaving and loss:

> I dreamed I gave birth a baby. The baby is big, two years old. I'm standing with him on a balcony whose guard-rail is missing two columns. I warn him that he might fall. He turns to me and starts to fall. I quickly run downstairs, grab him and save him.

It seems that the group that faces a risk (a fall, lack of protective guard-rail) seeks to return to the initial dyad unit, the security zone. But the dream offers another observation, too. The baby (the group) falls due to the lack of two columns in the balcony's guard-rail. A balcony is an architectural space on the seam, an intermediate space that is not totally public or totally private. It seems that the group feels itself standing on a balcony, in the borderline zone. It is as if the group is in an intermediate space located between grieving for what it has lost and will not be any more, and the recognition and acceptance of itself with the lack within it. Can a group that "miscarries" its participants save itself? Is the group therapist the missing rail, which fails to keep the baby safe, preventing it from falling? And maybe the balcony (the group) is a "third space" (transitional space) (Winnicott, 1971), where treatment and cure takes place, since, after all, the baby is saved.

With the end of the first working year, two new participants join the group. Their joining evokes waves of unrest, and leads to regression, which is expressed repeatedly by a re-examination of the group boundaries and the limits of holding. The attack on boundaries is exacerbated when a relationship of attraction–hatred evolves between Keren and Hadar (one of the new participants). This relationship reaches its peak when Keren announces to the group that she cannot attend the group meetings on Sundays any more, and asks me and the group to change the regular meeting day. Responding to Yaron's question, "What if we cannot change it?" she replies, "I will not be here." The request becomes a threat, and thought becomes "the thing itself", the action. Yaron replies, "I'm not changing." Keren gets up and leaves the room. The group and I are shocked and silent. Yaron is embarrassed, defeated, does not understand how he became the aggressor.

The group experiences feelings of rage towards Keren, and guilt and blame towards me for not preventing the escalation. Keren is absent from the group for two months.

During this time I am used as a bridge between Keren and the group. In one of the meetings, I ask the group about the message they would like to send to Keren. Yaron says, "Tell her that we love her." There is something honest and moving in this statement. Yaron is angry with Keren for evoking intolerance in him, and pushing his boundaries to the limit. Yet, at the same time, he is thankful for what she represents for him and for the group: the authentic presence, pain, vulnerability, and violence. He loves her for her integrity and bare neediness.

When Keren returns to the group, a routine conversation takes place that completely ignores the previous events. The participants talk lengthily about the boredom of their daily routines. I suggest that the group will take a look at the great effort they make to feel that everything is normal and routine continues. The group is furious with me for forcing them to face in the room what they are trying with great effort to keep out. I try to break the silence and turn it into speech, which at this stage is experienced as dangerous because it has the power to exclude.

In the following months, the group and I fight for a widening of communication and the possibility of discussing the most difficult emotions within the group. The group withstands its own destructive attacks, enabling growth within the group, expanding its boundaries, becoming the cause of its own cure. Several meetings after her return to the group, Hadar tells Keren, "I'm glad you returned to the group. I'm still afraid of you, but in a different way. I do not feel that you can destroy me. I feel that I can face your angry outbursts and your needs. We will be here as you need us. I also have learnt through you to understand what I need, and to say it here, without fear."

The "boundaries in the mind" of the group analyst

Years after I started to work with the group, I encountered these lines in a book: "When Kobi was born . . . I became a sieve, all of me, from top to bottom only holes . . . nothing is left in you inside . . ." (Shilo, 2005). I felt that the writer had written about me. In giving birth to a group, it is as if all your holes have been opened, and what was previously closed, safe, and familiar is exposed. I am aware that, though I hold, think, see, feel, ask, know, the holes do not close, links are impossible, and I often find myself losing the ability to think and understand (Bion, 1959). Sometimes, I feel that the group "is pouring through my fingers", as if the group maps all the holes in my body and pours out of them.

In the first two years, during a few meetings, the entire group is present as a whole. At every meeting something happens in the boundary zone. The group stubbornly and thoroughly examines my endurance, my readiness to devote myself to its "birth" and to raise it unquestioningly, without hostility or revengefulness because of it being a vulnerable and weak child in desperate need. In other words, the countertransference that took place at the time could be characterised by maternal preoccupation.

Leaving its boundaries perforated, the group makes me a damaged therapist, who fails to create and hold a safe space. Thus, the group entrusts to me the sense of its neediness and helplessness. And, perhaps, it also gets rid of feelings of envy in the full and complete motherhood they attribute to me by being the one who parented them.

Facing endless absences, I experience helplessness and inability. At one of the meetings, when Sammy announces his intention to leave the group, my whole body shakes uncontrollably through the entire meeting. In my body I know the anger, the hurt, the pain. It is the same trembling that the body experiences with unusual physical exertion. It is as if the group stretches my boundaries to the limit.

Within the transference, I am used as an object for projections. As such, sometimes I lose the knowledge of my boundaries. This loss is painful, and it seems that it makes me thicken the boundaries of my understanding and sensitivity to the needs of the group. A night after a group meeting, I wake up in a cold sweat, terrified. In my dream, my home is occupied, I escape into a nearby field and abandon my children . . . The dream is certainly related to the external reality of the second intifada, but also to the group and the feeling that I cannot save the participants. Perhaps, in the dream, I responded to the demand of the group (experienced then as aggressive) to suspend my boundaries and to devote myself totally to its needs.

Bosmat's leaving was especially difficult for me. It was if I could not make room for her pain and feelings of failure, since she could not make the group see her as a subject rather than a representation of the "Arab". Her leaving smashed my, and the group's, illusion that there was a possibility to repair the complex Israeli reality in the group togetherness. In retrospect, it seems that the special composition of this group testified to the existence of a manic reparation wish within me (Durban, 2003; Klein, 1988) to an internal and external damaged reality.

Over time, as work deepened, difficult and exciting feelings arose in the group, associated with envy and competition, the threat of one's place being taken, and the loss of the internal and external collective cohesion. Encountering these feelings brought the group back to a vulnerable and emotional discussion on boundaries. When the process became unbearable, the group ejected Keren, who settled (in the meantime) in the boundary zone between inside and outside, in the negotiations area (Oppenheimer & Benjamini, 2001). Keren and the group used me as a mediator and regulator of the exchange processes. Through me, the communication channels were kept open.

In my insistence to serve as a bridge between Keren and the group, I expanded the boundaries of my ability to contain my anger and hatred towards Keren, agreed to be the object of her rage attacks, and relieved any desire for revenge towards her and the group. I was used as an intermediate space for the group and for Keren. Thus, it was possible for the group to contain Keren and what she represented within it, and the group was contained and held within Keren's internal boundaries.

Gradually, we learnt the meaning of Yaron's statement about his love for Keren, despite her destructive attacks. Loving Keren meant loving the damaged, destructive, and persecutory part—which is, in fact, inside of me (either the group member or the group therapist). When I, the therapist, learn to recognise and accept my impotence, I learn to give up my omnipotence wishes and actually reduce the boundaries of my ideal reparation fantasy. At one of the meetings, I am asked, "Were you not angry with Keren? Were you not really disappointed in us . . .?" The question finds me at a quieter and safer place inside of me. It is a place where I can share with the group the internal process I underwent. These are exceptional moments when I feel that the group can contain both my and their feelings, and enjoy the motion of being therapist–participants in the group, which enables growth and development.

Discussion

Erlich (2001) argues that if everything that lies beyond the boundaries is foreign, alien, and unknown, then psychoanalysis always "sits" on the border. The term "boundary" in psychoanalysis and group analysis is central and critical to the understanding of intra- and interpersonal processes. It seems that this chapter demonstrates the importance of the issue and reflects the storm that takes place in the interior and exterior, real and phantasmal, boundary zone of the individual and the group in the therapy room.

The group's journey began in a stormy move of examination and definition of internal and external boundaries. The attempt to develop a primal shell, a collective group "skin" (Anzieu, 1989) encountered great difficulties. Perhaps it was due to uncertainty, alienation, and prominent diversity between the group participants, or perhaps because of the Israeli reality at that time.

The challenge facing the group and its participants was to succeed in breaking through the thick, stiff, and opaque boundaries that surrounded them, sometimes as protective shields and sometimes as barriers. It necessitated letting themselves be attached, helped, and touched—and that out of hope the analytic group would create an opportunity and a possibility for transformation of the border from a barrier to a thinner, more flexible and permeable boundary which was in a state of motion, enabling connection and touch (Urlic, 1999).

Bosmat's demand to change the setting at the first meeting and Anat's accepting a lift with another participant are actually the voices of the group as a whole reflecting its need to test and to attack the setting, structure, and law of the group: to break the boundaries and attack "the father function" (Resnik, 1999). It seems that boundaries in the group mind are not perceived as intended to protect, maintain, and enable, but as restricting, obstructing, and thwarting. They fight the boundaries as if to ensure their existence and ability to withstand reality and to survive it.

When the collective defence is not efficient enough and anxiety overwhelms, there is no choice but to take a more drastic step, such as leaving the group. It seems that, through the leaving of Uri and Bosmat, the group reduced its boundaries. At this stage, the group was unable to contain a variety of voices and variations, particularly those voices representing the other, which was perceived as an aggressor.

These are left inside it as undigested materials, beta elements (Bion, 1970), which do not transform in the group and are expressed in actions, one of which is dropping out. Through the group "drop-outs", it "throws up" what cannot be thought and digested (Biran, 1997). Thus, the group preserves the knowledge that evil, violence, aggression, envy, and competition are outside of it and avoids taking ownership and responsibility for the destructive forces within it (Nitsun, 1996). On the one hand, the group maintains itself, and, on the other hand, it attacks and diminishes the potential for being a cure object.

The desire and the need to expand the boundaries of Bosmat were perceived as an Intifada in the group itself, since permanence and continuity in the group space had not yet been created. The sense of threat to life, hatred and rage, along with hopelessness and despair, were, within the group, like gunpowder. Merely being close to it could have exploded the entire space. The explosiveness of the content did not allow communication and, ultimately, Bosmat left the group. The contained is an explosive material and the container throws it out (Hinshelwood, 1994).

The war on the external boundary enters the group and builds a barrier within it. This barrier is parallel to the Israeli security barrier, built through the length and breadth of the State of Israel for defensive purposes. Yet, this barrier blocks us from seeing the suffering and need for freedom of others. It splits, separates, and removes anything that threatens the interior.

In the first year, the drama of boundaries takes place on the axis of setting. In the second year, the central theme is related to the inability to contain and process the initial primitive emotions of the group, especially envy and competition, and to the way the boundaries are attacked as a major defence against the anxiety these intense emotions arouse. Sometimes, the anxiety is so intense that it seems that the group members cannot cope with it. Keren's leaving the group boundaries, and, at the same time, her remaining in the group and in my mind eventually enabled her return. It seems that this is what Foulkes meant when he spoke of the expansion of common ground and the persistent struggle for communications. Thanks to communication, Keren could eventually accept the group and the individuals within it as being separate from her, as subjects who, when they say no, do not reject her existence. And the group could contain and accept Keren and her otherness. Talking about the unbearable emotions returned the group's faith in its curing ability, restored the reflective space, and revived "free floating discussion" (Foulkes, 1964).

Epilogue

Summer 2014, when I wrote this chapter, there was another round of violent battle on Israel's borders. Once again there was no peace, and everything was tense and painful. I shut myself in my room, wrote an essay on the analytical boundaries, on intrapersonal and interpersonal boundaries, and found myself fighting with depression and the anxiety that eventually we will fail, and, in the end, the war on boundaries will overwhelm us.

The group continues for many years. It is clear to us all that the struggle to maintain the internal and external, overt and covert, boundaries is infinite. As long as there is life there is something and someone to fight for. The boundaries are intended to protect us, to ensure our survival and to maintain the essential mental work, even if, sometimes, the price is unbearable. Unlike in the past, the current round finds me more experienced and confident. I understand that all we have to do in the group microcosm space is try to "communicate" the storms, passions, fears, and fantasies that this attack raises. And we must all insist on this . . .

My journey and the group journey is not over. Neither is the journey to know boundaries, to recognise the right size, whether they are thin or thick, whether to stretch and expand them—but all within the safe and secure space the boundary provides—is the essence of the analytic group and the essence of this chapter.

References

Anzieu, D. (1989). *The Skin-ego*. New Haven, CT: Yale University Press.
Ashbach, C., & Schermer, L. V. (1994). *Object Relations, the Self, and the Group*. London: Routledge.
Barnes, B., Ernst, S., & Hyde, K. (1999). *An Introduction to Group Work: A Group Analytic Perspective*. London: Macmillan.
Bion, W. R. (1959). Attacks on linking. *International Journal of Psychoanalysis, 40*: 308–315.
Bion, W. R. (1962). A theory of thinking. *International Journal of Psychoanalysis, 43*: 306–316.
Bion, W. R. (1970). *Attention and Interpretation*. London: Tavistock.
Biran, H. (1997). Violence, jolt and tumult at large society and their reflection in the analytical group. *Mikbaz, 3*: 87–102 [in Hebrew].
Durban, S. (2003). The amendment: the third place. Lecture presented at the seminar "Between perfection and completion". Tel Aviv University, Department of Psychotherapy [in Hebrew].
Erlich, H. S. (2001). Otherness, borders and dialogue: reflections. In: H. Deutsch & M. Ben-Shoshan (Eds.), *The Other: Between Man Himself and Other* (pp. 19–37). Tel Aviv: Yediot Aharonot, Hemed Books [in Hebrew].
Foulkes, S. H. (1964). *Therapeutic Group Analysis*. London: Karnac.
Foulkes, S. H. (1975). *Group Analytic Psychotherapy: Methods and Principles*. London: Gordon and Breach.
Foulkes, S. H. (1990). The group as matrix of the individual's mental life. In: E. Foulkes (Ed.), *Selected Papers: Psychoanalysis and Group Analysis* (pp. 223–235). London: Karnac.
Handelsalz, M. (2004). He was not a gentleman, he was more than that. *Haarez*, 1 February. Retrieved from www.haaretz.co.il/literature/1.943324 [in Hebrew].
Hartman, E. (1991). *Boundaries in the Mind*. New York: Basic Books.
Hinshelwood, R. D. (1994). Attacks on the reflective space: containing primitive emotional states. In: V. Schermer & M. Pines (Eds.), *Ring of Fire* (pp. 86–106). London: Routledge.
Hopper, E. (2001). The difficult patient in group analysis: the personification of (ba) I:A/M. *Group, 25*: 139–171.
Klein, M. (1988). Some theoretical conclusions regarding the emotional life of the infant. In: *Envy and Gratitude and Other Works, 1946–1963* (pp. 71–80). London: Virago.
Nitsun, M. (1996). *The Anti-Group: Destructive Forces in the Group and their Creative Potential*. London: Routledge.

Oppenheimer, B., & Benjamini, D. (2001). About the concept of the border. *Organization Analysis*, 4: 39–46 [in Hebrew].

Resnik, S. (1999). Borderline personalities in groups. *Group Analysis, 32*: 331–347.

Rosenwasser, N., & Nathan L. (1997). What is group? Basic concepts in social psychology. *Group Facilitation Reader.* Jerusalem: Community Education Center Haim Zippori [in Hebrew].

Shilo, S. (2005). *No Gnomes Will Appear.* Tel Aviv: Am Oved [in Hebrew].

Urlic, I. (1999). Mirroring of psychogenic autistic barriers and neurotic boundaries. *Group Process, 32*: 535–546.

Winnicott, D. W. (1971). *Playing and Reality.* London: Penguin.

Yehoshua, A. B. (2002). The border duty. *Haaretz,* 2 February [in Hebrew].

CHAPTER ELEVEN

Combined therapy as a clinical tool: special focus on difficult patients

Pnina Rappoport

C ombined therapy is a clinical modality in which individual therapy is combined with group therapy. There are two basic forms of combined therapy:

1.   One therapist treats the patient in both individual therapy and in group therapy;
2.   Two therapists combine their treatment, one as the individual therapist and the other as the group therapist. This kind of treatment is known as conjoined therapy.

For the past fifty years, combined therapy has attracted a great deal of attention both in Israel and worldwide (Alonso & Rutan, 1982, 1990; Bernard & Drob, 1985; Caligor et al., 1993; Ormont & Stream, 1978). In 2007, a volume of *Group* was devoted entirely to articles about combined therapy (Ezquerro & Bajaj, 2007).

Many therapists see in combined therapy an optimal tool for providing a comprehensive picture of the patient's personality, since it enables the therapist to see the patient in multi-faceted life situations: individual, familial, social, and cultural. However, other therapists oppose combined therapy completely. They claim that it is only possible to provide optimal treatment in a group context and often cite Foulkes' claim that "by and large, the group situation would appear to be the most powerful therapeutic agency known to us" (Foulkes, 1964, p. 76).

My experience with combined therapy has exposed me to the various complexities that develop as a consequence of the patient–therapist relationship, especially to multi-level transference and countertransference. It is precisely these complexities that offer the therapist an opportunity to observe the most intricate parts of the transference process. Thus, combined therapy can be used as an efficient therapeutic tool, especially when dealing with difficult patients—the borderline and narcissistic personalities. However, the use of this therapeutic tool makes particular demands on the patient and on the therapist.

- What are the advantages and disadvantages of combined and conjoined therapy?
- What are the processes that the patient and the therapist experience during combined therapy?
- What are the goals of combined therapy and which insights does the therapist have to adopt in order to achieve them?
- Can combined therapy help difficult patients?

In this chapter, I try to answer these questions.

Vignette

Dana's mother referred her to me for therapy, with the complaint that no one could cope with her any longer. Her mother maintained that Dana was depressed, cried a lot, and could not sleep at night.

Dana, a pretty, twenty-eight-year-old successful manager of a large company, described herself in the therapy sessions as being completely helpless in regard to a pathological love for a married colleague. She claimed that she was unable to detach herself from him in spite of his demands to discontinue the relationship. In her transference towards me, she was the good daughter who never dared to compete with her mother. She exhibited extreme dependency and a need to meet me beyond the amount of sessions required. Between sessions, she flooded me with telephone calls that expressed her distress and anxiety. It was almost impossible to develop any other subject with her, other than her compulsive and impossible love. Since Dana remained in this condition for over a year, I thought she might benefit from group therapy.

Dana's entrance to the group was, in my eyes, extraordinary. She appeared assertive as well as skilled in social interaction and took responsibility for everything happening in the room. She took a "super-logical" stand, showing complete indifference towards me and yet, I noticed that she was trying to please me, as though she identified me as the authoritarian parent.

I felt that had Dana not entered the group, I doubt I could have recognised her inner strength or observe other components of her personality that had not been revealed in individual therapy, thus enabling a turning point in our relationship.

While witnessing this dramatic change in the therapy, I was reminded of other turning points from my own experience as a musician. I remembered the difference I felt while I was playing a theme alone, as opposed to playing the same theme with an orchestra, even while the other orchestra members played parts other than mine. In some way, I could feel now as a conductor who can identify the unique voice of Dana. Her voice joins the other voices of the group, while, at the same time, helping me to become a part of this magnificent moment. I could experience Dana with other shades that continue to develop through the group's influence. This unique musical ensemble comprises so many different voices.

Indeed, many times, we individual therapy practitioners can be imprisoned by our own countertransference and find it difficult to see the patient in a different light. The entrance of the patients to the group enables us to observe them in different relationships and identify different aspects of their personality. Often, this observation helps to break an impasse in treatment.

According to the group analysis, it is impossible to separate the intrapsychic axis from the interpsychic axis of the personality. Individual therapy focuses on the central axis and intrapsychic personality. Indeed, the therapist and the patient create an interpersonal relationship, but they are trapped within it. Conversely, in group analysis therapy, the voices of the other group members are also heard and a more diversified interpersonal relationship is formed. Thus, the therapist can observe the patient from various points of view, enabling the therapist to form a bridge between the intrapsychic axis and interpsychic axis, and to understand the complexity of the personality, which often cannot be expressed during individual therapy or in group analysis alone.

Difficulties in group analysis therapy

Foulkes, father of analytical group therapy theory, defines the group as the ultimate form of therapy. He frequently speaks of the total situation, the whole person and the group matrix, the network of communications, which is conceived as a whole:

> The matrix is the hypothetical web of communication and relationship in a given group. It is the common shared ground, which ultimately determines the meaning and significance of all events and upon which all communication and interpretations verbal and non-verbal rest. (Foulkes, 1964, p. 292)

> I held a conviction that the situation in which one works, the situation as a whole really decided all part processes and their meaning . . . naturally in a group the total situation is a group situation. (Foulkes, 1973, p. 73)

These words have guided many therapists and provided a source of confidence in the power of the group in solving personal, difficult situations. Yet, experience shows that some of Foulkes' concepts do not always provide a complete answer, especially when coping with difficult group situations or with difficult patients.

Nitsun (1996) raises the question about the validity of Foulkes' theoretical approach "in all situations" and "for all populations". He mentions Anthony, who suggests that anti-therapeutic processes are more inclined to occur in group analysis than in individual therapy. This happens because of the empowerment of the countertransference of the therapist, which causes sadism and envy towards group members, which are not constrained. Anthony also questions the claims that these anti-therapeutic measures become, eventually, therapeutic, since groups often contain extremely vulnerable members, with markedly fragile self-esteem and disturbed sensitivities, who might be hurt rather than healed by the process. Nitsun also claims that Foulkes' great emphasis on the total situation is, paradoxically, both a strength and a weakness. For example, although the concept of the group matrix is a generative concept, it can also obscure the dynamics of the group.

Foulkes (1964) advised us to "trust the group". However, can we really trust the group completely, especially when dealing with seriously disturbed patients? Nitsun (1996) agrees that in good groups and in a protected setting, this concept gives support and faith to the group conductor, assuring that the group will ultimately know how to treat itself. However, many group therapists do not conduct groups in ideal conditions. Often, the group is composed of people with serious disorders and ambivalence towards therapy. Some of the participants might experience a crisis that is difficult to deal with in the group framework.

Zinkin adds a different set of considerations to this question. In his article "Malignant mirroring", he refers to the damage that can be caused as a result of group mirroring. In severe cases, this mirroring can cause distractions in the group. He suggests that, in cases like this, "the conductor may, like the referee at a boxing match, have to part the combatants before too much damage is done" (Zinkin, 1983, p. 125).

According to my experience, one cannot always trust the group. In severe cases of "malignant mirroring", separating "combatants" is not enough. The perception of the self is so damaged that the patient could develop a "repetitive compulsive" behaviour of self-victimisation in other similar occasions as well. These difficulties can explain this need in combined therapy, meaning adding individual therapy to the group analysis. In the next section, I elaborate and add arguments with regard to the preference for combined therapy, especially when dealing with difficult patients.

Why combined therapy?

Caligor and colleagues (1993) contend that analysts who decide to add group therapy to individual therapy based their decision on their evaluation of the patient and their assumption that the group is likely to evoke unique reactions that might never occur in a dyadic interaction. According to them, joining a group amplifies individual therapy, because it provides an opportunity to re-experience issues from the patient's life that have come up during the individual setting. The group enables a practical working on various stages of the patient's life: separation–individuation stage, the oedipal stage, stages of envy and sibling rivalry, and stages of friendship and love.

Transference and combined therapy

Combined therapy allows the therapist to broaden the transference process and enables him to have a deeper and more significant acquaintance with the patient than in individual therapy alone. Whereas, in the first phase of therapy, transference is interpreted and worked through only in a dyadic system, in the second phase of therapy, the therapist may see the patient in different relationships that shows different aspects of the transference. The therapy moves from the relatively safe stage of dyadic therapy to the frustrating and anxiety-arousing atmosphere created by the group, which includes envy, rivalry, and triadic relationships. In this context, the transference towards the therapist is also different from that which occurs in individual therapy. These additional aspects of the transference process are a significant aid in understanding the patient, especially when dealing with difficult patients such as "borderline or narcissistic patients or patients with developmental deficits" (Kernberg et al., 1989, p. 19). Caligor adds that, in combined therapy, the patients bring behaviours and expectations to their treatment that differ from those presented by the traditional literature (Caligor, 1990).

Dilemmas in combined and conjoined therapy

Alonso and Rutan (1990) describe five major dilemmas in the decision of adopting combined therapy.

1.   Should there be a preference for combined therapy or conjoined therapy?
2.   An internal conflict that turns into an external conflict: when the patient projects an internal split of good and bad on to each of the

two therapy frameworks or on each of the therapists in conjoined therapy.

3. The dilemma of confidentiality in combined and conjoined therapy.
4. Groups in which only some of the participants are in combined therapy.
5. What is the correct timing to commence combined therapy?

These five dilemmas are explored in the sub-sections below.

Combined therapy or conjoined therapy?

Is combined therapy more effective when the therapist functions both as individual therapist and as the analytic group therapist, or is it preferable that two different therapists perform these two roles? The classical approach maintains a preference towards only one therapist, which enables the therapist to observe the patient in different situations, enlarging the transference towards the patient, and revealing different parts of the personality that could not be revealed in individual therapy or in group analysis therapy alone. On the other hand, those who recommend conjoined therapy argue that often the transference is so strong that it loses its usefulness, since patients might not overcome their feelings, and, as a result, might be held up in the therapeutic process.

An internal conflict that turns into an external conflict

The danger of conjoined therapy with difficult patients, especially borderline personalities, is that the patient might project his internal split of good and bad on to each of the two therapy frameworks. In some cases, he might express a wish to leave one of the therapists, which could become a difficult situation. The therapists must deal with their feelings of countertransference, which could arise as a consequence of being the focus of the patient's projection. I have witnessed some severe cases where the inner split of the patient caused an external split between the therapists themselves who, without intention, competed for the patient's attention and damaged their relationship. If therapists find it difficult to co-operate with each other, it is advisable that an external supervisor ensures the continued efficacy of the therapy.

The dilemma of confidentiality in combined therapy

Should the patient be encouraged to tell the group secrets that were revealed during individual therapy and caused him suffering and shame? To what extent should the therapist protect the patient? Some therapists insist that all information should be available for the group and that it should be dealt with in the group framework from different angles. In my own experience, it is highly important that patients feel secure and protected in the individual setting, and only then can they be encouraged to reveal things in the group. Generally, patients choose to open up when they are mentally prepared to handle a particular situation.

Groups in which only some of the participants are in combined therapy

In this situation, envy and rivalry might arise towards the "preferred children" in the group. These feelings themselves are not damaging and are material which can be used to work through similar phenomena in almost any family.

What is the correct timing to commence combined therapy?

1. Adding group therapy when the patient is in individual therapy and has a relationship with the therapist.
2. Adding individual therapy when the patient is, for some time, in group therapy.

    According to the first treatment model, combined therapy is similar to the stages of the child's development; for example, first the child stays at home with his mother, then the mother accompanies him to the kindergarten, and only then is the child able to play with his friends independently. The second treatment model is contrary to the stages of development and is expressed by regressive behaviour that is not always comprehended by the group. However, not all of the above dilemmas can always be resolved. Therapists who have faith in combined therapy realise there is a greater danger of denying the difficulties.

My own trust in combined therapy, especially for difficult patients, rest on five points which I will now examine in terms of:

1. A diagnostic tool.
2. A means for broadening the opportunities for working with transference processes which is also related to early stages in the development.
3. A means for dealing with the false self.
4. A method that enables the practical processing of the different stages of therapy.
5. A way of creating deeper, interpersonal communication between therapist and patient while supplying support, reflection, and additional enlightenment during the process experienced by the patient in the group.

Case study

Eran, fifty-one, divorced with two children, was a science professor and an associate of a start-up company. When he requested individual therapy, he showed great neediness. He spoke extensively about his loneliness, his wish for a relationship, and his feelings of helplessness. Almost immediately, he developed transference towards me as if I was an omnipotent parent. Our meetings appeared to give him the greatest insights into his life. He volunteered personal information freely, co-operated in working through materials, never missed a session, and was never late. He showed difficulty in terminating sessions and requested "homework" to think about. It was hard to understand the social isolation about which he complained. On the one hand, he tried his best to contribute to the therapeutic process and was a sort of "gifted patient" and, on the other hand, was there something fake and false in his personality?

Indeed, he described himself as a conflict avoider and always attempted to please everyone. His formal reason for turning to therapy was his difficult relationships with his twenty-year-old daughter and his ex-wife, who refused to speak to him, although he had no idea why. He did not understand why society, especially female society, rejected him. It was only at work that he received recognition and appreciation. In short, he succeeded in expressing his intellectual ability but was completely helpless whenever he had to rely upon emotional intelligence. The most salient feature was his sense of victimisation. According to him, his mother had never been supportive towards him. Instead, she would get angry if he showed independence. In the countertransference, he aroused in me maternal feelings and a wish to help him. After several months, during which we had built a trusting relationship, I thought Eran could benefit from combined therapy, where he could investigate the social aspect that he complained about.

In the group, Eran was a completely different man to the one I knew in the individual setting. He talked incessantly and displayed deep knowledge about almost every subject, but was completely disconnected from any emotional atmosphere in the group. In the first group session he attended, Eran confronted a female participant, who expressed her disgust with him: "You remind me of my father. He didn't know how to relate to anybody either." It was at this point that, for the first time, I could understand the feeling of being in a relationship with Eran.

At the end of his first group session, Eran announced to me that he intended to leave the group. He could not understand why I had put him in the group and claimed he did not need people apart from himself. What was happening in the group was a repetition of his usual social experience, especially his relationship with his wife and daughter: he gave all that he had to offer, but people rejected him anyway. I suggested that he should test himself in the group: if he could repair his relationship with two women in the group, he might be able to build different relationships with the significant women in his life.

Before the beginning of his second group session, Eran decided to stand on his head in revolt. His need for attention was extreme and abnormal in this context. The members of the group were angry with him, and with me, claiming that I was betraying them. I started to doubt my decision to bring him to the group. When things had calmed down and reflection was possible, his acting out could be translated as being that of a child, who felt that he had no other way to impress me. In his individual therapy, he had said that as a child he had been considered almost retarded. Since his mother did not consider his needs, she did not consider him at all, and only noticed him when he was doing something unusual. The group had enabled him to recall his parents' home, where he was recognised only when he excelled at his studies.

Over the next few weeks, Eran gradually spoke less in the group. The attacks he had drawn from the other participants diminished, and one of them even expressed admiration for his work. Nevertheless, he began to come up with strange, fragmented associations, mostly related to the fights going on at the Burma Road to Jerusalem, which were not always related to what was going on in the room. Innocently, I thought that these militant memories of war were related to his aggression and to his fight for his place in the group. However, a few days later, during individual session, he recalled a traumatic event from his military service where he was directly involved in a fatal accident. He was sent to trial and acquitted, but he repressed the whole subject, and claimed that he did not remember anything. During the court martial, he was referred to a psychiatric evaluation and probably treated with very strong drugs, since his post-traumatic reaction was expressed in loss of memory and loss of speech. Now it was possible to talk about his avoidance of the conflict, his fear of losing control, his feelings of guilt, his need to gratify those around him, and to reflect on the feelings his "false self" aroused in others. The group became a container within which he could work on his capacity to change. His archaic transference enabled him to reveal, in the group, primary feelings such as isolation, aggression, and a fear of loving. When this came up authentically in the group, Eran no longer felt so completely isolated from people, who could now identify with him. After a year in the group, when one of the female participants expressed affection for him, Eran almost started crying.

Today, Eran is in the process of beginning a relationship with a mother of three, and reports, for the first time, that he enjoys being part of a family. He still finds himself avoiding conflict, but the group encourages him to return to relatedness.

If one refers to the five points mentioned above, one can evaluate the enormous impact that combined therapy had on Eran's personality, and on me as his individual and group therapist. It is possible to see how combined therapy served me as an important diagnostic tool and assisted me in revealing parts of Eran's personality that were not revealed during individual therapy. In my countertransference, my feelings changed from anger towards Eran for trying to ruin the group and wanting to get rid of him to the loving feelings of a caring mother, who could accept him without him having to prove himself. His joining the group helped me to unfold archaic pre-oedipal parts of Eran's personality. By being a substitute mother for him, I could understand his need for attention better, a need that was so extreme that he felt he had to stand on his head in order to attract the others' attention and to please them, as well as his developing a false self which evoked negative feelings towards him in the group.

Above all, one has to remember that, in spite of the fact that Eran was in all kinds of individual therapy for many years even before coming to me, it was only thanks to the deeper interpersonal communication between us, in the individual and group therapy together, that he became aware of an important period of his life, which he had completely denied for thirty years and which had a huge impact on him. We were able to understand and deal with him in the present time.

One cannot conclude the subject of combined therapy without emphasising the important role of the group in helping the therapist in treating difficult patients, since the therapist could be imprisoned by his own countertransference, a situation that might cause a blind spot to appear in the therapy. As one could see in Eran's case, there was no way to understand what he was doing to other people, or to get acquainted with his anger and false self, without the help of the group. There is no doubt that the group should recognise its help to the therapist or, as Hopper puts it, "The Group as co-therapists" (Hopper, 2005, p. 103), illustrating how a group can help the analyst with troublesome processes which are ubiquitous in clinical work with difficult patients. I acknowledged that patients in a group can help their therapist, just as children can help their parents, in uncovering real emotions.

Last, but not least, the case history described in this chapter can also help to focus on the unique contribution of combined therapy in developing the personality and skill of the therapist, who learns to wear, at the same time, two hats: that of the psychotherapist in individual therapy and that of the conductor in group analysis therapy. Both these roles are essential to the therapist's identity and are a main source of power, since together they provide him with the ability to reflect intrapersonal and interpersonal parts and to integrate them. This quality highlights the power of therapy, especially when dealing with seriously disturbed patients who suffer, among other things, from fragmented thought processes and emotional splits.

References

Alonso, A., & Rutan, S. J. (1982). *Group Therapy, Individual Therapy, or Both?* New York: International Universities Press.

Alonso, A., & Rutan, S. J. (1990). Common dilemmas in combined individual and group treatment. *Group, 14*: 5–12.

Bernard, H. S., & Drob, S. (1985). The experience of patient in conjoint individual and group psychotherapy. *Group Psychotherapy, 35*: 129–146.

Caligor, J. (1990). A current look at transference in combined analytic therapy. *Group, 14*: 16–24.

Caligor, J., Fieldsteel, N. D., & Brock, A. J. (1993). *Combining Individual and Group Therapy*. Northvale N.J: Jason Aronson.

Ezquerro, A., & Bajaj, P. (2007). Combining individual and group therapy. *Group, 31*(1–2), Special Issue.

Foulkes, S. H. (1964). *Therapeutic Group Analysis*. London: Karnac.

Foulkes, S. H. (1973). The group as matrix of individual's mental life. In: E. Foulkes (Ed.), *S. H. Foulkes. Selected Papers* (pp. 223–233). London: Karnac.

Hopper, E. (2005). Countertransference in the context of the fourth basic assumption in the unconscious life of groups. *Group Psychotherapy, 55*: 87–113.

Kernberg, O. F., Selzer, M. A., Koenigsberg H. A., Carr, A. C., & Appelbaum, A. H. (1989). *Psychodynamic Psychotherapy of Borderline Patients*. New York: Basic Books.

Nitsun, M. (1996). *The Anti Group: Destructive Forces in the Group and Their Creative Potential*. London: Routledge.

Ormont, L. R., & Strean, H. S. (1978). *The Practice of Conjoint Therapy: Combining Individual and Group Treatment*. Oxford, England: Human Sciences Press.

Zinkin, L. (1983). Malignant mirroring. *Group Analysis, 16*: 113–126.

CHAPTER TWELVE

"Is there hope for change at my age?"

Bracha Hadar

M y patients often ask me this question, regardless of age. It becomes more fundamental when the patient is over sixty years old.

In this chapter, I talk about my group analytic group, started in 2010 for people over sixty. This group is the backdrop for the unfolding story of Azi, my eldest patient, who joined the group, aged eighty-five and left it aged eighty-seven, when he felt that he had finished his process.

Azi's history was very much connected to the establishment of the State of Israel in 1948. The significance that Erikson (1964), de Maré (1985), and others give to the historical–social forces which influence individual development, adds further understanding to the formative years of Azi's life.

The title of this chapter—"Is there hope for change . . .?"—is very relevant to my feelings about Israel at the moment. At the time of writing, it is August 2014, the war in Gaza continues, and is felt by many Israelis, including me, to be a deep national and personal crisis, which evokes similar feelings to those experienced during the Yom Kippur War. I am struck by the question—is there hope for real change in the Middle East?

Prior to joining the group, Azi had been in individual therapy with me in two phases which lasted many years. Although a deep working relationship had been created, he remained constricted within his narcissistic personality and had not changed much.

In this chapter, I discuss three points: highlighting the group's unique contribution to Azi's therapeutic process, calling attention to the issue of conjoint and combined therapy (Maratos, 2016), and debating the benefit of group therapy for older people.

Conjoint and combined therapy

This chapter describes the serial kind in which participation in a group follows individual therapy. My experience of conjoint therapy has taught me to use the serial kind, mostly in this direction, but I also have experience in the reverse way in which the group process enriches the individual therapy that follows it. I want to clarify that I never do it at the same time. None of the patients in my groups is my individual patient. Many of them were in individual therapy with me before they joined the group.

This is a controversial subject in group psychotherapy; while, in the beginning, Foulkes (1948) saw individual and group therapy as complementary, he later (1964) preferred to leave the group situation uncomplicated while the patient participates in the group.

A personal communication with Earl Hopper, one of the few group analysts from the founding generation who is still very active, taught me that in the 1960s and 1970s most of the group analysts were also psychoanalysts, and saw patients in groups following individual psychoanalysis or psychoanalytic psychotherapy. They were debating whether it would be better to follow individual work with group work or *vice versa*. Hopper (1982, 2003, 2005) writes about the serial kind, in which the members of his groups were in individual treatment with him for various periods of time ranging from six months to more than ten years.

Billow (2009) writes about the radical nature of combined psychotherapy.

Cohn (1986) prefers the double context (combined therapy). Weinberg and Ditroi (2007) give a wide range of considerations regarding the variations of this combination.

Group psychotherapy for older people: a brief review of the literature

Grotjahn (1989) starts his paper with the reality of how little space has been given in group analysis to the discussion of group therapy for senior citizens. This reality might be, still, under the influence of orthodox psychoanalysis, with the view that mental processes in the elderly are too rigidly established for favourable treatment results. Freud (1905a) held a pessimistic view of the ability of the over-forties to change in the analytic setting.

Ezquerro (1989), and Canete and colleagues (2000) conclude that psychotherapy can be especially indicated for the elderly population.

Grotjahn (1989) encourages group analysts to assist in accomplishing the task of integrating past life experience into final identity formation. The natural tendency of old people to look back and to meditate about past times and memories assists in the process of integration. The obsessive preoccupation with the shameful, embarrassing, or guilt provoking experiences is a difficult but analysable task. Old people, he says, may be old in body but ageless in spirit

My rationale for group psychotherapy for older people

Several years ago, I started to play with the idea of opening a group for people over sixty. I believe that my age at that time (around sixty) was a contributing factor in my decision. Perhaps, unconsciously, this was a way of dealing with my own issues of aging. This was my rationale.

The age of sixty onwards is the time when, theoretically, one can contribute to the world from what one has achieved until then. In reality most people reach this age without having completed the developmental tasks of the previous periods. In addition, they start to feel anxious about aging, dependence, fragility, and death. At the same time, there are new possibilities of accomplishing dreams and wishes for which there was no time beforehand.

It is common sense and universal wisdom that one should prepare oneself for this period. Group psychotherapy is a good space for this. It enables mental growth, finding meaning in one's life, separating from what has been lost, and the realisation that some things will never be the same.

This rationale resonates in Ezquerro's (1989) description of his group. In the first meeting, one of the members asked, "What do you think we should be doing here?" Another member answered, "We are facing a new opportunity to grow."

The birth of my group for older people

A serendipitous meeting with a new referral pushed me to open a group for older people. Rivka was a lonely woman, had never married, and had never had children. Her social life was very poor. In her story, I heard a crucial need to belong to a group of people who shared her age-related dilemmas. Soon enough, I had three other people, and we started the group.

In the first meeting, there were four members, three women and one man. At one point, Rivka shared her doubts as to whether she could still make a change in her life. She asked me and the group, "Is it not too late?"

In a relatively short space of time, three more members joined the group: two men and one woman. It was almost an optimal group in terms of the balance between men and women: four women and three men. Many important processes went on in this group, and yet, it was very unstable: People arrived late; absences from sessions were a regular occurrence. There was a constant oscillation between intimacy and alienation. Every intimate session was followed by absences, along with people expressing a wish to leave.

Azi joins the group

Azi joined the group ten months after we had started. He was eighty-five years old then, and much older than the other members, who were under seventy. He was the fourth man, now forming a group of four men and four women.

During this meeting, Martha talked about her decision to leave. She asked Azi why he joined the group and he answered, "I want to be in a place where people who carry pain in their life want to share it with others." In this session, two other members declared their plan to leave.

In the following sessions, I could see two parallel tendencies in the group: on the one hand, there was an intense use of defences which had served people all their lives: withdrawal from intimacy and the preservation of an independent way of life.

This tendency was reflected through Shaul, sixty-five years old, who had never experienced any kind of therapy. In a way, he was an ideal man: gentle, happy to help whenever necessary. He never needed anything from anyone. His ability to cope with the functional aspects of life was excellent.

Shaul was the only one for whom psychological language was new and strange. His attitude towards life was very concrete. Like Martha, he also said that he planned to leave, saying "I don't get any value for the money I pay." Yet, he became attached to some of the people and came willingly to the meetings.

Some of the women in the group were upset by his male chauvinist attitude. Other women, particularly Rivka, became attached to him because he helped her with advice and information. Apparently, his presence in the group helped her to feel less lonely in the world.

Rivka reacted to the prospect of people leaving with a dream:

My flat was occupied. I did not have a place to live because my father did not care enough to help me.

The dream correlated with events in Rivka's life, but I also heard her growing sense of "feeling at home" in the group, and the fear of this new "home" falling apart.

Azi reflected the other tendency in the group. Although it took him a whole year to find the courage to join the group, he eventually did, bringing all his positive energy and hope for making progress. At the end of his first session, on the doorstep, before leaving the room, he said, "I feel like a child in the group, compared to all the others who are adults."

Because of his narcissistic infantile personality, at the beginning he related to the group as an ideal self-object (Kohut, 1971), expecting an experience similar to the one he had with me. He expected the group to be a solid and safely existing entity for him, as it had been during his individual therapy. This tendency was very clear in his attitude towards crisis in the group.

Although the group was tenuous, with all the people wanting to leave, Azi continued to insist on his agenda: "I want to tell the group deep things that I feel ashamed about." I intervened with a remark that it was not possible to do that without, first, making relations with the other people in the group. In response, Azi suggested that each of them tell their life story. Shaul asked him to tell his story. Azi told the group about the unsatisfying relationship with his wife.

He went on to say how, after terminating his academic studies in the USA, he immigrated to Israel. A woman he met here took the initiative and turned the potential relationship into a fact and they married. He agreed because he was terrified of disappointing her. However, the truth was that he was never in love with her. Several days before the wedding, he contemplated cancelling the whole thing, but did not dare to say it out loud.

From then on he was unsatisfied in the relationship with his wife. Throughout his life he felt guilty that he had made her unhappy because he did not love her. It never occurred to him that she had her own part to play in their relationship. In spite of this, they had a good family life together, enjoyed raising their children, and, in old age, they had been enjoying their grandchildren.

Azi had a weak sense of separation–individuation (Mahler et al., 1975). He kept talking in "we" style about his life with his wife. She, too, did not see him as a separate person and kept criticising anything he did independently. In fact, he kept his individual therapy a secret because it was the only way he could feel separated from her. It was only when he joined the group that he told her about the group therapy. She reacted by saying, "You have lost my respect."

Secrets of shame

Beneath the surface of this story lay secret, hidden shame. In a letter Azi wrote to me after the first phase of therapy, he said, "I am haunted by memories from the past, when I was young and single, which I have never told anyone. I do not want to die without sharing them with someone. Can we meet for one session?"

I heard his plea in terms of the need for emotional work as part of the aging process (Quinodoz, 2010). There is a universal need to integrate memories into a coherent narrative. This can be difficult for people like Azi who have carried frustrations and disappointments throughout their lives.

This is why this one session was prolonged into eight years of individual therapy (second phase). The secrets Azi wanted to share all related to failed relationships with women when he was young. The truth was that nothing he talked about during the session was new for me.

He said, "I cannot come to terms with the man I was, and I will never be the man I want to be." Although he told me all his secrets, he felt the need to share them with other people as well. At that point, we began to discuss the option of joining the group.

I worked very hard to integrate Azi into the group. When he talked, it was as if he was on stage, speaking to an audience, not to individuals. Often, he did not hear and did not understand what was going on among other people. Once he said, "I cannot follow the interactions. I feel like an idiot, an outsider. What was the drama between Udi and Noga?" I made the following intervention, "This is your drama. When you are not at the centre of things, you do not understand what is going on."

I mentioned the three primary forms of speech that arise in the matrix of any group (Schlapobersky, 1995). These forms represent different stages of development that occur in the interaction with other people. At the most basic level is the monologue—a person speaks alone and he is both the speaker and the listener. The next level is dialogue—a conversation between two people. The third level is discourse, in which there is free interaction among the participants. In this situation, two people speak to each other in the presence of a third person. This is the basis for group communication. Azi did not know how to be the third person, and I had to teach him. Being very intelligent, and being motivated to change, he gradually learnt to talk differently.

Meanwhile, people kept talking about their desire to leave. Another man, Dan, who suffered from recurrent periods of depression, said, "I do not want to be in a place where people wish to leave because it makes me more depressed." Azi asked me if I felt like a failure, and I answered positively. He quickly tried to calm me: "What happens is not your fault." It was clear to me how Azi tried to preserve his idealising transference (Kohut, 1968), and I reflected to him his wish to "save" me from feeling ashamed of failure in front of the group. I said, "Sometimes it is important to acknowledge one's failure in the presence of others." In saying this, I also wanted to make a space for the group members to share any secrets of shame they might have.

Rutan (2000) highlights the importance of sharing shameful secrets with the group. In talking about the possibility of change, he writes, "Groups bring about change to the degree that they allow participants to speak about parts of themselves that are held to be 'unspeakable'" (p. 511).

Group in danger of disintegration

I did not succeed in holding all eight members within the group. Within a short period of time, five members left. I have many questions as to why, with no definite answers. Did Azi's arrival in the group, his infantile personality, and his intense need to be in the centre contribute to the disintegration of the group?

I found a part answer in Ezquerro's (1989) differentiation between two phases in the life span: late middle age and old age, with their quite different developmental tasks. "Late middle age is a specific developmental phase after mastery of middle age but before settling into old age" (p. 307). Ezquerro (1989) considers late middle age a critical period suitable for group psychotherapy. This is the age of the members in my group for older age people. Azi was older than all the others by almost twenty years and this could be part of the difficulty. Azi was settling into old age, and it was urgent for him to make some change.

Maybe I was too involved in my effort to help him become part of the group. I have no doubt that his age, eighty-five, was an issue for me as well as for the other members.

In hindsight, I believe that I was too preoccupied with holding this group together, not feeling free enough to think and reflect on processes within the group.

Only now, while writing, does Erikson's (1963) model of the eight ages of man come to mind. The last stage he writes about is old age, a developmental stage in which one can reach ego integrity, provided that he has successfully "adapted himself to the triumphs and disappointments adherent to being" (p. 268). The therapeutic work in the group can be an opportunity for the participants to reconsider their balance of failures and achievements, fulfilments and deprivations. When an old man reaches a stage of ego integration, death loses its sting. The lack or loss of this accrued ego integration is signified by fear of death. The one and only life cycle is not accepted as the ultimate of life. Despair expresses the feeling that the time is now short, too short for the attempt to start another life and to try out alternate roads to integrity. (Erikson, 1963, pp. 268–269)

Azi definitely felt that time was too short and he had to do his work on ego integration. I think that his old age, too close to death, was a source of fear for the others. Those who were not ready to deal with these issues dropped out from the group.

Despite the fact that five members left the group, I decided to continue with just three: Azi, Rivka, and Frida. Azi was the most motivated: "I feel that the group has something important to give me."

Although it was small, I felt, none the less, that it was a working group.

Azi brought more and more dreams to the sessions.

Azi: the dreamer in individual and group therapy

During the years of individual therapy, Azi had had thousands of dreams. In most he got lost, started contact with a woman, but never reached fulfilment. In most of the dreams the female figure was either his mother or his wife (both of them played interchangeable roles in his mind). Then, one day, there was a change. In one session, he brought a series of dreams in which he rebelled against his father, humiliating him. I said to him, "Your experience in the group has forced you to move away from the centre, where you had been a young, goody-goody child, and helped you begin to rebel against your father."

Azi never told the group that his father had been an important leader in the American Zionist movement. In individual therapy, we had spoken a lot about his father, who had not let him enter the world of men, and his mother, who treated him like a baby. As a youngster Azi thought that his childhood was paradise, and it was only later, as an adult, that he realised it had been a "golden cage".

When Azi became an adolescent, no one at home acknowledged that he was no longer a boy. Neither parent reflected any awareness of the change in his growing body. His father was always busy with the Zionist movement. He was an excellent speaker, with great char-isma. He had no time for Azi. Both Azi and his mother admired the father and "danced" around him.

In individual therapy, he denied any aggression towards his father. In his dreams, he did express hostility, occasionally accompanied by concrete movements and shouting that would wake up his wife, but his anger was not directed towards a particular person.

Change in Azi's transference during therapy

In the group, in contrast, he introduced dreams in which he was more aggressive and confrontational with his father.

In the individual therapy, where he was the centre of my attention Azi maintained his idealising transference towards me, and tried to impress me as to how brilliant, "good", and unaggressive he was.

In the group, however, the setting had changed. Gradually, he became one of the several members. He became a father figure to Rivka. He became a man attracted to Frida. His once strong transfer-ence towards me was now divided among the three of us. He could now move internally between being a child, a man, a father, and the elderly leader of the tribe.

In one session he told us a beautiful dream about him and Frida. In the dream they go to a kind of party and dance. Frida wears a white dress and looks very happy.

The dream was notable for what was missing. For the first time, there was no mention of his mother or his wife, or of any catastrophe. After talking about the dream, he turned to Frida and said, "If I were twenty years younger, I would court you." They went on to talk about male–female relationships, and about sex. They found certain similar-ities in their marital dynamics.

He became more self-aware and said, "I don't know how to differ-entiate between my need to impress and the knowledge of who I really am." He also admitted that it was difficult for him to let go of the "golden cage" of childhood, when he had been so admired. He talked about his difficulty in growing up and becoming a man. His wife had no small part in "castrating" him. Gradually, with the help of the others, he became able to resist her pressure to leave the group. On the other hand, and also with the help of the group, he could realise how painful it was for him to tolerate his wife's hostility with regard to his participation in the group.

Azi received a lot of warmth and loving affection from the two other women. Gradually, his self-object transference to the group was resolved. In its place, real loving relationships developed.

I can describe what happened in the group at that period in terms of Foulkes' (1948) basic law of group dynamics:

> The deepest reason why these patients . . . can reinforce each other's normal reactions and wear down and correct each other's neurotic reactions, is that collectively they constitute the very norm, from which, individually, they deviate. (p. 29)

Transformation

One day, Azi sent me a letter in which he wrote, "I think the time has come that I can leave the group. It has nothing to do with my wife. She does not know yet about this decision. I will only tell her after I have left. Lately I feel good in a way that I have never experienced in my adult years. I feel free and able to initiate things I always dreamt of. If I "fall", I am not so harsh with myself. I want to just "live" without having to report every week on how I feel. My heart is full of gratitude and love towards you for the ongoing work you did with me over the years. I will never forget you. I will remember you until the last day of my life."

I could sense between the lines of his letter the integrated man about whom Erikson writes in the following extract.

> It is the ego's accrued assurance of its proclivity for order and meaning. It is a post-narcissistic love of the human ego—not of the self—as an experience which conveys some world order and spiritual sense, no matter how dearly paid for. It is the acceptance of one's one and only life cycle as something that had to be and that, by necessity, permitted of no substitutions. (1963, p. 268)

Azi stayed in the group for two and a half years and left it when he was eighty-seven, feeling "free at last". Before joining the group, in one of the individual sessions, he had remembered Martin Luther King's famous words. As he spoke the words, he burst into deep sobs.

He could not have more clearly expressed his wish to be free from feeling anxious and depressed almost all his adult life.

He spent six years in the first phase and another eight years in the second phase of individual therapy, but his transformation and change happened during the two and a half years of his staying in the group.

Concluding discussion

Azi is a good example of Friedman's (2013) model of treatment of relation disorders in the group. My experience with Azi confirms Friedman's contention that group therapy space offers optimal possibilities to bring about change in multi-personal dysfunctions.

Azi belongs to a generation whose parents devoted their life's work to Zionism and preserving the state of Israel, instead of parenting their children. Usually, these "children" grew up to identify with their parents' project, and accepted childhood deprivation as a natural part of life. Azi was never able to present himself as being as important as the state of Israel. In addition, it seems that Azi's father needed to be the only man on stage. Azi gave up his development as an adult male, since there was no place for two men in the family. He paid a painful price for that throughout his adult life—in his career, his intimate relations with women, and his internal state of mind.

Erikson's (1964) contribution to child development in the context of historical–social change is relevant here. According to him, when we take the historical dimension into consideration in our psychoanalytic understanding of a person, "it implies a fundamentally new ethical orientation of adult man's relationship to childhood: to his own childhood, now behind and within him; to his own child before him; and to every man's children around him" (p. 44). Erikson urges the psychoanalysts to include actuality more deliberately and more systematically, in order to fill a gap in our understanding of historical as well as of infantile man.

Is there hope for change in the Middle East?

What does Azi's transformation in the group teach us about hope for change in the Middle East? I can find some similarity between the fate of Azi and the fate of Israel. Azi was chosen as the gifted child of the family. In his adult life, he could not find ways to get out of this role and remained stuck in his development as a child.

I think that we Jews pay a high price for the fate of being the chosen people. As with Azi, the role of the chosen one might hinder our self-image as a nation, as well as our actual relations with the world.

I have a dream of a group analytic group of nations, including Israel, in which each nation could explore its contribution to the difficulty in finding peace in the Middle East.

References

Billow, R. M. (2009). The radical nature of combined psychotherapy. *International Journal of Group Psychotherapy, 59* (*Special Issue: Models of Combined Psychotherapy: Current Trends*): 1–28.

Cohn, H. W. (1986). The double context: on combining individual and group therapy. *Group Analysis, 19*: 327–339.

Canete, M., Stormont, F., & Ezquerro, A. (2000). Group therapy—group analytic therapy with the elderly. *British Journal of Psychotherapy, 17*: 94–105.

De Maré, P. (1985). Large group perspectives. *Group Analysis, 18*(2): 79–92.

Erikson, E. H. (1963). *Childhood and Society* (2nd edn). New York: W. W. Norton.

Erikson, E. H. (1964). *Insight and Responsibility: Lectures on the Ethical Implications of Psychoanalytic Insight*. New York: W. W. Norton.

Ezquerro, A. (1989). Group psychotherapy with the pre-elderly. *Group Analysis, 22*: 299–308.

Foulkes, S. H. (1948). *Introduction to Group Analytic Psychotherapy*. London: Karnac.

Foulkes, S. H. (1964). *Therapeutic Group Analysis*. London: Allen & Unwin.

Freud, S. (1905a). On psychotherapy. *S. E.*, 7: 257–270. London: Hogarth.

Friedman, R. (2013). Individual or group therapy? Indications for optimal therapy. *Group Analysis, 46*: 164–170.

Grotjahn, M. (1989). Group analysis in old age. *Group Analysis, 22*: 109–111.

Hopper, E. (1982). Group-analysis: the problem of context. *Group Analysis, 15*(2): 136–157.

Hopper, E. (2003). The problem of context in group analytic psycho-therapy: a clinical illustration and a brief theoretical discussion. In: E. Hopper (ED.), *The Social Unconscious. Selected Papers* (pp. 103–125). London: Jessica Kingsley.

Hopper, E. (2005). Countertransference in the context of the fourth basic assumption in the unconscious life of groups. *International Journal of Group Psychotherapy, 55*(1): 87–114.

Kohut, H. (1968). The psychoanalytic treatment of narcissistic personality disorders—outline of a systematic approach. *Psychoanalytic Study of the Child, 23*: 86–113.

Kohut, H. (1971). *The Analysis of the Self.* New York: International Universities Press.

Mahler, M., Pine, F., & Bergman, A. (1975). *The Psychological Birth of the Human Infant: Symbiosis and Individuation.* London: Maresfield Library.

Maratos, J. (2016). Combined therapy—a group analytic perspective. In: J. Maratos (Ed.), *Applications of Group Analysis for the Twenty-First Century* (pp. 179–200). London: Karnac.

Quinodoz, D. (2010). *Growing Old: A Journey of Self-Discovery.* London: Routledge.

Rutan, J. S. (2000). Growth through shame & humiliation. *International Journal of Group Psychotherapy, 50*: 511–516.

Schlapobersky, J. (1995). The language of the group: monologue, dialogue and discourse in group analysis. In: D. Brown & L. Zinkin (Eds.), *The Psyche and the Social World* (pp. 211–231). London: Jessica Kingsley.

Weinberg, H., & Ditroi, A. (2007). Concurrent therapy, countertransference and the analytic third. *Group, 31*(1–2): 47–62.

CHAPTER THIRTEEN

"I still want to be relevant": on placing an older person in an analytic therapy group with younger people

Eric Moss

"And when old words die out on the tongue, new
Melodies break forth from the heart; and where the
Old tracks are lost, new country is revealed with its wonders"
(Tagore, 2013)

Introduction

There are those who argue on behalf of homogeneous groups, saying that members feel more comfortable opening up among other people like themselves, with similar emotional and functional problems, for example, over-eaters, drug addicts, bereaved spouses, etc. There are others who argue the opposite: that a heterogeneous therapy group more accurately reflects the composition of the society in which individual members must function. A heterogeneous group composition also offers a wider matrix of transferential relationships that can be analysed to the benefit of its members.

This debate can be related to age-related issues of the group composition. Specifically, it is relevant to ask, can older people benefit and contribute to other, younger members in an analytic therapy group? It is not so usual to place older people in such a group owing to myriad reasons, including cultural bias, the notion that older people cannot change and traces of Freud's original focus on the central importance of childhood experiences. And yet Foulkes, the founder of group analytic therapy, argued on behalf of placing people of different ages in a therapy group. He wrote that a mixed age group can greatly add to transferential reactions in both directions, that is, the older person for the younger and *vice versa*.

Anecdotes reflecting bias towards older people

Anecdote 1: what is in a word?

When I recently complained to my thirty-five-year-old son about getting older, he looked at me and said, "Dad, among my friends you and Mum are not old, you are *elders*." I instantly felt better.

Anecdote 2: who wants to work with older people, anyway?

I recently had occasion to take out a copy of my PhD dissertation, which I had completed forty years ago. It was on the subject of aging and mental health. Shortly after completing the dissertation, I had put it on the shelf and for decades ignored the whole subject—until recently, when I realised I had become old myself. I found myself wondering why I had not continued my work with aging people through the decades of my adult career.

Anecdote 3: older people prefer to be with other older people!

In many towns in Israel there are cultural centres, which offer many kinds of clubs, travel programmes, music, and other artistic events. I recently signed up for a class in one of these centres. During the first meeting, I looked around the room and saw there were no older people. I then looked across the hall and saw a room full only of older people, playing cards and bingo. I asked myself whether those older people really prefer to be with their own, or whether the age segregation I witnessed was simply an administrative decision based on common stereotypes and age prejudice, in Israel as elsewhere.

Introductory thoughts about psychology and aging

Mixed age groups and group analysis

In view of the cultural stereotyping and prejudice with regard to older people reflected in the above anecdotes, we can easily understand why a group analyst might be hesitant to place an older person (60–65 years of age and older) in a therapy group with younger people. To better understand this issue, it is important to recall that group analysis has particular rationales, criteria, and goals for placing someone in an analytic therapy group. These might be summarised as follows: (1) motivation for personal examination and willingness to make change; (2) an ability to show empathy towards others; (3) a willingness to look at earlier stages of one's life and relate early themes to present ones, particularly with regard to interpersonal engagement with others and involvement with groups; (4) an acceptance of and curiosity about the unconscious and its effect on one's life; (5) an acceptance of, and curiosity about, the role of transferential relationships as they appear in an intimate group of 6–8 people (Behr & Hearst, 2005). Can an older person, despite his or her age, meet these criteria?

Contradictory attitudes in Israel towards older people

In Israel, one can identify, on the one hand, a respectful attitude towards older people because of: (1) an awareness that many elderly people are Holocaust survivors and deserve a special sympathetic attitude; (2) Israel is a new country, and there is an awareness of a debt owed to the older generation of founding fathers. On the other hand, much of this very population suffers from relative poverty and neglect. This has been documented in many investigative reports in the news media and vociferous political and budgetary debates in the Knesset and other political platforms.

One explanation for this contradiction between a "politically correct" attitude towards older people and their harsher, objective situation might be connected to the fact that most of the early pioneers came to the country as young people, leaving their families behind. Later, many of those who remained in Europe were slaughtered by the Nazis. As a result of these factors, many "Sabras" grew up without grandparents and a "culture of grandparents" and of older people.

Introductory thoughts about psychology's views of older people

Perhaps Freud's major contribution was the discovery of the uncon-scious and its influence on our lives. In his investigations and writ-ings, he discovered that difficult childhood experiences, many of which had to do with what today are called sexual traumas, were repressed and then appeared in the form of dreams, slips of the tongue, jokes, etc., as well as certain pathological reactions and behav-iours. Because of these discoveries, his writings were perhaps skewed in the direction of childhood as opposed to later stages of life. Young adults could be helped to change, not older ones.

Jung took issue with Freud on this focus. Many of his writings, and those of latter-day Jungians, deal with phenomena occurring in adult development, particularly the important role of creativity in adult life. He and his followers scrutinised personal development in middle age and later (Jung, 1965). They found that many middle aged and older people come under great inner pressure to examine themselves (what Jungians call introspection). A prominent Jungian, James Hollis (1993), has pointed out that a critical factor leading to efforts to make changes in middle and later periods in life is that people become sometimes dramatically and frighteningly aware they will not live for-ever. Another Jungian, Erel Shalit (2011), examines classical literature, such as Dante's *Divine Comedy* and Homer's *Odyssey*, to name just a few, for reflections of introspection and personal change as heroes become older. In these archetypical tales of journeys through life, he finds examples of inner and outer conflicts that, if dealt with success-fully, can lead to what Jungians call individuation and personal growth.

The post-Freudian Erik Erikson (1950) developed a model of stages of psychosocial development throughout a person's lifetime, includ-ing the last stages. In his model, there are ample descriptions of the conflicts and challenges of later life. The challenge of the penultimate (seventh) stage is to leave behind experiences and personal conclu-sions that will outlast him or her and generate personal growth in others. The challenge of the last (eighth) stage, characterised by life review, is for the older adult to be able to look back and feel a sense of fulfilment with what he has done.

A question we might ask ourselves as group analysts is whether in his or her drive to help generate growth in younger people, is the older person truly open and sympathetic to the dilemmas of the younger ones? Or has the older person, in the certainty of all he or she has learnt in a lifetime, become preachy? Does he still have the modesty to be able to listen openly to the younger person? More so, does he have the humility to take in feedback about himself, as well as the desire to make changes? If so, he could be a good candidate for an analytic therapy group.

I myself wrote an article in which I compared groups of older people going to a lecture series on mental health subjects with another group that were in group therapeutic counselling (Moss & Davidson, 1980). I found that many of the older people were eager to participate in the therapeutic counselling group. It gave them more possibility of voicing their feelings about what they had or had not accomplished in their lives than did a lecture series.

We can see in the above citations, and others not cited here, that, in contradiction to a certain early psychological bias against psycho-analysing older people, there are ample later professional writings attesting to the fact that certain older people continue to function well in social situations and are motivated for self-examination (Behr & Hearst, 2005).

Furthermore, there are literary works: for example, James Agee's *A Death in the Family* (1957), films, *Cinema Paradiso*, for instance, and cultural traditions, such as the Jewish Passover ritual, family gatherings on Friday night, Sabbath evenings, emphasising the importance of older people in the lives of younger ones and *vice versa*.

In this chapter, I want to focus on what happens in an analytic therapy group in which there are one or two older people mixed in with a number of younger ones. I discuss how group analysis provides a framework for better understanding the interactions in such a group. I also discuss how, in a group analytic therapy group, older people can become important transference and reformative figures for younger ones and *vice versa* (Foulkes, 1975).

The therapy group and older members

Occasionally, an older person will want to join a therapy group. Or, sometimes, veteran members of a group simply become older, moving subtly into a newer stage as the group moves through time. Whatever, the presence of an older member can either present a problem for the group or a contribution, or something of both.

One problem is that the older person might need to deal with issues universal to old age and not shared by younger people. The most common of these are that the older member might become more frail and have to deal with deteriorating health and bodily functioning. A partner might die. Older children might move away. There could be an ominous, growing fear of death.

Younger people, busy with building and expanding their lives (e.g., separating from their parents, new love, present relationships, raising children, developing a career) might not have the time to think about these issues. Or perhaps they do, but because of the frightening and painful nature of some of these issues, would rather not think about them. In the therapy group, there might be resistance to examining them. The presence of an older person in the group might force the younger ones to think and talk about what they may not want to, which is what might be waiting for them down the road.

Even if the younger members are prepared to delve into these issues, the older person might not want to burden them, just as they do not want to burden their own children. Today, more than ever, there is a focus in society on youth and remaining attractive, dynamic, and healthy. In the face of this trend, the older group member could choose to remain silent, feeling that group time is better spent on younger members.

The silence of the group is a powerful voice. In its face, the older person might consciously or unconsciously interject members' projections and not speak. His silence could confirm an image of the older person as someone who does not want to, or cannot, speak about himself. The younger members then might simply ignore him, reinforced in the negative stereotyped view that older people are no longer introspective and neither do they particularly want to talk about themselves (i.e., a projective identification dynamic).

If there is more than one silent older member, a split could develop between them and the older people. The sub-group of older people has the potential of becoming an anti-group and, if not dealt with, this sub-group could subvert the whole group in myriad ways (Nitsun, 1996).

There are, though, more positive scenarios. For younger members, the older member can become the focus of negative transference reactions. The latter might seem to have the same negative character-istics as their own parents. In the group, there will be a therapeutic opportunity to process old, unworked through negative themes *in vivo*. Or, in contrast, the older person might be viewed as a good, "reparative" figure, an alternative to "bad" parents. Here, too, there are many opportunities for members, especially the older one and for the conductor, to help the young member realise he is "acting out" a desired, idealised figure.

Finally, the older person has many opportunities to learn from the younger ones. Listening to the struggles and dilemmas of the younger members could help him reconnect with earlier stages in his life and, thus, assist him with his personal life review. The older member, hear-ing the stories of the younger ones, has the opportunity to either vali-date his personal view that he has been a good parent and/or accept the mistakes he has made and move on. Ultimately, he might decide to make here-and-now changes based on what he has learnt from understanding the real and the transferential relationships of younger members towards him.

In all of these cases, he will become a valued and active part of the group. He will both gain from group feedback and add to the growth of other members. How this all works can be seen in the following case.[1]

Case study

A younger colleague turned to me for advice with a problem regard-ing his therapy group. He had been seeing a seventy-year-old patient, Ruth, in individual therapy. She was a retired social worker and having difficulties with her husband, an alcoholic. Some years earlier she had pressured him to join AA, and he had stopped drinking. But new problems, which had been hidden, then arose. Ruth knew that my colleague led a therapy group and asked to join. My colleague was hesitant and consulted me.

To his surprise, Ruth demonstrated an ability to internalise feed-back as well as to contribute to other members. She was flexible and resilient. She aroused conscious and unconscious maternal transfer-ences in several of the members, which were then analysed to the benefit of the whole group. She was able to enjoy, and grow from, members' responses. They challenged her to do things she had always been afraid to do. No less important, the group members urged her to develop new interests separate from the concerns about her husband, with whom, because of his drinking problem, she had become over-involved and an "enabler", not challenging his alcoholic behaviour.

One member was a forty-five-year-old married man who repeatedly claimed his wife was emasculating him. His pattern was to react with passivity and withdrawal. This isolating pattern angered Ruth. It reminded her of her husband and his passive–aggressive behaviour. She told him that by withdrawing and not being more assertive, he was not only hurting himself but was also a poor role model for his children. She encouraged him to deal with his wife in a more open and direct manner. He began to do so, and after months of working on this theme, he could report to the group that the relationship between him and his wife had much improved. At the same time, becoming involved in the younger man's marital problems forced Ruth to look at similar aspects of her own marital situation from a fresh, outside perspective.

Another member was a borderline woman in her mid-twenties, who was very impulsive and argumentative. Her character stemmed from highly unstable parenting. The older member had successfully raised three children, two boys and a girl. The two women liked each other and developed a mother–daughter transference, in which the older woman became a good maternal object for the younger one and the younger one brought out the best maternal instincts in the older one.

In one particular session, the younger woman complained she had just had a fight with her boyfriend. She shouted that she had had enough and was going to leave him the next day. Ruth responded in a calming tone, saying, "I know you're upset right now. But, try not to react so quickly. You're young. You have time. Tomorrow is another day." The younger woman listened and took in the advice. She remained with her boyfriend. The older woman had become a reparative figure for her.

Ruth, in her role of guide to the younger woman and, indeed, to the other younger members, might have been unconsciously processing her older issues, such as competition, female sexuality, depressive inferiority, grief, envy, and jealousy. She might have also been making up for guidance that she had never received as a youngster, perhaps because of the lack of grandparents in her life (see my earlier comments about the lack of a "grandparent culture" for many of the early "Sabras").

Also, on the unconscious level, despite the age difference, the older member seemed to arouse a sexualised, oedipal dynamic with several of the men, including the therapist. He recognised that the presence of the older woman, the age of his mother, was blocking certain sexual feelings in himself and also sexual discussion in the group. As a result, he realised that he had been unconsciously blocking sexual discussion. Acknowledging these sexual feelings in himself gave him better insight into the sexual feelings of group members, and he felt more able to bring these out for discussion (Moss, 1999).

Discussion

There are several factors to consider when debating whether or not to place an older person in a therapy group with mostly younger people. Several of the more important ones are described in the following subsections.

Personality and social functioning

It is a commonplace notion that as people grow older they continue to behave, think, and feel in many of the same ways as they did when they were younger. Outgoing, gregarious people will search for ways to continue to be socially active. Those who were loners might want to continue their social isolation in older age. Older people of the former kind might find a therapy group appealing. Those who had been loners for most of their lives might be more reluctant to participate in a therapy group. However, it is possible, too, that some of these might see going into a group as a last opportunity to change the way they relate to others and how they relate to the major issues in their lives..

Of course, people who have highly disturbed personalities might prove too disruptive for a group that needs a certain amount of stability to function well, but there are many fairly well-functioning people who, none the less, have what Friedman (2013) has called "relationship disorders". These kinds of people might gain from being in an analytic therapy group, one of the main tasks of which is to help members improve the way in which they perceive and behave towards others.

Introspection and life review

Another factor to consider in deciding whether to place an older person in a therapy group is the person's willingness and ability to examine himself in a deep way. Some older people are not particularly interested in investigating their lives. Their attitude is, "What's done is done." According to Yalom (1970), such unintrospective people— and this is not just true for older ones—are not good candidates for a therapy group. But, as we have seen above, other older people might be introspective and, therefore, react positively to a therapy group experience. It could be the last time in their lives that they have an opportunity to examine themselves and how they relate to others. As Erikson pointed out, life review is consistent with the eighth and last stage of a person's life. It might be facilitated by participation in a therapy group with younger people.

Age blindness in the group therapist

In considering how an older person might fit into an analytic therapy group, the conductor herself has a critical role. Her attitude towards aging and aged people will affect the way she relates to the older member and how active she is in urging the group to explore difficult issues associated with aging. As with others in the group, she might have a tendency to avoid looking at difficulties that might be waiting down the line (Yalom, 2011).

None the less, if she finds that the group is *not* talking about these issues, the conductor's task is to "push" for them. She might comment on the restless body language of certain members when issues of aging are brought up. She might ask the group directly why there is silence when these issues are brought up. Or she might ask the older member how he feels talking about being old. The point is that the conductor does what she has been trained to do: first wait to see if anyone brings up their own feelings about aging, and, if not, gently point this out. She might find that just a few comments or interpretations are enough to open up a floodgate of feelings. Or, perhaps the opposite: that her few well-meant comments are greeted by silence.

She will then have to find other ways to help members, old and young alike, to explore group resistance.

The above strategies will, of course, be familiar to most experienced group therapists, who must occasionally deal with group resistance. These strategies are valid not just for overcoming resistance to age-related problems but other kinds of problems as well (Moss, 1999). Perhaps, with regard to an older person in the group, it is less a matter of uncertainty about how to work therapeutically than overcoming a countertransferential resistance that may be blocking him and interfering with his work.

One must consider, too, the age of the therapist. As mentioned above, countertransferential resistance might be greater in a younger therapist, who could see the older patient as the same age as his own parent, with whom he might still have unworked out issues. An older therapist—especially one who has had a good personal therapy—might have an easier time relating to issues bothering older people, such as physical deterioration, retirement, the empty nest syndrome, and death.

This was true in my own case. At the time of writing this chapter, I was seventy-one years of age. Some years ago, I had been leading a group in which there were several members all over sixty. Each of them had had active vocational lives—one a film producer, one a clinical psychologist, and one a theatre director—and each, for different reasons relating to health, was no longer working. In each case, their health problems were related to getting older. Like Yalom (2011), who worked for years with cancer patients, I found myself quite open to encouraging these three to work on their feelings of loss—vocational, physical, and social—in the group. Unlike the "Sabras" who did not have a "culture of grandparents", I grew up in America, where all of my friends and I myself had grandparents. Not only was I not aware of having problems with age-related issues while leading my group, I felt, like Yalom, quite interested in the existential issues my older group members were facing.

Anecdote 4: age exclusion and prejudice in our own group analytic home

Age stereotyping and prejudice can affect the most sensitive and proficient group therapist. There follow some examples I have experienced in my own Israel Institute of Group Analysis.

Over the years, new and often younger people joined our four-year training programme and gradually took over important roles in the Institute. In one Large Group, there was much talk about problems that had arisen between students and teachers in the training programme. I had not been a teacher that semester and wanted to raise a subject closer to my heart. When I thought that enough time had been spent discussing the training programme, I spoke up and complained with obvious hurt that some of the "veterans", including myself, who in fact had been founding fathers, no longer had a role in the Institute. I anticipated empathic reaction, but none came. Instead, members continued to speak about problems relating to the training programme. I felt left out and unseen and had the uncomfortable feeling not just that people did not want to deal with the issue I had raised, but also did not want to relate to me personally.

These two episodes left me with mixed feelings. On the one hand, I felt hurt, ignored, and excluded, and started to sulk in silence. I developed a fantasy of setting up a group in the Institute just for older members. There, I would feel a full part of things. However, I then realised that this would accentuate a split between the older people in the Institute and the younger ones, which would go against the group analytic principle that splits should be worked against and divisive issues should be handled in the Large Group. So, I tried to ignore that fantasy and forced myself to talk about my feelings in the Large and Small Groups.

Summary and conclusion

Anecdote 5: the roots of age stereotyping

A short time ago, I was sitting in my wheelchair in a café. A little boy left his family at a nearby table and came over to me. He looked me up and down and then asked, "Mister, are you old? I was taken back, and asked, "Why do you think that?" "Because you are sitting in a wheelchair," he answered. I laughed, but later realised that that attitudes towards older people begin at the earliest age, with childish notions that later develop to stereotypes.

A mature group therapist must recognise his own stereotypical thinking about older people, which could be causing him to hesitate about putting an older person into a group. This might be reinforced by what we have learnt in our training about Freud's original focus on childhood trauma, repression, and the unconscious. Another reason might be the universal notion that older people are unable to change. Contemporary therapists do not necessarily agree with this view, but the old prejudice has not entirely gone away.

In fact, certain older people, with characters reflecting introspection, empathy, and a lifetime of social activity and social behaviours, or even more isolated older people who realise that they do not have too much more time to change themselves, may indeed meet the criteria for placement in a group analytic therapy group. They can both receive much from the feedback given them and also contribute to other, younger members. Some of this interpersonal exchange is on the concrete, in-the-present level. Moreover, with accurate interpretations by the conductor, these exchanges can also deal with the unconscious, transferential level.

The presence of an older person in a therapy group of younger people may, indeed, arouse very strong personal reactions in younger members, and they in the older person. The conductor who has worked through his own concerns and fears about aging can use these reactions to move the group and individual members forward in their efforts to grow.

Note

1.   My thanks to Dr Jeffrey Werden, psychoanalyst, New York City, and his group members for allowing me to use this clinical material from several of their group therapy sessions.

References

Agee, J. (1957). *A Death in the Family*. Knoxville, TN: McDowell, Obolesksy.
Behr, H., & Hearst, L. (2005). *Group Analytic Psychotherapy: A Meeting of Minds*. London: Wiley and Blackwell.
Erikson, E. (1950). *Childhood and Society*. New York: W. W. Norton.
Foulkes, S. F. (1975). *Group Analytic Psychotherapy*. London: Gordon and Breach.
Friedman, R. (2013). Individual or group therapy? Indications for optimal therapy. *Group Analysis, 46*: 164–170.

Hollis, J. (1993). *The Middle Passage: From Misery to Meaning in Midlife*. Toronto: Inner City Books.

Jung, C. G. (1965). *Memories, Dreams, Reflections*. New York: The Modern Library.

Moss, E. (1999). The hysterical group and the hysterical analyst. *Group Analysis, 32*: 559–568.

Moss, E., & Davidson, S. (1980). The development of a psychiatric rehabilitation service. *International Journal of Rehabilitation Research, 3*: 45–55.

Nitsun, M. (1996). *The Anti-Group: Destructive Forces in the Group and Their Creative Potential*. London: Routledge.

Shalit, E. (2011). *The Cycles of Life: Themes and Tales of the Journey*. Carmel, CA: Fisher King Press.

Tagore, R. (2013). *Gintanjali: A Journey to Infinity to Discover Yourself*. New Dahli: Gintanjali Press.

Yalom, I. (1970). *The Theory and Practice of Group Psychotherapy*. New York: Basic Books.

Yalom, I. (2011). *Staring at the Sun: Overcoming the Terror of Death*. London: Piatkus.

CHAPTER FOURTEEN

The patient, the group, and the conductor coping with subtle aggression in an analytic group

Rachel A. Chejanovsky

Introduction

I have been prompted to write this chapter by my recent experience with aggression in my analytic therapy group. I am concerned with a subtle form of aggression, one that is almost silent. In some ways, it cannot be seen, and is as quiet as a lullaby, but as insidious as drops of water slowly wearing away a stone. This form of aggression can occur every day, and it can have serious consequences for personal development. Some patients are unaware that they have suffered, or are suffering, from such aggression, as though they learnt long ago to accept it as an ongoing fact of their life, which they accommodated and even took for granted, as "given" (Hopper & Weinberg, 2011, p. xxxv). Their experience of aggression was often accompanied by feelings of guilt or shame. For example, a woman who was born into a family characterised by continuing aggression towards her told the group, "My mother had a hard time giving birth to me; I was a difficult child." On hearing this, I thought, "What kind of mother would blame her child for a difficult birth?" In my eyes, this was an example of extraordinary, but unrecognised, aggression.

Such aggression is hidden in expressions, gestures, attitudes, etc., in daily interaction among individuals. It can become persistent and continuous, and even seem to be a "normal part of life". When it appears at a stage of dependency, such aggression can deform the individual who is on the receiving end of it, especially if this occurs in a relationship characterised by an absence of mutuality and equality.

I call such aggression "subtle aggression". It is similar to the concept of "micro-aggression", which is often used in reference to the experience of marginalised populations in their everyday life (Pierce, 1970).

Freud (1920g) defined as "traumatic" "any . . . excitations which are powerful enough to break through the protective shield", and which "are bound to provoke a disturbance on a large scale in the functioning of the organism's energy and to set in motion every possible defensive measure" (p. 27). The shield to which he refers is future consciousness or ego functioning. Khan (1986) discusses

> the mother in her role as protective shield over the whole course of the child's development, from infancy to adolescence in all those areas of experience where the child continues to need the mother as an auxiliary ego to support his immature and unstable ego-functions. (p. 122)

Khan's ideas on the concept of cumulative trauma are relevant in this context. Thus, subtle aggression will especially affect the ego functioning of the individual who experienced it persistently and continuously at a stage of dependency.

How does subtle aggression influence psychic life? What effects does it have on psychosocial functioning? What special conditions will an individual who suffered from subtle aggression need in order to be helped in a therapeutic group?

A theoretical frame of reference

Ogden (1992) attempted to integrate some of the ideas of Freud, Fairbairn, Winnicott, and Bion into his own object relations perspective. He suggests that the internalisation

> of an object relationship be thought of as necessarily involving a dual subdivision of the ego. *Such a dual split would result in the formation of two new sub-organizations of the ego, one identified with the self in the external object relationship and the other thoroughly identified with the object.* (pp. 149–150)

Both aspects of the split will find expression in interactions with the other.

Friedman's (2007) perspective on what he calls "relation disorders" can also widen our understanding of the deleterious effect of subtle aggression. He writes, "Relationship disorders are mainly the result of . . . mis-containment" (p. 257). A containing person in the child's environment is one who helps the child by "taking the child's conflicts on him/herself". Mis-containment refers to a pathological situation in which there has been no one in the child's environment to take on his difficulties. This will contribute to the child's later development of a relationship disorder.

Ogden's and Friedman's views are relevant in helping us better understand the group's function as container and as antidote against the insidious effects of subtle aggression, as seen in the following case history.

A short case history

Tammy came to the Mental Health Centre following two minor car accidents. Neither she nor any of her passengers was injured, but she could not drive any more. This limited her ego functioning, and was an expression of breakdown. In a way, she was signalling that she was having difficulty in being in charge of her life. Her loss of control was an indication of the effect of subtle aggression on her psychosocial adjustment. The aggression that was absorbed during her lifetime came out in unelaborated ways: loss of control and diffuse anxiety. In her family life, Tammy was locked in an idealisation–devaluation relationship, especially with her mother, on whom she was over-dependent, and, to a lesser degree, on her brother, whose academic success she deeply envied. Her mother had repeatedly declared that she (the mother) had not been mature enough to have children when she gave birth to Tammy, and that from the beginning she felt uneasy towards her daughter. During her childhood and adolescence, Tammy was criticised for her learning difficulties. When she was twelve years old, she was given a formal diagnosis of "learning disabilities", which the parents had not detected before because of the split in their views of her involving devaluation and idealisation.

The insidious effects of this family pattern on her external and internal life was reflected in the results of a battery of psychological tests carried out during therapy, in which marked suicidal tendencies were noted. However, on one level, Tammy was trying desperately to grow out of her dysfunctional patterns. One of the signs of her efforts was that she had left home to live with her boyfriend, far away from her parents.

I shall now present highlights from the group therapy, tracing a picture of this patient, her specific difficulties, and her development within the group.

Some vignettes that highlight the group process

First vignette

At the beginning, Tammy was usually very quiet. Group members had to draw her out. It took time for her to make a place for herself. She seldom brought themes to the group, but occasionally joined in after someone else introduced an issue. Eventually, Tammy told the group about her parents and her brother, presenting them as perfect people. As for herself, she had always been an outsider, an under-achiever. She could not learn in the same way that her brother could. Neither could she have a perfect relationship with her boyfriend, like the one that her parents were thought to have experienced together. These views were an expression of her pervasive low self-esteem and of the split views that the members of her family had of her, which she had come to have of herself.

As much of this dynamic was unconscious, it was difficult to address it directly. However, by sharing in the group, she did two things: she was telling her story and, at the same time, declaring that she belonged to the group, and was asking to be understood. "The child feels sheltered when he feels understood" (Yogev, 2012, p. 64). In fact, the group offered her the understanding that she needed. Members tolerated her symptoms by accepting her and her feelings without criticism. They related to her with serious attention and responsiveness.

As the group progressed, members began to challenge the view that she came from a perfect family. Hearing their feedback, for the first time ever, she began to doubt her idealised view of her family.

The group helped her to realise that she no longer had to accept the family's devaluation of her. This realisation happened in stages. At the beginning, members accepted and tolerated Tammy's idealistic appraisal of her family. Yet, in time, members gradually formed a view of the family that was more compatible with reality (Foulkes & Anthony, 1984). The group's mirroring and resonating enabled a new view of the family to emerge, and this, in turn, allowed her to explore alternative ways of viewing herself.

Second vignette

During another meeting, Tammy talked a lot about being nervous and impatient. I understood this to be a consequence of the subtle aggression in her childhood. She told the group about having gone to buy a present for a friend. When she arrived at the store, it was being cleaned, and she was asked to wait. She became agitated and angry and walked out. When she told her husband, he suggested that she take some "natural" pills to calm herself down.

At first, members joined her by talking about their own medicine. A young man said something about his capacity to think and be rational, and that this, and not medicine, was his way of coping with his nerves and frustrations. This was an expression of hope and trust in the group and in the process.

After some time had passed, I asked Tammy whether there was anything in her inner life that she could draw upon to calm herself down. Tammy thought for a moment and then said that she could make more of an effort to have a sense of proportion about things. There was something in the tone of her voice that prompted a participant to say to her that she was reciting slogans! She smiled shyly, as though she knew what he was talking about. The member said that he thought maybe she was trying to please me, the conductor and authority figure. The member confronted her with a reflective negative mirroring (Pines, 1998) followed by an accepting explanation, which again shows the sensitivity of the group towards her.

We then explored her transference towards me. She saw me as she saw her mother, an almighty woman with whom she had to comply even when this meant submerging her "true self" (Winnicott, 1960). We saw that this was a defence that was impeding her from genuinely thinking. The fact that a group member, and not me, had commented on her attitude made it easier for her to reflect upon her situation.

Despite all the difficulties inherent in this exchange (Foulkes, 1990), participants did not criticise her lack of patience. Their lack of criticism was a mutative experience for her.

Third vignette

However, Tammy, on the other hand, lacked empathy towards the participants. In one session, a young woman who was in a doctoral programme (and whom she envied) talked about her doubts in her relationship with her partner. During a pause in the discussion, Tammy spoke about the wonderful vacations she had with her boyfriend. The group did not comment on her story, ignoring Tammy's subtle aggression towards the other member and her lack of empathy.

This expression of envy and aggression reflected the lack of containment she had experienced during her childhood. The aggression was an expression of beta elements (Bion, 1962, pp. 308–309); her mother did not fulfil a transformative function in her psychic life, so these elements were expelled into words without awareness of their meaning except in a very literal sense. Outside the analytic group, these responses can elicit anger and aggression, reinforcing an endless vicious circle.

At this point in time, the group had crystallised as a good object for participants. Thus, it was a good womb for her, offering her a secure and accepting space. It was able to survive her attacks and contain her (Winnicott, 1950). This containment was a great help for me. When she expressed herself, I could not empathise with her. She was diminishing a peer in the group. This was a conflictual moment for me. The group, on the other hand, was able to go on.

Fourth vignette

During the third year of work, Tammy began to speak with affect and in more personal ways. She talked about her self-criticism and her fear of experiencing joy. Before a short break, she said that she hoped to survive the lack of meetings. Tammy had developed a dependency upon the group, a regressive state that paradoxically was helping her to find herself. She had come to belong to the group; it became a containing environment for her (Schlapobersky, 2015, p. 428).

Final vignette

Some months later, during one particular meeting, Tammy was very quiet. She was invited to share what she was experiencing. At first she refused, but later she told members that she had been thinking about having a child. She felt ready! But, she said, there was a problem—her job. She was concerned that if she had a child, she would be under pressure to leave work. Her worry was odd because, just a few days before, she had received a letter of recognition from her bosses commending her for excellence in service to a client. I stopped her, wondering why we were again talking about concrete problems. She said that dealing with work was her way of surviving each day. It helped her to pay less attention to her intense despair. She did not know why she was on earth and doubted that anyone would ever love her.

The group was moved and someone asked her what happened. She explained that she had been an unwanted child, that her mother had had a hard delivery because of her, and that later she had been a difficult child. Now that she was planning to become pregnant and would need her mother, her mother had told her that she was not ready to become a grandmother and asked her to defer the pregnancy. The group members were shocked and angry on her behalf. They suggested that she ignore her mother and live her life. They offered practical advice and emotional holding. This theme was elaborated upon during later meetings. After this exchange, she became more open and began to bring more intimate issues to the group, such as her relationship with her own body.

This final vignette offers an overview of the difficulties of this young woman both in her psychic self and in the actual relations with her family, and her mother in particular.

Tammy was acting out her identification with that part of her ego that identified with the self in the external object relationship (Ogden, 1992). She was expressing unsatisfied needs that arose in the context of an earlier mother–child relationship. She attempted to repair the damage that arose within this early relationship (Hopper, 2005, p. 96) by continually seeking containment and understanding. She was locked in a clinging relationship to an all-mighty mother representation. In real life, she was still hoping for her mother's help in becoming a mother herself (a normal hope). All this was happening in parallel within the group. She wanted to see if the group could contain her. The group and I were responsive to her plea. This triangulation of the situation (Tammy, the group, and myself) allowed her transference to be elaborated. In the countertransference, I felt uncomfortable with her (which is the response of the internalised mother representation). For example, as described in the vignette, I stopped her at the outset in a rather ruthless way. I felt frustrated by the turn her explanation was taking. This moment of contact with my own aggression found expression in an observation that moved the process forward, but my complementary countertransference feelings (Racker, 1991, p. 135) echoed the self-hatred in her internal object relations world. I felt at odds with myself at that point and retreated, thinking that my feelings were not in accordance with the situation that unfolded at that moment. The group, on the other hand, remained loyal to her needs. They could listen to her distress and respond accordingly, stimulating strength and not assisting deficiencies (Friedman, 2007). This was what allowed changes to take place in her life. Group members were dependable in a way her mother had never been, and perhaps I was unable to be at that point.

Discussion of the case

Tammy participated in the group for the whole period it functioned. During this period, her boyfriend proposed to her, she married, and became pregnant. She not only stayed in her job, she received a formal recognition of excellence. Later, on her own initiative, she decided to leave her work and took a course leading to a degree in assisting "special needs" teachers. Subsequently, she obtained a job as teacher's assistant. These are very concrete achievements. In the words of Haley (1986, p. 40), she got "past a stage in the life cycle", a humble yet important goal in therapy. These outer changes may have reflected developmental changes in her inner life.

Close to the end of the group, members challenged her in a warm and playful way, especially when she touched topics in too concrete a manner, such as asking, "How should a couple behave?" Members would then move her to more emotional grounds in a way that would not make her defensive. Her attitude towards them grew warmer.

In my view, Tammy did not complete the process of separation from her family, especially from her mother. This is why I am cautious in my appraisal. None the less, it seems that the deep dependence she experienced inside the group strengthened her ego and her self-esteem. The group offered her an opportunity to create a healthier distance between her and her family, as well as protection from the deep envy towards her brother.

What facilitated the group's level of acceptance?

It is possible that the clear boundary around the group-as-a-whole enabled the group to be so tolerant of differences and diversities (Van Der Kleij, 1983). The group met continuously in a stable and safe place, a quiet and large room that did not suffer from interruptions during the hours of encounters. It was a slow-open group that functioned for a period of three years. During this period, a number of participants came and left. What was remarkable was the basic and profound acceptance that every member felt towards Tammy. For a long time, I was puzzled by the gap between the group's acceptance of her and my own discomfort. There were moments when my own feelings lacked empathy towards her, and the group helped me with my blind spots (Hopper, 2006, p. 556).

At the same time that Tammy was going through her experience, each member was involved with his/her own problems. These individual processes were interwoven with the development of the group-as-a-whole. The relations in the group were complex and dynamic. There were all kinds of events: discussions, disagreements, confrontations. But, all in all, there was a deep feeling of camaraderie and sharing, an overall feeling of acceptance of each member towards the others.

Foulkes' "basic law of group dynamics" states that "The deepest reason why patients . . . can reinforce each other's normal reactions and wear down or correct each other's neurotic reactions, is that *collectively they constitute the very norm from which, individually, they deviate*" (Foulkes, 1948, p. 29). This was the reality in the group's weekly encounters. Each participant was a unique person with a particular point of view. In the group, there was fruitful exchange on myriad levels of communication. This brought conflicts and new understandings to the fore. The communication also brought about changes that are harder to be accounted for with certainty because they belong to the area of feelings, attitudes, etc.

Members not only listened attentively and tried to understand each other, but the group became a reliable space where a member could be sincere and honest and expect the same from the others. This meant that members learnt to be open to different points of view and also discovered unpleasant facts about themselves. The exchanges in the group promoted self-awareness in each individual. Members' capacity for insight and integration was expanded (Foulkes, 1990).

Another contributory element might have been the external circumstances in which the group took place for part of its three-year duration. Between the first and the second year, there was a war in the north of the country. It began in the last month of our first year, when we were close to the summer break. Members shared their deep fears about what was happening and where the war would lead. Some of them had relatives or acquaintances in the north or in the army and used the group to express their worries. The group could maintain a reasonable dialogue within clear boundaries, when the world around them felt unsafe. Brown's (1998) view is that boundaries "provide a partially illusory psychic 'envelope' (Anzieu, 1984) that strengthens self-identity and a sense of we-ness". It is possible that the external circumstances reinforced the group's cohesion and enabled a more consistent position of acceptance of participants towards each other. It seems to me that, in times of extreme stress, the contrast between the group and the environment invites participation and brings a deep sense of belonging.

Tammy presented a real challenge for the group. She was unempathic and aggressive at times. This was a result of the subtle aggression she received from her family. The group members provided Tammy, perhaps for the first time in her life, with support and empathy, honest mirroring, and sincere care: that is, alternative modes of relating (Brown, 1998). It seems to me they were attuned in a very realistic way to her needs. There were harsh responses to her from members and from me. However, they were realistic, specific, and measured, so it was possible for her to accept them. They did not diminish her, or become overwhelming, as subtle aggression can become over long periods of time. Such sensitive responses can promote change from tenuous to fuller connectedness, not only with the self but also with others (Dolan et al., 1997).

It was surprising and instructive to hear members express observations and understandings that I had not thought of. In the case of

Tammy, their deep acceptance of her, in the light of my own occasional discomfort, was significant in helping me better understand the dynamics that she facilitated in the group.

"Psychoanalysts and group analysts now accept that they are deeply involved participant observers in the interpersonal field of the therapeutic matrix in which we immerse ourselves" (Brown, 1998, p. 400). In this respect, it seems to me that, through projective identification, I was bearing her self-hating parts within myself. Holding these parts inside myself—when the group was identified with her and her needs—provided her with the "good enough environment" in which the *"full course of an experience is allowed"* (Winnicott, 1941, p. 67).

An addition

The processes and ambience of the group were a relief for me. This was the first group that I conducted after completing my training. In a way, I was going it alone. Of course, I had the backup of the Institute, but, all in all, I was working by myself and checking the value of the learning period. I had a very good experience during my training, and I was willing to see how it worked. Could I trust the group, follow it, as Foulkes (1990) proposed? Would it work? I think it did, and my belief in this approach to therapy and my capacity to articulate it was significantly reinforced.

References

Anzieu, D. (1984). Group phantasies. In: *The Group and the Unconscious* (pp. 100–128). London: Routledge & Kegan Paul.

Bion, W. R. (1962). The psycho-analytic study of thinking. *International Journal of Psychoanalysis, 43*: 306–310.

Brown, D. (1998). Foulkes's basic law of group dynamics 50 years on: abnormality, injustice and the renewal of ethics. *Group Analysis, 31*(4): 391–419.

Dolan, B., Warren, F., & Norton, K. (1997). Changes in borderline symptoms one year after therapeutic community treatment for severe personality disorder. *British Journal of Psychiatry, 171*: 274–279.

Foulkes, S. (1948). The group analytic situation. In: *Introduction to Group Analytic Psychotherapy* (pp. 25–34). London: Heinemann.

Foulkes, S. H. (1990). On interpretation in group analysis. In: E. Foulkes (Ed.), *Selected Papers. Psychoanalysis and Group Analysis* (pp. 187–196). London: Karnac.

Foulkes, S. H., & Anthony, E. J. (1984). Some group phenomena. In: *Group Psychotherapy. The Psychoanalytic Approach* (pp. 152–161). London: Maresfield Library.

Freud, S. (1920g). *Beyond the Pleasure Principle. S. E., 18*: 7–65. London: Hogarth.

Friedman, R. (2007). Where to look? Supervising in group analysis. A relations disorder perspective. *Group Analysis, 40*(2): 251–268.

Haley, J. (1986). The family life cycle. In: *Uncommon Therapy. The Psychiatric Techniques of Milton H. Erickson, M.D.* (pp. 41–64). New York: W. W. Norton.

Hopper, E. (2005). Countertransference in the context of the fourth basic assumption in the unconscious life of groups. *International Journal of Group Psychotherapy, 55*(1): 87–113.

Hopper, E. (2006). Theoretical and conceptual notes concerning transference and countertransference processes in group and by groups and the social unconscious: Part I. *Group Analysis, 39*(4): 549–559.

Hopper, E., & Weinberg, H. (2011). Introduction. In: E. Hopper & H. Weinberg (Eds.), *The Social Unconscious in Persons, Groups, and Societies. Volume 1: Mainly Theory* (pp. xxiii–lvi). London: Karnac.

Khan, M. (1986). The concept of cumulative trauma. In: G. Kohon (Ed.), *The British School of Psychoanalysis* (pp. 117–135). London: Free Association Books.

Ogden, T. H. (1992). An object relations theory of internal objects. In: *The Matrix of the Mind* (pp. 133–149). London: Maresfield Library.

Pierce, C. M. (1970). Offensive mechanisms. In: F. Barbour (Ed.), *The Black Seventies* (pp. 265–282). Boston, MA: Porter Sargent.

Pines, M. (1998). Reflections on mirroring. In: *Circular Reflections. Selected Papers on Group Analysis and Psychoanalysis* (pp. 17–40). London: Jessica Kingsley.

Racker, H. (1991). *Transference and Counter-Transference*. London: Maresfield Library.

Schlapobersky, J. R. (2015). On making a home amongst strangers: the paradox of group psychotherapy. *Group Analysis, 48*(4): 406–432.

Van Der Kleij, G. (1983). The setting of the group. *Group Analysis, 16*(1): 75–80.

Winnicott, D. W. (1941). The observation of infants in a set situation. In: *Through Pediatrics to Psychoanalysis* (pp. 52–69). New York: Basic Books.

Winnicott, D. W. (1950). Aggression in relation to emotional development. In: *Through Pediatrics to Psycho-Analysis* (pp. 204–218). New York: Basic Books.

Winnicott, D. W. (1960). Ego distortion in terms of true and false self. In: *The Maturational Processes and the Facilitating Environment* (pp. 140–152). London: Karnac.

Yogev, H. (2012). The development of empathy and group analysis. *Group Analysis*, 46(1): 61–80.

CHAPTER FIFTEEN

Foreigner in your motherland, foreigner in your chosen homeland: Jewish cultural identity

Suzi Shoshani

One purpose of this chapter is to illustrate processes of equiv-alence (Hopper, 2003) with respect to the unconscious mean-ings of immigration. Such meanings range from personal experiences (growing up in a country feeling that this is not a home-land but only a temporary place of residence) to the experiences of the Jewish people during their entire history with respect to being uprooted and having to make new beginnings in new lands. There-fore, the group analyst in the Israeli context must always be sensitive to a large range of meanings in understanding clinical experiences in groups (de Maré, 1991), both personal and contextual processes.

Man is born into a culture. He carries within him the human cul-tural heritage. The historical foundations of the human race, like the Holy Scripture, the myths, the common legends and stories that accompany past events, which man absorbs from birth, all contain cultural symbols. Some of them are passed unconsciously and some of them are acquired during man's development. Thus, issues of belonging to different national cultures are central, affect our person-ality, and shape our identity, consciously or unconsciously. We are meeting and dealing with them in group analysis.

Human identity is related to the culture in which we live (Christopher, 2001). Culture gives meaning to the social world of man since it provides understanding of his life. Human beings live in a world of meaning. Therefore, one may say that the cultural identity provides meaning to the society in which we live, act, and develop, and is an integral part of our entire identity.

Social systems have culture and patterns of communication of which the members of the system are, to varying degrees, unconscious, even though they have both co-constructed these cultures and patterns of communication, internalised, shared, inherited, and transmitted them (Hopper & Weinberg, 2011)

In Israel, the population is mainly composed of immigrants from different countries and cultures. Therefore, there is great importance to the understanding of the Jewish cultural identity. Similarly, in group analysis, it is important to understand the development of the cultural identity of the individual and of the entire group. This understanding enables the group's members and conductor to explore and understand their world and change themselves accordingly. This matter is particularly evident in the early stages of absorption in the group, and, later, in situations of conflict and aggression. We enter a group with our cultural identity and soon confront the cultural identities of others. We have to learn, accommodate, and sometimes change according to these experiences. Sometimes these cultural identities are in conflict, as is often the case in times of immigration.

This chapter deals with some aspects of the formation of a Jewish cultural identity. Using Abraham's fundamental myth and my own personal experiences, which shaped my identity as a Jew in Romania, my motherland, and in Israel, my chosen homeland, I will illustrate some characteristics of the Jewish cultural unconscious that defines the Jewish self-identity and their component in group analysis in Israel.

Identity

First of all, let me emphasise the connection between the individual and the society in the identity formation process.

According to Erikson, identity "connotes both a persistent sameness within oneself (selfsameness) and a persistent sharing of some kind of essential character with others" (1956, p. 109). Identity is the sense that "I am somebody". A person's identity is a collective of identities, organised by the developing personality, and organising and directing it. The identity presents man to himself and to society (Erikson, 1968).

In Laing's opinion (1961), man's identity is formed by his relationships with others. The individual's identity depends on the identity given to him by others, the identities he attributes to others, and the identity that, in his opinion, is attributed to him by others. Therefore, self-identity is a synthesis of me seeing the others seeing me.

In Foulkes and Anthony's view, "man is primarily a social being" (1965, p. 234). The primary impetus is to belong to a group and to have influence on it (Dalal, 1998; Maslow, 1954). In fact, personal identity is constructed within a group.

Kernberg (1976) argued that personal identity derives from complex intrapsychic and interpsychic processes, conscious and unconscious. Personal identity is constructed during the course of one's life by cultural values and identifying with the social environment. Identity is formed out of differentiation from the other, and this process is constantly evolving.

Cultural identity

The society into which man is born has a crucial role in his development and functioning during his life: "Individual's identity develops within a cultural framework and cannot be separated from it" (LeRoy, 1994, pp. 180).

Foulkes uses the term "foundation matrix" to explain that "strangers being of the same species and more narrowly of the same culture share a fundamental mental matrix" (1990a, p. 228). Cultural identity is the sum of the skills and customs, the internalisation of values, norms, and other essential elements acquired by a man as a member of the society to which he belongs. Every society has typical patterns of culture that shape the individual's values and beliefs, and influence them.

One might say that cultural identity is a process that is built through the link between the inner individual's identification group and his external group, the society. Those aspects of the culture system are part of the social unconscious of the society in which the individual is born and develop. The social unconscious is based on transgenerational cultural inheritance through a variety of institutions such as education, child-rearing practices, and socialisation more generally (Hopper & Weinberg, 2011). This process is mostly unconscious, passed from generation to generation and always forming and changing.

Foulkes (1990b) claimed that, in group analytic view, by analysing the social unconscious we meet the cultural inheritance.

The unconscious cultural identity may become conscious and visible in a group in which the boundary between "me" and "you", "us" and "them", is crossed and transgressed.

People become aware of their cultural identity when they are alone in a strange cultural context (LeRoy, 1994), after they arrive in a foreign country or join a therapeutic group (Bledin, 2003). A therapist must be aware of this when introducing a new participant to the group.

Changing cultural identity

Many authors have studied the identity crisis of immigrants, emphasising the crisis of moving from a man's motherland to his chosen homeland. Most of them show that the loss of the mother(land) disturbs the structuring of the emigrant's identity and requires a period of mourning and readjustment (Garza-Guerrero, 1974). Emigration means leaving behind the familiar world of external objects and often the internal world of objects as well. Like a child who needs to separate from his mother in order to constitute self-identity, the immigrant must resolve the earliest crisis of separation from his mother(land) in order to move on to a relatively functioning autonomous ego in his chosen homeland.

The immigration of Jews to Israel in the nineteenth and twentieth centuries had a unique aspect regarding their cultural identity. The cultural heritage of Jews around the world was imprinted over thousands of years, through Biblical myths, traditions, behavioural norms, perceptions, way of life, and common historical events. This cultural heritage of leaving the motherland and yearning for the Promised Land became an ideal and appears prominently in stories of survival, heroism, and victories of the Jewish people. We met those aspects in our groups.

The immigrant's myth

Most of the people who immigrate to Israel have a strong Jewish cultural identity and a sense of closeness to the Promised Land, which stems from the Jewish social unconscious that was constructed in their motherland. Even immigrants who arrived in Israel unavoidably and were displaced from their motherland because of persecution, pogroms, and lack of personal security—such as Holocaust survivors, immigrants from Muslim countries, and the former Soviet Union—have a cultural Jewish identity, partly unconscious. This cultural identity helps them to overcome the crisis of emigration when they arrive in Israel. Based on the founding Biblical myth, I will illuminate this aspect: "Now the Lord had said unto Abram, Get thee out of thy country, and from thy kindred, and from thy father's house, unto a land that I will show thee" (Genesis 12, 1).

Shortly after the creation of the world, God tells Abraham, the founding father of the Hebrew nation, to leave his land, his motherland, and his father's house and to move to another land that God will show him. In the early days of the Jewish nation, there is already a myth of uprooting and wandering but, at the same time, one can also see in this myth an encouragement to explore and discover what is beyond the narrow boundaries of the surroundings. This is the foundation matrix of the Jewish nation and perhaps even the postulate at the basis of globalisation. The process of leaving the old and familiar world and going to the unknown in order to find identity is essentially a process of separation–individuation. This is an unconscious motivation for Jewish people. This force leads to progress and development but can also be destructive. Perhaps this is also the base of the myth of the "wandering Jew", who is always exiled from his motherland, and when he returns to it, he longs for the land he left and is sentenced to bear forever the pain of the two homelands.

The myth of immigration and repatriation reappears in the story of immigration to Egypt and the Exodus. The separation–individuation of Moses from the Egyptian people, the war of the few against the many, and the survival in the journey to the Promised Land, are myths of heroism that unite the Jewish people.

In our times, the attempt to explore and to discover new worlds is not only a dream but also reality: economy is universal, the boundaries blur, transportations are easy, and the communications through the internet create for all of us a global network. However, and perhaps because of this, there is a constant wish for self-determination, for finding one's own unique identity that separates him from the other and determines his belonging.

Other myths, originating in the social unconscious that form the cultural Jewish identity, seek to answer the question as to what caused Abraham to obey God.

> And I will make of thee a great nation, and I will bless thee, and make thy name great; and thou shalt be a blessing (Genesis 12, 2).

> And I will make thy seed as the dust of the earth: so that if a man can number the dust of the earth, then shall thy seed also be numbered (Genesis 13, 16).

> And I will establish my covenant between me and thee and thy seed after thee in their generations for an everlasting covenant: And I will give unto thee, and to thy seed after thee, the land wherein thou art a stranger, all the land of Canaan, for an everlasting possession; and I will be their God. (Genesis 17, 7–8)

God's promises to Abraham ranged from those that are trivia and minor to those which are major and significant. He recognises that man cannot live without a homeland, and, therefore, he undertakes to provide one in his last promise. The uprooting is a temporary process required to obtain a new and eternal homeland.

God's words contain an unequivocal and irreversible promise for a secure future and a covenant between God and Abraham from which derives the uniqueness of the Jewish people. At the basis of the Jewish nation, in the transference between the generations, in the social unconscious, there is a strong element of uprooting that entails suffering, anxiety, and fear of the future: leaving the known and familiar. Yet, at the same time, in order to overcome these feelings, there is a promise of greatness, success, uniqueness, and ascension to the highest level of "a covenant with God" and of a home, a permanent residency to the Jewish people, for all generations. One can say that departure, separation, and uprooting from the familiar are enabled through defences and fantasies such as omnipotence, grandiosity, patronisation, and supremacy: "we are the chosen people". These conscious and unconscious defences and fantasies have a symbolic value, which enables the uprooting of the Jewish people and an ability to cope with the pain and suffering that comes from immigration while maintaining their cultural identity.

In the course of centuries in which the Jews lived in exile, they suffered from the results of lack of belonging and a sense of strangeness, rejection, exclusion, inferiority, humiliation, discrimination, helplessness, and loss of a "containing object" (Bion, 1970), which is man's homeland. They learnt to overcome these effects through a mental compensation such as pride, spiritual and moral supremacy, segregation, and an idealisation of the desired Promised Land, of which they could dream and belong to in order to continue Abraham's dynasty.

Self-experience

The stories of the Torah, their explanation, and the historical events of the Jewish people that were accompanied by myths of heroism and a covenant with God are transferred by the parents, consciously and unconsciously, to the Jewish child from birth. In the Jewish cultural heritage, parents have, for generations, used "chosen glories".

Chosen glories are shared mental images of pride and pleasure evoking past events and heroes that are recollected ritualistically. Past victories in battle and great accomplishments of a political or religious nature frequently appear as chosen glories. Chosen glories are passed on to succeeding generations in parent/teacher–child interactions and through participation in ritualistic ceremonies. They link children of a large group with each other and with their large group, and the children experience increased self-esteem by being associated with such glories (Volkan, 1988).

To illustrate the experience of forming a cultural Jewish identity, I shall share with you my childhood's experiences in my motherland, Romania.

I became aware of these myths only at a late stage in my life. As a little girl, I remember asking my mother, "Why can't you buy me a golden cross like my friend Anka has?" I also wanted a Christmas tree in our house with presents. I did not understand why I could not have those lovely Easter eggs and break them open while playing with my friends and say, "Long live Christ the King". When we travelled on the bus and passed by a church, why could I not be like everyone else and make the sign of a cross? The church wedding ceremonies were so beautiful, and I wanted to take part, listen to the organ music, and hear the voices of the choir filling the church space. Why did my friends tell me I could not come in? Instead, I went with my parents, three times a year, to some gloomy two-storey house (only later did I realise that it was on Rosh Hashanah, Yom Kippur, and Passover). Its ground floor was designated for men in black clothes with big hats, and its small and crowded first floor was intended for women wearing elegant clothes, peeking below through the curtains, babbling, not interested in what was going on. There was no music, and one could hardly hear the chanting of the prayer from the ground floor. Everything was so plain and uninteresting. There was no joy, no excitement, and mostly it was boring. I did not have any friends to play with, except for my two cousins. I also understood, although my parents did not tell me so explicitly, that I must not tell my friends from school where I had been. It was not a holiday they could understand, and at school we were not taught about Jewish holidays. I concluded that I was different, strange, and did not belong; I must hide. My motherland was not my land and I lived, partly, in a ghetto.

Yet, parallel to these feelings, my memory was also imprinted with heroic tales that I was told about my people: wars in which Eretz Israel (The Land of Israel) was conquered several times during history, David's victory over Goliath, Samson's stand against the Philistines, Bar Kokhba revolt, the Return to Zion, the War of Independence, etc. I also heard stories about the Jewish wisdom, like the story of Joseph the dream diviner, Moses and the Exodus, King David's wisdom, and the mothers' trial by King Solomon. I was acquainted with some important musicians, authors, artists, and scientists, such as Einstein, Freud, Mahler, Mendelssohn, and Soutine. Although I was part of a minority and despite the feelings of inferiority, alienation, and rejection that I felt in my motherland, I began to feel that I belonged to something else, something unique. Gradually, I understood that I was in a transitional land, following a path that would eventually bring me to the desired Promised Land—Israel, my ideal object.

Now the question arises: how can we miss something we do not know? Do the words "next year in Jerusalem", said at Passover dinner, mean something, or are they empty words? Not for a little girl. I could fantasise about my grandmother's house in Israel (she left when I was three years old), and the streets of Tel Aviv leading to the sea; imagine the synagogues and the great temple, which was, for me, the king's palace and I was his princess. All these fantasies about the chosen homeland filled the cold and lonely space of feeling that I did not belong to the land where I was born.

The years have passed and the reality of my motherland became more complex. School expanded my world and introduced me to an additional emotional burden, which forced me to hide my skills and my wisdom. It was not easy to cope with an anti-Semite mathematics teacher, who did not like the fact that I was the only one who got nine at the first exam in sixth grade, and had no other choice but to send me, as the class representative, to the school's contest. When I was chosen, thanks to my good memory, as one of five children who were supposed to represent their school in the town competition, I aroused great jealousy and objections in my school. The fact that I was chosen to represent my school in the final was not received with enthusiasm.

My success raised anger, insults followed, along with cries of contempt, "Yid", and the abuse. My injury was not easy. The hostile surroundings presented many obstacles along my path to success, and sometimes even managed to push me off my track. In the end, I "broke" my arm a day before the race, I flunked the mathematics test, because I wrote $2 \times 2 = 5$, and the teacher managed to pull me off the school team, claiming that only boys could compete against a school which had an all-girl team. I sat in the audience, knowing all the answers to the questions, and painfully watched my school lose.

Nevertheless, as an antidote to these difficult experiences, I always felt an inner satisfaction, which was nurtured by my family, whether consciously or unconsciously, regarding my Judaism, wisdom, and superiority. These myths helped me overcome the dismal external reality. Thus, leaving my motherland was not experienced as being so traumatic. It was as if I was being freed from the ghetto, from the need to hide or to diminish myself. It was as if I had a license to be who I really was. Actually, it was a fulfilment of a dream.

On the way to Israel, I became afraid of the new and unfamiliar world that was full of unknown customs, a foreign language, and a different way of life. Many questions arose: will I manage to adjust? Will I be able to contain all the new information? Will I become a part of the new country that, along with my parents, I chose to live in and to raise my family, or will I be different again?

I was surprised to encounter, once again, feelings of inferiority, alienation, humiliation, and not belonging to the country I had dreamt about. In Israel, I was the Romanian, the new immigrant. I did not know anything about religion, did not know who Ben Gurion was, or the difference between Mount Tabor and Mount Herzl. I dressed funny, stood when the teacher entered the classroom, and said please and thank you. I knew how to ballroom dance but was completely helpless when it came to folk dancing, which was popular in Israel at that time. And mainly, I heard the children in the class giggling and telling jokes about the "Romanian thief".

Was this not similar, in a way, to the feeling of alienation I felt in Romania? Perhaps in Romania I felt more rejection and in Israel more exclusion, but in both cases I was a stranger, I did not belong. Immigrants from Middle Eastern countries underwent similar experiences. The images were different, but the essence was the same. Instead of "Romanian thief" they heard "Moroccan knife", "Persian miser", etc. They, too, had to hide and deny their culture that the "sabras" and the immigrants from Western Europe considered to be inferior. They, too, felt devaluated regarding their customs and culture, tried to distance themselves from their inner heritage, and glorified Israeli culture. On the one hand, they had to adjust to Israel, and, on the other, to Western culture. Their feelings of humiliation and inferiority were greater. Most of us reduced the use of our mother tongue and we were often ashamed of our parents.

At the beginning of acclimatisation, these immigrants experienced a devaluation of their norms and customs. Their behaviour was perceived as being in opposition to "sabra" behaviour, which was characterised by heroism, the sanctity of the army, a direct and patronising speech, and confident and rude behaviour. The immigrants were required to adopt these values and even to renounce their culture. Sometimes, in order to protect themselves, they used mechanisms of splitting, detachment, and supremacy: "I'm elite, I belong to a higher culture, I have knowledge in mathematics, music, languages, philosophy, and culinary talent that you, the 'Sabra' do not have". And sometimes they felt inferior.

How can one overcome and escape feelings of alienation and inferiority and create a new identity while adopting a chosen homeland? I believe that the common Jewish cultural identity, which was built partly in the Jew's social unconscious around the world, over many years and out of different experiences during history, helped the immigrants to adapt to Israel and deepen their cultural identity.

"Arise, walk through the land in the length of it and in the breadth of it; for I will give it unto thee" (Genesis 13, 17). This is what God says to Abraham and meant that Abraham should walk around the country and conquer it in all aspects: geographically and spiritually, in order to identify with the new homeland and to make it part of him. That is what most of the new immigrants did at the beginning of their journey in Israel. They travelled through the length and the breadth of the land, learnt Hebrew, literature, and the Bible, and studied Zionism and the history of the state of Israel. All these helped them to develop a sense of belonging to Israel and shape their new identity. Gradually, through processes of separation–individuation and a deepening of their roots in Israel, immigrants found a way of building a unique and balanced identity that combined past and present and was suited to their needs. The more "conquering" the "Sabra" culture was, the more was there a place that enabled the integration of the motherland's culture and allowed the creation of a new identity.

Immigration and group analysis

Human cultural identity determines behaviour in the analytic group. This identity influences the interpersonal relations of the patient and develops and changes constantly during treatment. A new participant who joins the analytic group feels like an alien and does not belong. He must learn a "new language", new codes of behaviour, and the spoken and unspoken rules of the group. He must internalise the history of the group and its members. The group also refers to the new participant as an alien and a disturbing factor that might change the structure and customs of the group. Between the group and the patient there are, simultaneously, attraction, avoidance, and even rejection. These relations are accompanied, sometimes, by anxiety and aggressive responses. Sometimes, the new participant demonstrates detachment from the group's members and patronises them, and sometimes the members of the group exclude the new participant, creating a split between them. In his book co-authored with Foulkes, Anthony claims that the stranger in the group "feels the rub of strangeness until he finds acceptance and can blend with his surroundings . . . it is disturbing to the self-satisfaction of the group, and they must deal with it either by assimilation or extrusion" (1965, p. 159).

The difficulty in accepting the other is also expressed during group analysis and not just at its beginning or with the joining of a new participant. To illustrate this, I shall describe a short vignette from one of my analytic groups.

A relatively new participant, originally from Germany, who converted to Judaism, constantly criticised Israelis' lack of manners, as well as their aggressive and invasive behaviour. She was furious when someone was late, even by two minutes, checking her watch all the time, and could not accept any exceptions to the fixed time of the beginning or the end of the meeting. She arrived at meetings with the precision of a Swiss watch, did not drink anything, and left exactly when the meetings ended, without saying a word to the other members of the group. She lived in Israel alone and was rather lonely. Another "Sabra" participant, second generation to the Holocaust, invited her for Passover, against the rules of the group, when she heard that she was going to be alone during the holiday. The German immigrant refused the invitation and hardly said "thank you", because she interpreted it as an invasion of her life. After a while, when they argued about something else, the "Sabra" woman said to the German woman, "You think that you are superior with your manners and European education. You think the Israelis are inferior, but actually we are better then you. You don't know how to behave, what warmth and love is, and what politeness really is. You were not touched by my invitation to celebrate with my family and didn't thank me properly. So, maybe we push and drive horribly, we talk loudly, shout, we are impolite and late sometimes, but we are real and more human than you. We care about the other."

The group identified with each of the women and the participants expressed their dual feelings, and tried to understand the pain of both viewpoints, indicated by the way in which the attack was also a defence: the aggressor, as well as the victim, feels hurt. They mentioned that both women wanted to belong and to be recognised in their personal identity.

The "us" and "them" division is, as Berman et al. (2000) claim, a universal structure that is at the basis of cultural identification and is part of the group analysis process. This structure includes a superior–inferior hierarchy. This is one of the defence mechanisms that operate at the beginning of the rebuilding process of an identity in general, and a cultural identity in particular, which appears at the commencement of the adjustment process to a new culture, as well as during group analysis. The task of the therapist is to contain all cultures, and to find the differences and similarities between them without valued hierarchy, and to help the group's members to find their own uniqueness and to shape their cultural identity.

References

Anthony, E. J. (1965). The phenomenology of the group situation. In: S. H. Foulkes & E. J. Anthony (Eds.), *Group Psychotherapy: The Psychoanalytic Approach* (pp. 157–160). London: Karnac.

Berman, A., Berger, M., & Gutmann, D. (2000). The division into us and them as a universal social structure. *Mind and Human Interaction, 11*(1): 53–72.

Bion, W. R. (1970). *Attention and Interpretation*. London: Tavistock.

Bledin, K. (2003). Migration, identity and group analysis. *Group Analysis, 36*: 97–110.

Christopher, J. C. (2001). Culture and psychotherapy: toward a hermeneutic approach. *Psychotherapy, 38*(2): 28–115.

Dalal, F. (1998). *Taking the Group Seriously: Toward a Post Foulksian Group Analytic Theory*. London: Jessica Kingsley.

De Maré, P. (1991). *Koinonia. From Hate through Dialogue to Culture in the Larger Group*. London: Karnac.

Erikson, E. H. (1956). The problem of ego identity. *Journal of the American Psychoanalytic Association, 4*(1): 56–121.

Erikson, E. H. (1968). *Identity. Youth and Crisis*. London: Faber and Faber.

Foulkes, S. H. (1990a). The group as matrix of individual's mental life. In: E. Foulkes (Ed.), *S. H. Foulkes: Selected Papers* (pp. 223–233). London: Karnac.

Foulkes, S. H. (1990b). Problems of the large group. In: E. Foulkes (Ed.), *S. H. Foulkes: Selected Papers* (pp. 249–269). London: Karnac.

Foulkes, S. H., & Anthony E. J. (1965). *Group Psychotherapy: The Psychoanalytic Approach*. London: Karnac.

Garza-Guerrero, A. C. (1974). Culture shock: the mourning and vicissitudes of identity. *Journal of the American Psychoanalytic Association, 22*: 408–429.

Hopper, E. (2003). *The Social Unconscious*. London: Jessica Kingsley.

Hopper, E., & Weinberg, H. (Eds.) (2011). *The Social Unconscious in Persons, Groups, and Societies. Volume 1: Mainly Theory*. London: Karnac.

Kernberg, O. F. (1976). *Object Relations Theory and Clinical Psychoanalysis*. New York: Jason Aronson.

Laing, R. D. (1961). *The Self and Others*. London: Tavistock.

LeRoy, R. J. (1994). Group analysis and culture. In: D. Brown & L. Zinkin (Eds.), *The Psyche and The Social World* (pp. 180–201). London: Routledge.

Maslow, A. H. (1954). *Motivation and Personality*. New York: Harper & Row.

Volkan, V. D. (1988). *The Need to Have Enemies and Allies: From Clinical Practice to International Relationships*. Northvale, NJ: Jason Aronson.

PART III

APPLICATIONS OF GROUP ANALYSIS

Group analysis goes to academia: therapeutic approach and professional identity in graduate studies of psychology

Shulamit Geller and Eran Shadach

A s we wrote this chapter, we found ourselves responding both to its theoretical aspects and, to a significant degree, to its personal and emotional aspects. On one such occasion, during conversation, we each experienced a surge of early memories.

Shulamit: Once, when I was five years old, I met my parents returning from the cinema. I asked them how the film was, to which they answered that they had not understood a thing. I asked, with natural astonishment, "Why, was there no translation [Hebrew subtitles]?" Their response was a burst of laughter, yet no one offered to explain why my question had been so funny. In my family, in the post-Holocaust 1960s, the act of entering a room full of adults talking—even laughing—and discussing matters I was fully aware I was not supposed to know, using a language I was unable to understand, was a very palpable experience. I recall my huge curiosity and determination to understand, along with a fear of what I might discover. Much later, during my group analysis training, I was excited to discover that these were coded messages that were now given validation by the group members and conductor. I felt as though I had found a "dictionary" which could be used to translate and observe my own self and my parents, and to find my bearings in a territory that had, hitherto, remained sealed.

Eran: I grew up in a Kibbutz belonging to Hashomer Hatzair, in a communal child-rearing system with relatively limited adult presence. In order to survive and develop socially, the children depended to a large extent on their ability to exchange information in an efficient and easily grasped manner, and so each scrap of information we possessed individually became a part of our group's shared property. Years later, during my group analysis training, memories of these experiences resurfaced, and were replicated to a large degree within the group. I was able to draw upon the strength of mutual support in a group of equals, while once again experiencing formerly repressed feelings of danger and isolation, and longing for an interpretative and protective authority.

As we wrote the chapter, it became clear to us that each of our memories revolved around the central role and importance that the family holds as the primary group which an individual encounters (Foulkes, 1990a), and as an organisation which is supposed to supply the resources to cope with fear of misunderstanding, isolation, and disenfranchisement (Rouchy, 1995). Our memories indicated a pronounced deficiency of these family functions, but, while the first memory called attention to the importance of learning a new language and grammar in a cultural context (Zavos, 2005), the second memory involved the absence of a traditional family structure and of parental authority figures, and demonstrated the unique features of the group of equals. According to Meltzer and Harris (1976), the family mediates between the individual and the community, moving between progressive and regressive conditions of existence. The family (or the group) is, thus, seen as an outlet for feelings of love and hope, hatred and pain. It fosters the ability to think and to develop. In the following seminar description, we emphasise the link between the language of group analysis and the development of thinking abilities, which is a prerequisite for all therapists, including group therapists.

Group therapy training is an essential, yet scarce, aspect of graduate studies in psychology. Recently, therapy services in Israel have granted group therapy an ever-expanding role, perceiving it as an important component of every therapist's professional profile. Nevertheless, the scope of these studies is limited, and the thrust of the training in the various therapeutic disciplines is primarily orientated towards individual therapy (Ward & Crosby, 2010).

Current group therapy training programmes, in both Israel and worldwide, are mostly provided by extra-academic institutions (e.g., the Israeli Institute of Group Analysis), or as part of postgraduate university programmes (e.g., the School of Social Work at Tel Aviv University).

Therefore, we also received our official group therapy training in the Group Analysis Diploma Course only after finishing our clinical internship. We met as lecturers in the Department of Clinical Psychology at the Tel Aviv-Yaffo Academic College, the first college in Israel to run a graduate programme for clinical, rehabilitational, and medical programmes, all three of which offered adult and child sub-specialisation. Our reunion sparked the idea to introduce a seminar for group therapy into the curriculum, which would present the principles of group dynamics and could supplement the students' identities as psychologists and group therapists. Initially, the seminar's theoretical background comprised approaches such as those of Yalom and Leszcz (2005) and MacKenzie (1997), while applying the heterogeneity principal (Foulkes, 1975) as well as the concept of learning from experience (Bion, 1962). This concept refers to a double movement: on the one hand, movement towards the foundation experience which is acquired while learning, and, on the other hand, the need to let go of previous experiences in order to allow new learning to occur (Gampel, 2004). Later on, we expanded the theoretical background to include major group-analysis concepts.

The seminar structure

Despite differences in structure and in scope, intended similarities exist between the current course and our training programme at the Israeli Institute of Group Analysis. The seminar was designed to follow the unique and shared features related to group therapy training programmes in general (e.g., Furr & Barret, 2000; Kobos, 2010; Stone, 2010) and those of group analysis approach in particular. It was comprised of four basic elements: theory, practice, supervision, and observation (Behr, 2010; Nathan & Poulsen, 2004).

Twenty-four second-year graduate students from the six therapy programmes participated in the seminar. Group composition was balanced for gender and for programme affiliation to achieve maximal in-group heterogeneity (Foulkes & Anthony, 1957). The students' primary task in the first semester was "to experience and understand the role of a participant in a group". Applying the fishbowl paradigm (Knight et al., 2010), the participants were divided into two equal-sized groups. Throughout seven sessions, the working group, co-led by the seminar lecturers, was positioned in the inner circle, while the remaining twelve students were instructed to be attentive to the processes and dynamics of the working group in order to reflect on these aspects after the session. After seven sessions, the groups switched. At the conclusion of each session, all participants convened for thirty minutes of supervised discussion in the form of a median group (De Maré et al., 1991).

The students' primary task in the second semester was "to experience the role of a group therapist". The group was divided into two new twelve-person groups. Each group experienced self-conducting for a period of six sessions. Each session was led by a different pair of students according to a task-centred theme (e.g., parenting, authority, and competition), while the remaining members of the group acted as participants. At the same time, the second group was seated behind a one-way mirror (Hobbs, 1988) accompanied by the seminar lecturers. After six sessions, the two groups switched roles. At the conclusion of each session, as in the first semester, all students convened for supervised discussion to conceptualise and theoretically understand the co-conductors' work in the form of a median group. The repeated transitions between roles and identities of participant, observer, trainee, and conductor allowed the participants to investigate the meaning of foundation matrix and dynamic matrix concepts, as well as to experience processes such as "ego training in action", "exchange", and "translation", which group analysis considers central to the operation of therapeutic work.

Foundation matrix and dynamic matrix

Group analysis puts a stress on the importance of the context in which a group exists. This context includes the organisation of the wider society inside which the group operates, which is termed the "foundation matrix", and which includes elements such as language, social status, and education (Foulkes, 1975). In the seminar, the foundation matrix was the basis of the Israeli identity, which included many common denominators, such as most of the participants being native-born Jewish Israelis who have served in the army and, ultimately, the fact that they were all students undergoing training which they had arrived at after successfully passing an extensive and complex process of selection. The foundation matrix also takes into account the differences between members of the group, which, in the seminar, included, among other things, differences of gender, religious affiliation, ethnic origin, and family background. In the common shared ground of the foundation matrix of the seminar, lecturers and participants occupied the nodal points (Foulkes, 1990b), which, according to sub-system NOS conceptualisation, make "meeting people" possible: that is, ". . . the function of connecting the individuals with each other to form bigger units . . ." (Ormay, 2012, p. 189).

An expression of the foundation matrix may be seen in the use of the idiom "equal burden", in a session that dealt with the theme of parenthood. The theme was first processed on the level of the personal responsibility each of the participants bore to take care of their aging parents, as compared to their siblings' share of responsibility: ". . . how do you feel when you become your parent's carer, and who shares the burden with you?" This developed into a discussion of a typically Israeli concern with sub-groups which do not carry their equal share of the burden (of taxes, work, and army service) and the compensation for those who do: "On the other hand, you stand on the frontline, but also receive the medals . . . I recently saw *Band of Brothers*, an amazing series . . .". It is possible to understand these associations and the discussion which developed later as an expression of the Israeli "soldier's matrix" (Friedman, 2015)—a matrix which propagates an ethos of brothers-in-arms and of battle glory, essentially meaning that we are never truly released from army service. Therefore (and since the social context at the time involved heated political debate on the topic of Orthodox Jews' army service), by conceiving parent care as a form of service, the soldier's matrix revealed its significance as a template that bestows value, but also becomes a burden.

The dynamic matrix that emerges from the foundation matrix (Foulkes, 1964, 1990b) is the organisation of the group itself. It included professional and personal ambitions, as well as individual striving towards competence and success that are typical of psychology graduate students. Accordingly, the subject of sharing the burden was present in the "here and now", an example of which can be seen in the words of one female participant: "As I was sitting in the sun before we started . . . I wanted someone to take the burden of the group upon himself." Referring to the soldier's matrix, this statement might reflect the conflict between identification with the need to rise with honour to the demands of the "fire line", and the anger and fatigue accompanying the same need.

Ego training in action

Foulkes' expression of "ego training in action" refers to the process in which each patient both experiences and observes the dynamic processes produced in the immediacy of the group, which are then analysed openly by the group members and the conductor. Thus, intrapersonal dynamics ("vertical" interaction) become available to the entire group, which can then utilise them for the purpose of interpersonal action ("horizontal" interaction) (Foulkes & Anthony, 1957). In this manner, each participant in the group becomes more aware of the dynamic struggle taking place within himself or herself (Foulkes, 1975), as well as of the fact that meaningful psychological processes take place within the context of an interactive social net and not in isolation. In one of the self-conducting sessions, the participants defined the seminar lecturers seated behind the one-way mirror as the "real conductors", while the students, who were, in fact, conducting them, were designated "babysitters". Since the conductors identified strongly with this label, they were left paralysed for some time.

In the following supervised discussion, the student-conductors shared with the group the conflict they had experienced between the need to respond to the group's expectations that they remain a part of it, and the need to shift into the role of conductor. The supervised discussion's settings provided the conductors with an opportunity to view themselves through others' eyes, to receive feedback about the way they were perceived, and to maintain an ongoing interaction on this subject (Foulkes, 1964). In this manner, the participants were invited to investigate how forces external to the individual, such as social status, shaped their identity. They were encouraged to have a dialogue with it, and allowed to understand its significance. In this way, the supervised discussion permitted the group to move from dealing with *insight* to dealing with *outsight*, a function related to professional and social affiliations (De Maré et al., 1991).

During a session led by the seminar lecturers, a participant who, in a previous session, had experienced feelings of being invisible to one of them shared these feelings with the group. In the course of the discussion that developed, this participant reported similar feelings that he had experienced in the past in different groups, during which he had felt that his capabilities were not perceived or appreciated by others. In post-Foulksian terms regarding "ego training in action" (Brown, 1994), the work in this session followed a circular and spiral movement pattern. The movement begins with a more complete unveiling of the participant's inner world, which, through sharing, becomes more fully integrated with his self-image. Such discoveries allow the participant to discern the difference between old internal object relationships and new ones in the "here and now". As a result, the session is no longer merely an automatic reconstruction of past experiences, but an opportunity for the participant to learn to attune himself or herself to other people's experiences and to apply meaning to them. In the current example, through subjective and reciprocal interaction with other group members, the participant was able to undergo an emphatic encounter with similar experiences others had testified to, and this helped to free him of the passive silence which had characterised him to that point and, subsequently, to become an active member of the group.

Exchange

Exchange is one of Foulkes' unique group-specific therapeutic factors (Foulkes, 1964). It is made possible through free-floating discussion in the group, creating a network of social interaction, and, as such, is a central mechanism in the formation and development process of identity (Dalal, 1998). Exchange demands a balance between resembling the other and differing from him, through which a communication network of mutual interpersonal relations comes into existence, and the dynamic matrix is constructed (Foulkes, 1975, 1990b). Four elements must be present in the group for a significant exchange to happen: "Free exchange of information and explanation . . . between people who see one another as equals . . . [and] build up a common pool of knowledge and culture . . . in the interest of all participants" (Zinkin, 1994, p. 105). We may understand the recurrence of the idiom "equal burden" in a later session as a reflection and an expression of the participants' need to test their different identities through exchange. The Israeli identity (e.g., mandatory army service, combat duty), the family identity (e.g., family status, responsibility towards parent caring), and the group identity were all expressed in this discussion. In this way, each participant contributed his personal experience to the shared pool of the group and created an opportunity for both the participant and the group to be relieved of their personal isolation (Foulkes, 1948, 1990b).

One of the interesting references to exchange comes from the conceptual sphere of materialistic society as an expression of the prism of "fair play" (Zinkin, 1994, p. 110). According to this approach, the conductor should analyse the group activity in terms of a "marketplace of commodities", which operates under the rule which maintains that the entire group benefits from information that is in possession of the individual. In other words, each participant in the group is a kind of equal-rights merchant, while the emotions, thoughts, and other emotional material in the group are viewed as merchandise communally owned by the collective. In this way, it is possible to view any group activity whatsoever as a kind of social co-operative in which a constant bustling and productive trading of ideas, emotions, and relationships takes place, over which both giver and receiver have ownership rights and from which both are able to benefit. Traditionally, conductors tend to deal with conflict material in the group through the deciphering of transference (Bion, 1961; Hopper, 2007). Comparably, the language of exchange invites both a sharing of contents and the acceptance of ownership over them, in which case, we may refer to a language of giving, taking, and sharing, as well as borrowing, and even theft and robbery. Exchange contributes to the group on the condition that each individual in the group owns something that the others need. Thus, a successful exchange is one in which by way of sharing, the private becomes public, and what was shared by individuals with the group is not lost, but joins the cache of common property, while the group becomes more aware, communal, and therapeutic (Zinkin, 1994).

The following example from the supervised discussion illustrates the use of exchange in the teaching process. The discussion began with the intervention of an observer who presented his own emotional analysis of what had just happened in the group. In response, he was accused of intrusiveness and a lack of sensitivity. As conductors, we interpreted the working group's angry reaction to the observer as a transference manifestation towards us for our intrusiveness. In retrospect, had we used the terminology of exchange, we would also have been able to show the group that the observers had shared an emotional experience that had been a result of their observation. This intervention would have allowed the group to appreciate the way in which they had been perceived and the emotions the observation had aroused. Making this information a property of both groups would have raised awareness of differences, which would have served "ego training in action" and advanced acquisition of the group's new language. It might even have allowed the participants to experience a profit shared by both groups and softened the experience of intrusion and injury.

Translation

During one of the supervised discussions, a participant said that she felt the group was speaking an unfamiliar language, and that she could not understand a thing being said, which made her feel paralysed and detached from the discussion. Her words evoked many responses from the participants, which alternated between identification and interpretation. Towards the end of the session, the participant felt that she understood what had been going on previously and could join the discussion again.

Foulkes and Anthony (Foulkes, 1964; Foulkes & Anthony, 1957) regard translation as a tool which can be used to provide the "autistic" symptom with meaning, both in the traditional manner of raising the unconscious into consciousness and as a means of communication within the group from the aspect of intra- and interpersonal communication (Pines, 2000). Since the conductor's role is to identify the basic ties between the participants' various languages based on their shared mental matrix (Foulkes, 1973; Pines, 2000), developing the students' ability to assign meaning to incidents within the group, to interpret them, or to translate them, is an essential part of teaching group therapy. In the seminar, the students frequently practised the act of translation, both in the supervised discussions, and in their self-conducting sessions. Looking at the latest example, the "dictionary" which the group "wrote" offered the withdrawn participant an opportunity to feel a restored relatedness (Ormay, 2012) with her identity and with her experience of capability as a member of the psychologist sub-group. Regarding our personal memories earlier in this chapter, the new dictionary offered by our groups opened a gate for us to connect to a past of immigration, authority, exclusion, and inclusion. In both cases the translation offered a "zone of contact" between the translating culture (the group analytic language) and the foreign (Venuti, 2000), which had now become familiar.

In a session on the theme of siblings, one of the student conductors offered the following interpretation: "The group's dwelling on the generational issue wasn't a coincidence, since the session took place immediately after Holocaust Memorial Day, which provokes thoughts of presence and absence in relation to the previous generation which is now disappearing." The following session dealt with leadership and took place after the Memorial Day for Israel's Fallen Soldiers. At the beginning of the session, one of the participants said, "Leadership is a dangerous thing and this is connected to Memorial Day: commanders usually sacrifice their lives and what is left? What for?" During the supervised discussion, we translated the statements in both meetings as expressions of the hidden relationships and values of the foundation matrix of the contextual society (Zinkin, 1994), which, when uncovered, have the potential to provide a group with a common language (Pines, 2000). In our discussions, the themes that emerged were related to the collective identification with the state of "living under threat" (Friedman, 2015), as well as with the Holocaust and resurrection.

Stressing the Israeli foundation matrix created a more mature communication process within the group as a whole, which, in turn, promoted the individual maturation of the participants as well (Pisani et al., 2005). It is important, none the less, to stress that translation, while creating a shared language, does not enforce homogeneity, but enables communication and a renewed interest in the proceedings beyond gaps and differences, without ignoring the existence of conflict and struggle (Foulkes, 1964; Zavos, 2005). In the group that dealt with the theme of leadership, when certain participants treated the conductors as "instructors", the conductor suggested that this term assigns alienation to the role of "conducting", and might reflect the group's attitude to the changing conductors, diminishing their professional value. The conductor's intervention demonstrates her role as the translator who provides accessibility to the hidden codes that the participants are communicating unconsciously, translating into a coherent language (Pines, 2000).

Concluding remarks

In this chapter, we have demonstrated the usefulness of group analysis theory in teaching group therapy, and its contribution to the formation of psychology students' professional identity. The seminar invited the participants to investigate themes such as authority, leadership, and sibling relations, stressing the struggles, the doubts, the similarities and differences which appear and are expressed in the group's "here and now". This investigation, which made room for feelings of belonging and success, as well as feelings of exclusion and failure, contributed to the formation of a sense of professional belonging and to the internalisation of the norms of group therapy (Burck, 2010; Friedman, 2007).

An important measure of the seminar's success was received during the course evaluation, a process performed routinely at the college. The feedback questionnaires which the students submitted as a regular part of the teaching programme evaluation process (Nathan & Poulsen, 2004) gave the seminar a general average score of 6.41 and a score of 6.06 for its theoretical contribution in a score range of 1–7, where 7 represents the highest evaluation. These evaluations were supported by verbal feedback provided by the students, which indicated a significant learning experience as participants and as co-conductors, matching satisfaction in similar training programmes (Sunderji et al., 2013).

Israeli society is a society of immigrants, highly concerned with group affiliation and questions of identity. Correspondingly, our students may be described as individuals who "migrated" to the seminar from different programme affiliations and from different stages in their lives. Conceivably, this choice of "migration" was a means to fulfil their need for a group in which they could feel a sense of belonging (Bledin, 2003). People derive their common identity from the groups they belong to (Elias, 1939; Frosh, 2010) and this identity becomes a powerful force in their lives (Dalal, 1998). Therefore, it is possible to define the professional identity as multi-faceted in its connection to different belonging groups (Stacey, 2005), facets of which appeared in the seminar as those of psychologists and group therapists operating within the Israeli matrix.

Finally, in the course of the eight years during which we have given the seminar, there have been changes in the way we understand, conceptualise, and deliver it. Drawing on our training programme, we have learnt to apply the language, the theory, and the concepts of group analysis as described in this chapter, so that our current style of teaching allows for more exchange and "ego training in action". Group analysis has become a significant element for us as psychologists lecturing in academic institutions, into which we introduce our unique private identities. The seminar teaching and our ongoing mutual dialogue have reinforced our understanding that identity is not a static state which can be captured at any given moment, but a process (Frosh, 2010) which is simultaneously inclusive and particular, unceasing and transformative (Stacey, 2005).

References

Behr, H. (2010). Malcolm Pines et al.: the art of teaching group analysis. *Group Analysis*, 43: 241–252.

Bion, W. R. (1961). *Experiences in Groups*. New York: Basic Books.

Bion, W. R. (1962). *Learning from Experience*. London: Karnac.

Bledin, K. (2003). Migration, identity and group analysis. *Group Analysis*, 36: 97–110.

Brown, D. G. (1994). Self development through subjective interaction. A fresh look at "ego training in action". In: D. Brown & L. Zinkin (Eds.), *The Psyche and the Social World: Developments in Group Analytic Theory* (pp. 80–98). London: Routledge.

Burck, C. (2010). From hazardous to collaborative learning: thinking systemically about live supervision group processes. In: C. Burck & G. Daniel (Eds.), *Mirrors and Reflections: Processes of Systemic Supervision* (pp. 141–162). London: Karnac.

Dalal, F. (1998). *Taking the Group Seriously: Towards a Post Foulkesian Group Analytic Theory*. London: Jessica Kingsley.

De Maré, P., Piper, R., & Thompson, S. (1991). *Koinonia: From Hate, through Dialogue to Culture in the Large Group*. London: Karnac.

Elias, N. (1939). *The Civilizing Process*. Oxford: Blackwell.

Foulkes, S. H. (1948). *Introduction to Group Analytic Psychotherapy*. London: Karnac.

Foulkes, S. H. (1964). *Therapeutic Group Analysis*. London: Allen & Unwin [reprinted London: Karnac, 1984].

Foulkes, S. H. (1975). *Group Analytic Psychotherapy, Methods and Principles*. London: Gordon and Breach [reprinted London: Karnac, 1986].

Foulkes, S. H. (1990a). Psychoanalytic concepts of object relations theory: comments on a paper by Fairbairn. In: E. Foulkes (Ed.), *Selected Papers of S. H. Foulkes: Psychoanalysis and Group Analysis* (pp. 107–117). London: Karnac.

Foulkes, S. H. (1990b). The group as matrix of the individual's mental life. In: E. Foulkes (Ed.), *Selected Papers of S. H. Foulkes: Psychoanalysis and Group Analysis* (pp. 223–233). London: Karnac.

Foulkes, S. H., & Anthony, E. J. (1957). *Group Psychotherapy: The Psychoanalytic Approach*. London: Penguin [reprinted London: Karnac, 1984].

Friedman, R. (2007). Where to look? Supervising group analysis: a relations disorder perspective. *Group Analysis, 40*: 251–268.

Friedman, R. (2015). A soldier's matrix: a group analytic view of societies in war. *Group Analysis, 48*: 239–257.

Frosh, S. (2010). *Psychoanalysis Outside the Clinic. Interventions in Psychosocial Studies*. London: Palgrave Macmillan.

Furr, S. R., & Barret, B. (2000). Teaching group counseling skills: problems and solutions. *Counselor Education and Supervision, 40*: 94–104.

Gampel, Y. (2004). Prologue. In: Bion W. R. (2004/1962). *Learning from Experience*. Book Worm [in Hebrew].

Hobbs, M. (1988). From behind the scenes: the psychodynamic implications for an analytic psychotherapy group of being observed through a one-way screen. *Group Analysis, 21*: 235–248.

Hopper, E. (2007). Theoretical and conceptual notes concerning transference and countertransference processes in groups and by groups, and the social unconscious: Part II. *Group Analysis, 40*: 29–42.

Knight, E. B., Barth, P. A., Fink, A. H., Cunningham T. J., Vaughn, C. A., & White, R. E. (2010). Baylor College of Medicine group psychotherapy training. *Group, 34*: 301–308.

Kobos, J. (2010). A laboratory learning approach to teaching group psychotherapy. *Group, 34*: 293–300.

MacKenzie, K. R. (1997). Clinical application of group development ideas. *Group Dynamics: Theory, Research, and Practice, 14*: 275–287.

Meltzer, D., & Harris, M. (1976). *The Educational Role of the Family. A Psychoanalytical Model*. London: Karnac.

Nathan, V., & Poulsen, S. (2004). Group-analytic training groups for psychology students: a qualitative study. *Group Analysis, 37*: 163–177.

Ormay, A. P. (2012). *The Social Nature of Persons: One Person is No Person*. London: Karnac.

Pines, M. (2000). Interpretation: Why, for whom, and when. In: D. Kennard, J. D. Roberts, & D. A. Winter (Eds.), *A Workbook of Group Analytic Interventions* (pp. 138–145). London: Routledge.

Pisani, R. A., Colangeli, G., Giordani, A., & Popolla, P. (2005). The median group: training and supervision. *Group Analysis, 38*: 537–548.

Rouchy, J. C. (1995). Identification and group of belonging. *Group Analysis, 28*: 129–141.

Stacey, R. (2005). Organizational identity: the paradox of continuity and potential transformation at the same time. *Group Analysis, 38*: 477–495.

Stone, W. (2010). Introduction to the special issue on training in group psychotherapy. *Group, 34*: 277–281.

Sunderji, N., Malat, J., & Leszcz, M. (2013). Group day: experiential learning about group psychotherapy for psychiatry residents at University of Toronto. *Academic Psychiatry, 37*: 352–354.

Venuti, L. (Ed.) (2000). *The Translation Studies Reader*. London: Routledge.

Ward, D., & Crosby, C. (2010). Using an observation model for training group therapists in a community mental health setting. *Group, 34*: 355–361.

Yalom, I. D., & Leszcz, M. (2005). *The Theory and Practice of Group Psychotherapy*. New York: Basic Books.

Zavos, A. (2005). (Im)possible translations: challenging therapeutic authority through textual practices. *Group Analysis, 38*: 115–128.

Zinkin, L. (1994). Exchange as a therapeutic factor in group analysis. In: D. Brown & L. Zinkin (Eds.), *The Psyche and the Social World: Developments in Group-Analytic Theory* (pp. 99–117). London: Routledge.

CHAPTER SEVENTEEN

Working with a multi-cultural group in times of war: three metaphors of motion and mobility

Ravit Raufman and Haim Weinberg

W hen Ludo, the protagonist of Romain Gary's novel *Kites* (*Les Cerfs-volants*, published in 1980) was asked to describe in one single word what characterises grace, he recalled his Polish lover named Lila. "I thought of my little Polish, her neck, her arms, her flickering hair, and I answered without hesitation: the movement." This quotation from Gary's masterpiece novel illustrates one central idea of psychoanalysis, that the foundation of life and mental health is related to the experience of being in motion. While object relations theories emphasise motion and mobility in the individual's psyche, group analysis theories emphasise these processes within the group space.

In this chapter, we discuss three metaphors of motion/lack of motion, manifested in a multi-cultural group in Israel during wartime. Themes from the Israeli social unconscious (Hopper & Weinberg, 2011) resonated with the complex and challenging climate in which the group took place. Each group was held within the framework of a training programme for group facilitators at an Israeli university. The group processes were accelerated due to two events occurring a year and a half apart: the first was the military operation in Gaza in 2012. The second occurred in 2014, with the death of the Israeli former

Prime Minister, Ariel Sharon. We also describe a bi-national group, which started a few days after the opening of the second operation in the Gaza strip during the summer of 2014. These events triggered experiences associated with three metaphors of motion and mobility: moving in and out, moving up and down, and whether or not to be in motion. Although these images of movement and motion have sexual connotations, we focus here on their more general connotations. Fundamentally, being in motion is being alive. Total absence of movement equals death.

The group's transitional space is usually a place for playfulness and creativity; being alive and in motion is strongly associated with creativity. Winnicott (1971) viewed creativity as enabling us to experience life as something that is worth living for. According to him, the opposite of creativity is a submissive and passive attitude toward reality, where the world is perceived correctly, but only as something to which to adjust oneself. Winnicott viewed creativity as a universal state, as being alive in a continuous psychic mobility and motion. Children tend to attribute life to moving objects, which are, therefore, perceived as breathing and alive. Many expressions in our daily language reflect this idea, such as "how are things going?", "what's up" (expressing something alive and developing) in contrast to "I am stuck", associated with lack of movement. One task of the group conductor is to enable the group mobility, to set it in motion. This idea is highly related to Winnicott's concept of "going on being" (Winnicott, 1958).

The idea of moving forward, refusing to get bogged down in the past, is strongly related to the notion of hope. Hopper (2001) argues that where there is life, there is hope, virtually by definition. For every individual person, hope can only be understood within his social, cultural, and political transgenerational context, in which he attempts to make creative use of traumatic experience, involving reparation, restoration, and restitution. Keeping hope alive allows people suffering from trauma to move towards post-traumatic growth (Tedeschi & Calhoun, 2004), which is a positive psychological change that occurs as the result of struggle with a highly challenging, stressful, and traumatic event. However, as we see in the following group vignettes, when the political and social situation becomes too stressful and traumatic, the space for elaborating and working through painful events collapses and all hope disappears.

How can the (group) analyst be of help in those situations and not become himself entrapped in such a frozen, motionless, and hopeless state of affairs? Symington (1983) argues that the analyst unconsciously acts, thinks, and feels according to issues belonging to his patients' unconscious mind. As long as the analyst unconsciously identifies with what is projected on him, he is limited, entrapped in a lasso. The ability of the therapist to free himself from this limiting lasso is called by Symington "an act of freedom". However, the therapist cannot intentionally initiate this act. He has to be patient and wait for the right moment when a psychic motion occurs inside, followed by the ability to verbally express it freely, outside the projective lasso. It is only from this new, free position that the therapist develops a relationship that has the power to create change within the patient. These mechanisms are especially powerful in a group, because the group analyst is entrapped not only in the projections of one patient, but in the group's matrix that can be accelerated in the social context.

First group

The group consisted mostly of women. Half of the participants were Israelis (including three Muslims), and the others came to Israel from different countries. The group was conducted in English, the mother tongue of about half of the participants. The mother tongues of the other participants were Spanish, Hebrew, Chinese, Arabic, and various European languages. This created diversity in their ability to express themselves fluently, and in "feeling at home" with the language.

First event: a struggle for territory—moving in and out

In the opening session, we realised that our room was mistakenly assigned to a different group at the same time. As we had already started the meeting and the other group arrived late, the second group's facilitator was asked whether she would be ready to hold the meeting in another room. This short unplanned negotiation was done spontaneously. The second group leader responded willingly and things were quickly and easily resolved. Ostensibly, this was not an unusual event requiring special attention, but later on participants related to this event either as an example of a good way to bridge conflicts, or as an example of the inevitable aspects of conflicts between groups.

In the Israeli–Palestinian reality conflicts are highly associated with territorial struggles. The interpretation of this event has changed over time according to the context in which it was mentioned. Obviously, this event touched several layers, including how the conductor copes at the beginning of the first meeting with issues of authority and power struggle. However, as immigrants arrive to Israel from all over the world, fighting for territory is one of the cornerstones of the Israeli social unconscious. One of the main issues in Israeli process groups is the question of borders and territory (Teplitz, 2005). The struggle for living space and group boundaries (both in terms of space and time boundaries) can be identified concretely as well as symbolically in almost every Israeli group.

In terms of motion, we can refer to the dialectic movement between "in" and "out"[1]: The main dilemma became who goes out and who remains inside, meaning who is included and who is excluded, or "exiled". Belonging and exclusion are fundamental issues in the Israeli habitus (Weinberg, 2009). Thus, it is not surprising that this event reflected the tension around this dialectic of exclusion/inclusion. In retrospect, it became clear that this event resonated throughout the life of the group, as a kind of foreshadowing key issue. In the opening session, one of the Muslim participants immediately declared that she did not define herself as a Palestinian, but, rather, as an Israeli. Another Muslim participant could hardly speak until the end of the meeting. When she spoke, she said that once her Muslim friend had identified herself as an Israeli and not as a Palestinian, she felt she had no place in the group, since her "sister" left her alone. While others saw the conflict resolution around the room issue as an example of a good democratic solution, for her the fact that the other group left quietly did not necessarily indicate that they were happy. On the contrary: she interpreted the organised and peaceful way in which they left the room as a testimony of their submission, muteness, and inability to express their needs. We found ourselves dealing with questions such as who has a place in the group, who does not, and what are the processes involved in this dilemma?

The social unconscious of Israelis is inextricably linked to the Jewish history. Any struggle for territory also incorporates historical significance, reactivated in the "here and now" of the group. This common event might have been charged with meanings and associated to one of the most significant events in Jewish history, the Holocaust. Volkan (2001) used the term "chosen trauma" for a traumatic historical event, living in the collective memory of a nation or society. Such a trauma becomes a template in the national memory, preserving the experience of existential threat in order to avoid a sense of complacency in the future, serving as a mental representation of massive trauma, from which the ancestors of the group suffered. It exists unconsciously in the "mind" of the large group and in social regression situations, such as wartime, it is reactivated to support and strengthen the threatened identity. There is no doubt that the generation now living in Israel is under the influence of the Holocaust, as reflected in almost every Israeli group dynamic. The image of the persecuted Jew in exile is one of the basic components of the Sabra myth, the antithesis to the persecuted Jew in the Diaspora. Expressions of weakness or submission are regarded as existential threats. Weinberg adds that because this myth included the image of Israel as a wilderness, a land with no people (that the Sabra and the pioneer settlers came to flourish), inevitably the existence of the other, who had settled on the land for centuries, was ignored.

Within this context, any struggle for territory (room, for example) might acquire the meaning of exclusion and conquest, as one group, organising a living space for itself, inadvertently takes the place of another group, who also has the right to the same space. The group discourse following the statements of the Muslim participant clearly expressed this issue. The Israeli expression "I'm not a freier" ("I am not a sucker"), reflects an unconscious assumption behind everyday behaviour of Israelis to the effect that they would do anything not to feel exploited (Roniger & Feige, 1993). The centrality of this assumption calls for explanation, given that Israeli society has traditionally emphasised collective goals and self-sacrifice. Perhaps the deep need "not to become a sucker" is a response to centuries during which the Jews submissively lived under the reign of the Gentiles. In Hebrew, the word "freier" describes a person who is naïve, a kind of "loser" who might find himself giving up his wishes too easily. Staying in the room and not giving up might be perceived as a refusal to become a loser, a defeated person. On the other hand, since the protest against the passivity of the group who left the room was raised by an Arab participant, we can speculate that the social unconscious of Palestinians was activated, echoing the memory of their Nakba trauma, perceived by Palestinians as their national tragedy, being forced to leave their homes during the War of Independence of Israel in 1948 (Tali, 2017).

Shadowed by this reality, it is tempting to think that the right thing to do was to find an appropriate democratic solution to the room issue. The Israeli conductor, who became a representative of the conquering and excluding entity, found herself attacked by the Muslim participant, whose first reaction to the event was silence. One of the challenges of the conductor, considering the place of motion in the group's life, was not to be narrowly entrapped in the projective processes, enabling the motion between "in" and "out", and exploring the potential dynamics involved. The silence of the Muslim participant can be understood not only as representing one pole of the Israeli–Palestinian conflict, but also as choosing "not to be in motion" or "not to be in a dialogue". As soon as she could verbalise this difficulty, the group dynamic changed. As mentioned, a central goal in the process of achieving mental change, whether in individual or group therapy, is related to the possibility of mental motion.

Second event: moving up and down

In November 2012, one month after the opening of the semester, the military operation "Amud Anan" started in the Gaza strip, creating an enormous tension in Israel and around the world and having a strong impact on students who came to study in Israel from different countries. The tension in the university programme increased as one of the supervisors of the programme left Israel for the USA in the middle of the semester because of the insecure situation. Her act was in contrast to the students coming to Israel during that stressful time.

Friedman (2010) describes group work in times of war and points out that, whereas in the past the therapeutic endeavour focused on war victims, since wars in Israel are directed towards citizens, their direct influences penetrate into the here and now of the group. The supervisor who left and the other conductors who chose to stay in Israel posed two contradicting possibilities: does the military operation and the insecure atmosphere in Israel violate the group's safe space? Or perhaps this threat has the potential to echo and encourage a discourse about existential anxieties, as well as desires and fears and what Israel represents for the participants in the group?

Considering the Israeli culture, we should emphasise the emotional meaning of "Aliya" (the Hebrew translation of going up/mount, which refers to Jews who immigrated to Israel from abroad) and "Yerida" (the Hebrew word for descend, which means the opposite of Aliya—emigration from Israel). While processing the above event in the group, the value preference of the movement "up" (Aliya) upon moving "down" (Yerida) became clear, as the word "down" is associated with concepts such as withdrawal, inferiority, and so forth. In the multi-cultural context of the group, it attains additional meanings. Israel is a melting pot for Jews from the Diaspora, who immigrated to the "promised land". Aliya (mount/rise) and Yerida (descend, emigration from Israel) are not neutral terms, but, rather, carry deep norms and values. Bergson (1998) pointed out that it is possible to gather all the movements and forces in the universe into two basic poles: one is moving upward, and the other downward. The first one is composed of all the objects in the universe, the one that created life and keeps articulating it. This is the motion behind any developmental process. The other is the one that decomposes all objects in the world and is familiar as the second rule of thermodynamics. It is easy to notice the similarity between this idea and Freud's life and death instincts, noticing how "moving up" is identified with life, whereas descending is identified with destruction. In the group's context, these metaphors were associated with the Israeli ethos, not necessarily representing all the group participants.

Third event: the Prime Minister's death

A dramatic event in the group's life happened one day before the termination session, in January 2014. This was the death of the past Prime Minister, Ariel Sharon, after being in a coma for several years. Naturally, termination sessions evoke many feelings, unfinished business, hopes for a good closing, desires, sadness, separation anxieties, and so forth. His death was a meaningful event in Israeli society, however, it was different from the death of other leaders: in part, it was also a kind of relief after his being in a coma for years. It finally enabled grief, mourning, and separation. The relevance of these aspects to the group's termination session goes without saying. Outside of the group, his death was an opportunity for a retrospective reflection upon his achievements, as well as his ideology and decisions that were controversial in Israeli and international society. Inside the group, this complexity enabled a potential space to process issues associated with termination and saying goodbye, with all desires and fears involved. It was the Muslim participant who identified herself as an Israeli (and not a Palestinian) who brought up this topic for discussion. She did it in the most personal way, by mentioning that her father, who was a central figure in her community, had a close relationship with Ariel Sharon. Even though she chose a personal way to talk about this topic, the group was intrigued by the fact that the mourning response was brought to the group by a Muslim participant. Her personal way of talking was perceived as something that had the potential to blur boundaries, and flex the dichotomy between Israelis and Palestinians in the group, similar to the Prime Minister's condition in recent years before he died—a condition that blurred the lines between life and death. This liminal situation, existing between two oppositional poles while striving to violate clear borders, challenged unequivocal differentiations creating more of a continuum. Paradoxically, the personal tone of the Muslim participant created blurred boundaries between the personal and the political, enabling a transitional space for ongoing interaction. The death of a leader is also the point in which society, or the group, goes on without them, and, therefore, it was especially symbolic at this specific time. His death also closed a circle, marking the possibility of continuing with life. In this respect, it marked the transition from a static state into motion.

Lakoff and Johnson (1980) related to the central role of relativity in the process of creating metaphors. Concepts such as "high", "low", "long", "short", and others, taken from experiencing sensations and the way in which human beings perceive themselves in space, function in metaphoric expressions to describe various life situations. Lakoff and Turner (1989) stated that all existential experiences could be described in one metaphor: "Life is a Journey". This metaphor refers to life as something that is always associated with the ability to move from one state to another. In respect of Ariel Sharon, it is possible to say that the opposite of life is not death, but, rather, the lack of movement, including the lack of the option to die, to separate, to mourn, and to internalise. The parallelism between his death and the group's termination evoked questions associated with the relations between inside and outside, the penetration of the Israeli reality into the group's realm, and the experience of motion and mobility in the group.

Bi-national group of Palestinian and Jews

This group consisted of Israeli Jews and Palestinians and included "bibliotherapeutic" experiences. Bibliotherapy (Zoran, 2000) is a clinical therapeutic method in art therapy, in which the literary text serves to enhance and facilitate therapeutic processes (the text is in the centre of the therapeutic dialogue). Literary texts acquire therapeutic qualities and serve as a transitional area. This text functions as a "third voice", in addition to the voices of the patient and the therapist, and takes part in the dialogue as an autonomous interlocutor.

The group took place in the summer of 2014, two weeks after the beginning of the second operation in Gaza, in which many relatives of the Jewish participants took part. The participants came to the group in the middle of storming battles in Gaza and some of them brought their children with them in order not to leave them at home when sirens signalled rocket attacks. On the first day of the war, the brother of one of the students was killed and it was questioned whether to continue the group at all. The group room was flooded with the external reality and the participants could barely work with symbolisation. This difficulty is especially meaningful in a group dealing with literary texts focusing on the uniqueness of symbolic literary representations, and the transitional areas with which they are identified. Whereas mixed groups of Jews and Arabs are always complicated, during the days of that military operation it was almost impossible to tolerate the intense conflict. The symbolic space has been attacked, while the real space is being concretely bombed. Every poem or short story brought to the group quickly led to emotional meltdown and tears. The students questioned the discussion of poems and stories while a cruel war continued outside. Dealing with literary texts was perceived as a luxury and the group leader was criticised as inflexible in her persistence in conducting the group on such days. One of the extreme events, emphasising the lack of playfulness and the destruction of potential space between concrete and symbolic experiences, as well as between external and internal realities, occurred when a participant introduced one of Tagore's poems, usually associated with playful experiences. The poem includes one line that describes transitional space: "on the seashore of endless worlds, children play" (Tagore, 1916).

This quotation describes the borderline between worlds. The point at which the limited encounters the endless is the place of playful experiences—the transitional area. Winnicott (1971, p. 112) used this poem as the introduction to his work on transitional objects and transitional phenomena. However, in the group, this poem attained a horrifying turning point. On the day it was introduced to the group, Palestinian children, who had been playing on the seashore of Gaza, were killed by Israeli bombing. The participant who brought the poem to the group could not imagine the meaning attributed to this poem in the new context of the war. Beside the thematic aspect of children at play, what happened in the group was, in fact, an attack on the metaphoric aspect of the poem. This is extremely powerful when we deal with a poem that strives to describe transitional experiences. The playful quality was dismissed and the poem became a horrifying, cynical, and ironic description of the military reality, an enactment of anxieties related to situations of war and conflict, in which survival does not allow for playful experiences. This situation can be marked as an inability to move or "lack of motion". Apparently, we had good reason to cancel this group meeting. The reaction to Tagore's poem strongly posed the basic dilemma as to whether the group can survive or not. However, in spite of this situation, the participants showed up at every meeting and were determined not to miss any sessions. Although they said it was absurd to show up on those days, actually, in their behaviour, they also ensured how important it was for them. They kept bringing literary texts—a fact that was both ironic and rescuing. They reacted to these texts with intense emotion, whether the texts echoed experiences of pain and distress, or a wish for a life of love and compassion. One of the participants brought the poem of the Finnish poet, Eeva Kilpi (2000, translated for this edition):

> Really, as though there (actually) must be in me
> Such an amount of pain
> If not in the soul then in the body
> If not in the leg then in the rib
> If not under the heart then in the knees.
> Weakness resides in me courageously
> Struggling for its existence.

> Perhaps it is a choice never tested
> Another form of life, that in our great efficiency
> We have destroyed and thrown away
> A delicate manner of being, sensitive
> Crying within us.

The poem opens with a kind of an oxymoron, "really, as though", connecting the real with the imagery ("as though"), describing two modes of existence: the concrete one and the one connected to the experience of "as though", or "as if". The poem strives to locate the pain, enables it to move inside the body, from the leg to the rib, the heart, the knees, evacuating a place for weakness and bravery, for the struggle for existence. The poem's solution, so relevant to the group, finds an alternative space in which we can be vulnerable, weak, gentle, sensitive, a place that enables crying.

Discussion

Stern (2004) suggested a micro-analytic view of understanding motion in therapy. He shows how the present moment is the one enabling motion. These moments are relational moves, operating within the consciences of the participants in that motion. "This is a present moment in which the two parties achieve an intersubjective meeting. At this moment the two become aware of what each other is experiencing. They share a specific mental landscape . . ." (p. 151).

Movement in therapy groups occurs when there are enough moments of meetings of the kind that Stern described, and the task of the therapist is to encourage the emergence of those moments. Ostensibly, the group is the ideal place for creating such moments of meetings, as that shared "mental landscape" inevitably comes to life with the creation of the group matrix and the group interpersonal encounter. However, in times of conflict, the creation of such a space is challenged and threatened by the external reality. Loewald (1960) described movement in therapy as the promotion and utilisation of *controlled* regression. However, when the political–social situation outside the group is too stressful, it penetrates the group boundaries, so that regression becomes uncontrolled.

When the world outside the group is dangerous and threatening, external reality is likely to enter the group's space. The group members cannot focus on the here-and-now experience and have difficulty in symbolisation. This might be explained partly through equivalence phenomena (Hopper, 2003). The integrity of the group container becomes extremely important, because this container is attacked and challenged from the inside as well as the outside. The events described in this chapter illustrate how much this container can be threatened and attacked. The outside attacks led to inner ones. The processes around Tagore's poem exemplified how the entire metaphoric space had been attacked. Working with this poem actively illustrated the playground that was bombed and attacked. As the example of Tagore's poem about children playing on a beach shows, during such times the ability for symbolisation disappears, the "group play" freezes, movement stops, and the connection between group members is blocked.

Motion in this complicated space becomes impossible and the group feels stuck within it. In times like this, despair overwhelms hope.

When motion returns to the group, new playful interactions between the real and the imagery are enabled and experiences such as those described in Kilpi's poem allow authentic communication:

> Really, as though there (actually) must be in me
> Such an amount of pain . . .

As Weinberg (2015) has written,

> The group therapist should stay attuned to the sounds of pain beyond the expression of anger and sometimes rage, and bring those sounds to the forefront. It is a difficult and delicate task to help people who suffer, to open their mouth to express their hurt, to open their ears to listen to the suffering of the other, to open their eyes to see the subjective experience of the other, and especially to open their hearts to acknowledge and recognize the other's pain. (p. 49)

Note

1.   The notions of moving in and moving out have a military connotation, so relevant to Israel, and also found in sporting metaphors and hunting metaphors, for example, move in for the kill.

References

Bergson, H. (1998). *Creative Evolution*, A. Mitchell (Trans.). New York: Dover.

Friedman, R. (2010). The group and the individual in conflict and war. *Group Analysis*, *43*(3): 281–300.

Gary, R. (1980). *Les Cerfs-volants*. Paris: Gallimard.

Hopper, E. (2001). On the nature of hope in psychoanalysis and group analysis. *British Journal of Psychotherapy*, *18*(2): 205–226.

Hopper, E. (2003). *The Social Unconscious: Selected Papers*. London: Jessica Kingsley.

Hopper, E., & Weinberg, H. (Eds.) (2011). *The Social Unconscious in Persons, Groups, and Societies: Vol. I: Mainly Theory*. London: Karnac.

Kilpi, E. (2000). *Butterfly Cross the Road: The Collected Poems 1972–2000* [in Finnish]. Helsinki: Söderström.

Lakoff, G., & Johnson, M. (1980). *Metaphors We Live By*. Chicago, IL: University of Chicago Press.

Lakoff, G., & Turner, M. (1989). *More Than Cool Reason: A Field Guide to Poetic Metaphor*. Chicago, IL: University of Chicago Press.

Loewald, H. W. (1960). On the therapeutic action of psycho-analysis. *International Journal of Psychoanalysis*, *41*: 16–33.

Roniger, L., & Feige, M. (1993). The freier culture and Israeli identity [in Hebrew]. *Alpayim*, *7*: 118–136.

Stern, D. (2004). *The Present Moment in Psychotherapy and Everyday Life*. New York: Norton.

Symington, N. (1983). The analyst's act of freedom as agent of therapeutic change. *International Journal of Psychoanalysis*, *10*(3): 283–291.

Tagore, R. (1916). *Gitanjali* [*Song Offerings*]. Calcutta: Macmillan.

Tali, S. (2017). The Palestinian social unconscious. In E. Hopper & H. Weinberg (Eds.), *The Social Unconscious in Persons, Groups and Societies: Developments in the Theory of the Matrix in Group Analysis* (*Volume III*). London: Karnac, in press.

Tedeshi, R. G., & Calhoun, L. G. (2004). *Posttraumatic Growth: Conceptual Foundation and Empirical Evidence*. Philadelphia, PA: Lawrence Erlbaum.

Teplitz, M. (2005). Thoughts about authority, role and boundaries. *Organizational Analysis*, *8*: 32–38 [in Hebrew].

Volkan, V. (2001). Transgenerational transmissions and chosen traumas: an aspect of large group identity. *Group Analysis*, *34*(1): 79–97.

Weinberg, H. (2009). The Israeli social unconscious. *Mikbaz, the Israeli Journal of Group Psychotherapy*, *14*(1): 11–28 [in Hebrew].

Weinberg, H. (2015). The group as an inevitable relational field, especially in times of conflict. In: R. Grossmark & F. Wright (Eds.), *The One and the Many: Relational Approaches to Group Psychotherapy* (pp. 38–56). New York: Routledge.

Winnicott, D. W. (1958). Primary maternal preoccupation. In: *Collected Papers: Through Paediatrics to Psychoanalysis* (pp. 300–305). London: Tavistock.

Winnicott, D. W. (1971). *Playing and Reality.* London: Tavistock.

Zoran, R. (2000). *The Third Voice* [in Hebrew]. Jerusalem: Carmel.

CHAPTER EIGHTEEN

Co-constructing a common language: aspects of group supervision for the multi-disciplinary staff of a psychiatric ward

Ido Peleg

The ward as a matrix

Group analytic thinking believes that, at his core, man is a social being. He needs a group and a feeling of belonging in order to exist and to develop. The experience of isolation is the basis of emotional difficulties. In order for the group to include otherwise isolated individuals, it is necessary to expand the group's common zone of communication and its ability to tolerate diversity (Foulkes & Anthony, 1965).

Improving the capacity to relate to others and feel supported by them is central to group therapy with psychotic patients, in both inpatient and outpatient settings. This also applies to groups that combine psycho-educational and behavioural elements in their work (Cook et al., 2014; Deering, 2014; Kanas, 1999; Urlic, 1999). Skolnick (1999) writes that he has

> tried to make the case that an understanding of group dynamics, enabling the psychotic to rejoin the group as an emotionally alive contributing person rather than an objectified thing to be repaired, is essential to all meaningful treatment. (1999, p. 79)

Can a psychiatric department as a whole serve a similar function to patients who have lost the ability to function in their social environment and have had to be hospitalised?

Foulkes' and his colleagues' work at Northfield during the Second World War inspired the development of the therapeutic community movement and the introduction of its ideas within psychiatric hospitals (Pullen, 1999). Central to this approach is a democratic and egalitarian attitude towards patients and the use of group work. Main (1983) suggests that the hallmark of the therapeutic community "is not a particular form of social structure but a culture of enquiry into personal and interpersonal and inter-system problems and the study of impulses, defences and relations as these are expressed and arranged socially" (p. 217).

This is a particularly complicated endeavour in a psychiatric hospital, where patients might have been hospitalised against their will. This might have happened when they and their social environment cannot maintain the understanding and communication necessary to work together to alleviate mutual suffering. Subsequent to hospitalisation, communication difficulties might manifest themselves in the ward as well. Thus, it is common to see splitting, projective identification, and acting out. These manifestations affect the staff and lead to the development of basic assumption culture (Bion, 1961) in the ward as a whole. Members of staff have a tendency to use coping strategies such as control, silencing, and even unneeded aggression towards patients (Hinshelwood, 2004; Novakovic, 2011). These negative behavioural patterns could infiltrate the relationships among staff members as well. Hinshelwood (2001) probably had this in mind when he suggested that maintaining a reflective space in a psychiatric ward actually entails "thinking under fire".

The psychiatric ward may be conceptualised as a large group consisting of two main sub-groups—staff and patients. A main goal of the staff group is to expand the "common zone" of communication in the ward. Hospitalised patients suffer fragmentation of thought and language, and difficulty of attaching meaning to words. Therefore, there is a need to co-construct a common language that will enable better communication and understanding among patients, between patients and staff, and between staff. This is a complex task, for members of staff come from different disciplines (physicians, psychologists, nurses, social workers, etc.), and hold different professional languages and attitudes concerning the main goal of their work.

The tension between attentiveness and coercion is most prominent in closed wards. Not only has the patient to cope with the ramifications of his compulsory hospitalisation, but staff, who are forced to treat him, must attend to his needs while, at the same time, cope with the patient's fury at being treated against his will. The task of maintaining mutual attentiveness in these circumstances reminds one of Benjamin's formulations: she sees the therapeutic process as a movement from an intersubjective state of mutual control to a state of mutual recognition (Benjamin, 2004; Peleg, 2012).

Staff supervision in a psychiatric ward

Sensitivity, support, or supervision groups to the entire, multi-disciplinary staff of psychiatric wards are a relatively common practice (Bolton & Roberts, 1994; Bramley, 1990; Jackson & Cawley, 1992; Johnston & Paley, 2013). Such groups are used to solve acute crises among the staff, to give staff ongoing, emotional support, to promote experiential learning and even treat staff or individual members. Most writers suggest interventions that deepen the understanding of the relationships and mutual influences among staff members, patients, and the organisation. Identification of projective processes in the ward is central to this task. This is especially true in closed wards, where one has to cope with compulsory treatment and social exclusion. In this chapter, I suggest that the main focus of supervisory groups for the entire ward staff is the development of a common language and mutual attunement between staff and patients.[1]

Supervision helps to construct a common language

Ogden (1997) states that

> the analytic task of helping the analysand become more fully human involves facilitating the patient's efforts (albeit ambivalent ones) to experience a greater range (and play) of thoughts, feelings, and sensations that are felt to be his own and that are generated in the context

of his own present and past relations with other human beings, including the analyst. (pp. 10–11)

In order to achieve this, the therapist helps the patient to "train his ear", that is,

help him enhance his capacity for attunement to the subtlety of language as well as his capacity to use language in a way that more fully captures/creates his thoughts, feelings, perceptions and so on in the analytic discourse. (Ogden, 1997, p. 6)

Ogden (2005) conceives of the analytic supervisory experience as a form of "guided dreaming" (p. 1265). He sees dreaming as

the unconscious psychological work that the individual does (both while asleep and in waking life) with his lived emotional experience . . . The supervisory experience is an experience in which the supervisor attempts to help the supervisee dream the elements of the experience with the patient that the analyst has been previously only partially able to dream (his "interrupted dreams") or has been almost entirely unable to dream (his "undreamt dreams"). (p. 1266)

Ogden sees inability to dream (and think and attach meaning) as a central phenomenon in schizophrenia (Ogden, 1980).

A therapist who cannot dream about the patient is liable to develop a psychosomatic disorder, a psychotic countertransference, or be pulled to violate boundaries. This difficulty becomes more pronounced in a psychiatric ward, in which a group of patients are all living together in a crisis state.

Berman and Berger (2007) expand on this perspective in the supervisory group. They recommend inviting the group to enter a reverie (Bion, 1970), or common state of dreaming while suggesting "free floating" discussion. Such discussion is based upon participants' associations to a segment of a group session that has been brought to supervision. This "group dreaming" helps the supervised group formulate and understand its own experience as well as the experience from the session brought to supervision.

In addition, the authors emphasise that a main aim of group supervision is the development of empathy between the therapist and his group/patients, and between participants in the supervision itself, a perspective suggested by Moss (2008) as well. Application of these ideas to group supervision of a whole staff of a psychiatric ward facilitates the formulation of the experience in both the ward as a whole and in therapy sessions brought to supervision. This helps to construct an attentive culture in the ward, attuned to the feelings of both patients and staff.

Clinical anecdote: controlling and listening

Community meetings are held twice a week on closed wards. All the patients are invited to the meeting. It is a time for patients to raise requests and demands about a variety of subjects, both concrete, such as lack of toilet paper in the bathrooms, and less concrete, such as problematic personal interactions on the ward. The community meeting is meant to provide an opportunity for the staff and the patients to deal with problems in the ward together. It provides an opportunity to experience the freedom of expressing opinions in public (or in the presence of the authority, as will be seen shortly), and of simply being heard.

The hospital was getting ready for elections to the Knesset (Israeli parliament). As part of the build up, the conductors raised the issue of elections for discussion during the community meeting. A new patient, who had undergone compulsory hospitalisation, protested that he could not leave the ward to vote. Several patients joined in, claiming that they were second-class citizens whose political opinions were muted. Not only were they locked up in the ward, but they were not allowed to voice their opinion and vote. Several patients asked whether all those who had been compulsorily hospitalised indeed had to be.

There were other complaints about life in a compulsory ward: showers that were open for limited periods; hot drinking water that could not be boiled, etc. The discussion became stormy, and the conductors left the group as upset as the patients. The disturbing experience in the community meeting was subsequently brought to the supervision group of the ward.

While associating to the description of the community meeting, some members of the staff supervisory group discussed the meaning of freedom and what freedom of expression meant specifically for them. They talked about the importance of the elections, and someone said they touched on questions of life and death. Some described arguments in their families about political questions, and the central place of these issues in their lives. Some discussed memories of life under regimes in which there was no freedom to vote, or to express opinions. These and other members of staff said that their experience in the closed ward was painful for them. They sometimes hurt others in ways they would not want to be hurt themselves.

The participants went on to deal with questions about their freedom of expression while the ward director was present. What if some members of the staff thought that a locked-up patient did not have to be kept locked up any more? Or, maybe he or she should be allowed to go out of the ward and vote, but the ward director thought otherwise? Would their voices be heard? Could they have any impact at all? Could everyone have the same influence?

In response, the head of the ward talked about his feelings. He spoke about the fact that it was important for him to give the patients the maximum amount of freedom, but that it was also his duty to look out for them. And, perhaps, he was not totally free either. He was under the authority of the directors of the hospital and of the district psychiatrist. Everyone was preoccupied with the question of just how much freedom existed in the hospital organisation.

Influenced by the discussion, the ward director and the staff began to examine whether there was any possibility of changing the ward's plans for election day. Were there patients in this closed ward whose status could be changed to allow them to leave, accompanied, in order to vote? Would it, perhaps, be possible to find additional hospital staff to work on the ward on election day? Could they consider additional arrangements with the hospital directors?

In response to these thoughts, the staff members who presented the community meeting for supervision reported that some patients had said "This is all a waste of time! The staff do not really listen to us". This comment led to a closer examination of the supervisory meeting. It became clear to everyone that the remarks made in the community meeting were taken seriously by the members of the supervisory group. The patients truly had an influence. The community meeting was a place in which the patients could air their thoughts about the ward and influence what was happening. Even if they did not realise it, they would discover this with the passage of time.

This fact was reflected in a comment that the principal nurse of the ward made. She talked of how, during community meetings, there were fewer and fewer complaints by the patients and more of a feeling of closeness and tolerance towards others.

Discussion

This supervisory session is an example of the place of supervision expanding the communication matrix, as well as broadening empathy between staff and patients, and among staff. The all-encompassing public event—election time—was very significant for both staff and patients. The unavoidable limitation of some patients' freedom to vote, because of their chaotic emotional status, was difficult for the staff because it was in contradiction to their basic democratic social values. They chose to bring up this subject in the community meeting, making it clear they were open to discussion. However, they introduced it after decisions had already been made on how to organise election day. As a result, the subject of compulsory hospitalisation and a feeling of being "controlled" was on everyone's mind.

Subsequently, introducing to the supervisory group what had happened in the community meeting enabled a second look at the subject. Inviting the ward staff to participate in a reverie *a là* Berman and Berger (2007) allowed participants to get in touch with the feelings of patients as well as their own feelings—an awareness of which many had avoided until then. Talking about personal experiences of oppression in their lives and about limitations of their own freedom and influence in the ward enabled them to articulate some of the patients' experience in this closed ward.

In addition, the supervisory meeting enabled staff to test and expand the amount of freedom of expression in the ward, and also the degree to which they had influence on the ward and in the hospital. The willingness of the head of the ward to freely share his feelings regarding the election arrangements helped to forge an experience of partnership and open communication. This was "a moment of meeting" (Stern et al., 1998) between staff members. This experience with the ward head facilitated the extending of similar communication with patients by helping staff to better understand their feelings.

Attentiveness to patients' feelings and doubts presented a move towards "mutual recognition" (Benjamin, 2004) in an organisation in which coercion was an unavoidable part of its culture. In addition, the therapeutic and supervisory work strengthened the notion of the ward as a relevant space, in which there was a balance between reflection and action (Hinshelwood, 2001). One has to bear in mind that, in many ways, the community meeting reflected the culture and climate of the ward as a whole.

Clinical anecdote: attaching meaning and constructing a common language

A meeting of a small dynamic group of psychotic patients was brought for consultation to a staff supervision group. A few weeks before this meeting, there was tension among the staff's different ethnic groups. Both the dynamic group meeting and the supervision meeting were held during the season in which all three main religions in the country—Judaism, Islam, and Christianity—coincidentally held their major holidays. The spread of ethnic groups and religions was reflected in the makeup of staff and patients.

The following is an excerpt from the group, which was brought to the supervision group.

The reader should be aware that the participants all had psychotic thought disorders, and so their comments may sound scrambled occasionally. Names and details have been changed for reasons of confidentiality:

Yevgeni: I think it would be simpler if you think, at 7.00 p.m. we made it like a birthday party here, all the world watching TV: Moti, Yerucham, Yevgani. All the religions will be together, with no violence. It'll be easy. In the evening I'll be ready.

Sharif: He's saying we should just take it easy.

Yevgeni: My father taught me not to be afraid. Everything will be fine. All families will have a big celebration, and it will be perfectly okay.

Sharif: I think what he is saying is that we can celebrate together, all the religions. No one is allowed to beat anyone else.

Samir: Why am I being kept here? The people support me! No, You're not going to control us. There isn't enough power and land for two nations.

Yevgeni: There is only one God. We're his children. A good father has no children. All the nations are his children. You don't need borders and you don't need fear.

Halim: You can be positive through fasting. This is how a person can find his way in life. I shouldn't tell people about my illness. It will make me unhappy.

David: I'm married and have a child, I love my family, I came with a friend of my own free will and then I was forced into this hospitalisation. Today is a happy day for me because the doctor gives me a holiday.

Sharif: I miss my life. That is where I belong—my home. My brothers and sisters don't answer me when I call on the phone. In my home they do everything. Why do they abandon me?

Maged: In another week we have a holiday. I want to know if this is going to be a hospitalisation like the one in 2009—like being in jail.

Sharif: (turning to the conductors):   Help us! In everything: in social rehabilitation, in the medical treatment. We also have to take some responsibility. Someone has to do the work. We—it's not fair! "Dead checking" by the families. You are the responsible ones here. Redeem us!

Yosef: We should be respected.

Maged: Let's stand up. It's hard to be locked up. To have to stop eating Arab food and start eating hospital food—what kind of normal person would do such things?

Sharif: Respect! I beg of you. I just want a few little things.

The fragmented thought process reflected in what the patients say is obvious. Still, a central motif in work with these patients and in this kind of group can be discerned, which is the transformation from primary communication to a language that enables thinking and the finding of meaning (Bion, 1959; Ogden, 1980; Hinshelwood, 2004). When treatment is given in the wider space of hospitalisation, there is value to understanding the group themes as they relate to the ward and the hospital. Supervision is meant to help the conductors and staff members identify these themes.

With regard to Ogden's (2005) and Berman's and Berger's (2007) recommendation, the staff in the supervision group were invited to "dream" the patient and supervision groups by introducing free

associations to the presented material. On invitation from the supervisor, several associations about the recent holidays were introduced,
some of which were about the holiday experiences in their homes.
Others brought their recollections of the warm atmosphere among
staff when a holiday toast was given. Someone else mentioned the
feeling of "togetherness" experienced at the opening of the supervisory meeting.

One staff participant recalled that, during the toast, some of the
patients had stood outside the room in which the ceremony took place
and tried to come in. Another spoke about the unpleasant feeling of
"being outside", which the patients had spoken about in the dynamic
group, and about the fact that he, as a staff participant, had felt so bad
excluding them. Yet another participant said that there were members
of staff who had not felt welcome during the celebratory toast. Several
staff members said that it was upsetting to hear that he had such
thoughts. They assumed that everyone had felt welcome—as they did.

Another participant, who, in the prior supervisory meeting, had
expressed her feeling that there was covert racism in the ward, said
that there was a hidden wish to exclude her because of what she had
said. People were embarrassed. The supervisor reflected that there
might be an unconscious wish to get rid of difficult feelings, such as
fear, aggression, and hopelessness by excluding people—patients and
staff members alike—who represent these feelings. By doing so, they
also get rid of the embarrassment which the raising of these themes
caused.

A participant expressed his wish to let the patients to go home over
the holidays and how difficult it was for him to be in a position in
which he had to deny some of them a home visit. Another staff
member described the experience of being hospitalised. How indeed
is it that "You do not have the possibility of choosing anything and
your freedom has been limited? You have to eat unpleasant food, not
of your choice. You cannot choose the hour you eat, or even how much
time you have to sit at the table. You have to wait for someone else to
light up your cigarette. You have to learn to get along with strangers
under unpleasant conditions."

A woman talked about her feelings as a therapist in these conditions: "What kind of feeling is it to give a patient an injection under
force? I learnt to be a compassionate nurse, and here I am doing things
that the patient does not want. What kind of nurse am I?"

Discussion

The narrative that developed in the supervisory group began with a discussion of the closeness at holiday time that was clearly felt in the supervision room, inspiring a feeling of safety. It evolved into a discussion about the exclusion of those disruptive people who wanted to spoil the fun—patients and staff alike. The subject of exclusion was connected to the feeling of repression and prejudice expressed in the protocol of the patient's dynamic group, and which had also been present among the staff. This might well be connected to the Israeli socio-political background: tensions between ethnic subgroups, the Israeli–Palestinian conflict, etc.

The supervisor's intervention about a desire to exclude people that represent difficult feelings did not lead to a deepening of the discussion and possibly even blocked it. Perhaps the intervention of the supervisor was too threatening, or exposed a reality and emotions in the staff group that were too difficult to touch. The difficulty in dealing with this subject is parallel to the absence of patient discussion about their aggression in their therapy group, and their tendency to see themselves only as victims. This might have been particularly applicable to the group under consideration, which consisted of members who had been compulsory hospitalised because they had been violent to those around them.

It also might have been due to the fact that the staff had to tolerate the patients' violence, as well as their own aggression, on the ward. Perhaps talking about the patients' experience was an unconscious attempt by staff to present themselves in the best light. Perhaps it was a defence against the supervisor's invitation to deal with themes of aggression, and his efforts to facilitate a serious examination of staff relationships and their influence on patients.

Despite this, after the supervisor's intervention, the staff members were able to talk about some of their difficult and ambivalent feelings regarding the influence of their decisions on the patients and their existential conditions. This was an opportunity to better understand the patients' experience on the ward and the patients' experience with them, the staff. This included being seen as evil, arbitrary, and repressive. It was parallel to better understanding what it is that patients have against their families and, indeed, society. Staff members could deal openly with the inherent tension between care and attentiveness and coercion in their work.

The supervisory meeting helped the staff to develop a new language that enabled the examination of patients' experience with staff and *vice versa*. It also helped the conductors who presented the patients' group to formulate clearly the feeling of prejudice and exclusion in the group, thereby enabling them to reflect these feelings in the next group meeting. The difficulty in coming into contact with aggression and violence was not processed enough, and there was a need to work more on this in the coming supervisory meetings.

The two clinical vignettes point to the centrality of power–weakness and inclusion–exclusion configurations (Friedman, 2007) in both patient groups and the ward as a whole. This is a consequence of the forced distancing of patients from their social environment and their stay in a medical organisation that uses coercion. Nevertheless, it is deeply connected to the patient's fragmented inner worlds, their persecuting experience, and the social environment in Israel, with its socio-political tensions.

These socio-political tensions are clearly seen in the psychotic group's dialogue in the second vignette. Compulsory hospitalisation and occupation, psychiatric treatment and salvation, longing for peace between Arabs and Jews are all present in the here and now of the group and the whole ward. These tensions affect staff members as well, who live with the Israeli conflicts in their everyday lives. One cannot really explore the matrix of a ward as a whole in Israel without paying attention to these subjects. However, staff members usually avoid open discussion of these tensions, since they fear that it will be destructive to their relationships and lead to an eruption of aggression between them. The courage to speak about the dynamics of exclusion, discrimination, and racism in the supervisory meeting gave birth to a moment of hope. It could be possible to deal honestly with the core conflicts of our lives in Israel, at least in a psychiatric ward.

It is suggested that the supervisory process, with its emphasis on attunement and understanding, helps to transform configurations of power–weakness and inclusion–exclusion in the ward. It enables true "moments of meeting" (Stern et al., 1998) and "mutual recognition" (Benjamin, 2004) to emerge. This is of utmost importance when treating patients for whom "The lack of trust, fear of engulfment and the wish for relatedness create a tenuous situation which sets the stage for personal relationships that continually cause pain, withdrawal and failure, occurring in a context of thought disorder, etc." (Della Badia 1999, p. 307).

Note

1.   In writing this chapter, I build on my involvement as developer and co-ordinator of a group supervision programme in the wards of a psychiatric hospital in the north of Israel over the past five years.

References

Benjamin, J. (2004). Beyond doer and done to: an inter-subjective view of thirdness. *Psychoanalytic Quarterly, 73*: 5–46.

Berman, A., & Berger, M. (2007). Matrix and reverie in supervision groups. *Group Analysis, 40*: 236–250.

Bion, W. R. (1959). Attacks on linking. *International Journal of Psycho-analysis, 40*: 308–315.

Bion, W. R. (1961). *Experiences in Groups.* London: Tavistock.

Bion, W. R. (1970). *Attention and Interpretation.* London: Tavistock.

Bolton, W., & Roberts, V. Z. (1994). Asking for help: staff support and sensitivity groups re-viewed. In: A. Obholzed & V. Z. Roberts (Eds.), *The Unconscious at Work* (pp. 156–168). London: Routledge.

Bramley, W. (1990). Staff sensitivity groups: a conductor's field experiences. *Group Analysis, 23*: 301–316.

Cook, W. G., Dobson, L. A., & Arechiga, A. (2014). Brief heterogeneous inpatient psychotherapy groups: a process-oriented, psycho-educational (POP) model. *International Journal of Group Psychotherapy, 64*: 181–208.

Deering, C. G. (2014). Process oriented inpatient groups: alive and well? *International Journal of Group Psychotherapy, 64*: 165–180.

Della Badia, E. (1999). Supervision of group psychotherapy with chronic schizophrenic patients. In: L. Schermer & M. Pines (Eds.), *Group Psychotherapy of the Psychoses* (pp. 301–323). London: Jessica Kingsley.

Foulkes, S. H., & Anthony, E. J. (1965). *Group Psychotherapy. The Psychoanalytic Approach.* London: Karnac.

Friedman, R. (2007). Where to look? Supervising group analysis—a relations disorder perspective. *Group Analysis, 40*: 251–268.

Hinshelwood, R. D. (2001). *Thinking about Institutions: Mileux and Madness.* London: Jessica Kingsley.

Hinshelwood, R. D. (2004). *Suffering Insanity. Psychoanalytic Essays on Psychosis.* London: Routledge.

Jackson, M., & Cawley, R. (1992). Psychodynamics and psychotherapy on an acute psychiatric ward. The story of an experimental unit. *British Journal of Psychiatry, 160*: 41–50.

Johnston, J., & Paley, G. (2013). Mirror mirror on the ward: who is the unfairest of them all? Reflections on reflective practice groups in acute psychiatric settings. *Psychoanalytic Psychotherapy, 27*: 170–186.

Kanas, N. (1999). Group therapy with schizophrenic and bipolar patients: integrative approaches. In: L. Schermer & M. Pines (Eds.), *Group Psychotherapy of the Psychoses* (pp. 129–147). London: Jessica Kingsley.

Main, T. (1983). The concept of the therapeutic community: variations and vicissitudes. In: M. Pines (Ed.), *The Evolution of Group Analysis* (pp. 197–217). London: Jessica Kingsley.

Moss, E. (2008). The holding/containment function in supervision groups for group therapists. *International Journal of Group Psychotherapy, 58*: 185–202.

Novakovic, A. (2011). Community meetings on acute psychiatric wards: rationale for group specialist input for staff teams in the acute care services. *Group Analysis, 44*: 52–67.

Ogden, T. H. (1980). On the nature of the schizophrenic conflict. *International Journal of Psychoanalysis, 61*: 513–533.

Ogden, T. H. (1997). Some thoughts on the use of language in psychoanalysis. *Psychoanalytic Dialogues, 7*: 1–21.

Ogden, T. H. (2005). On psychoanalytic supervision. *International Journal of Psychoanalysis, 86*: 1265–1280.

Peleg, I. (2012). Oppression, freedom and recognition in analytic therapy group: Group and therapist interaction from relational and group analytic perspectives. *International Journal of Group Psychotherapy, 62*: 437–458.

Pullen, G. (1999). The therapeutic community and schizophrenia. In: L. Schermer & M. Pines (Eds.), *Group Psychotherapy of the Psychoses* (pp. 359–387). London: Jessica Kingsley.

Skolnick, M. R. (1999). Psychosis from a group perspective. In: L. Schermer & M. Pines (Eds.), *Group Psychotherapy of the Psychoses* (pp. 43–82). London: Jessica Kingsley.

Stern, D. N., Sander, L. W., Nahum, J. P., Harrison, A. M., Lyons-Ruth, K., Morgan, A. C., Bruschweiler-Stern, N., & Tronick, E. Z. (1998). Non-interpretive mechanisms in psychoanalytic therapy: the 'something more' than interpretation. *International Journal of Psychoanalysis, 79*: 903–921.

Urlic, I. (1999). The therapist role in the group treatment of the psychotic patients and outpatients: a Foulkesian perspective. In: L. Schermer & M. Pines (Eds.), *Group Psychotherapy of the Psychoses* (pp. 148–180). London: Jessica Kingsley.

CHAPTER NINETEEN

Analytic group for the children of the Holocaust and the second generation: a construction of belonging to the injured self through mutual recognition processes

Enav Karniel Lauer

Prologue

"Everyone has a name / given to him by God / and given to him by his parents" writes Zelda, an Israeli poet, and expresses the idea rooted in Judaism: remembering the man who passed away, giving him a name and recognising him. Remembering and naming serves as a metaphor for recognition of the existence of a man as a separate individual, as well as part of a community. The "Name" provides value, place, and commitment to be remembered and included in a group. By that, there is a response to the chilling testimony of Yehiel De-Nur in the Eichmann trial:[1]

> I was there for about two years. Time there—was not like it is here on earth. Every fraction of a minute there passed on a different scale of time. And the inhabitants of that planet had no names, they had no parents nor did they have children . . . they were not born there and they did not give birth . . . they did not live—nor did they die— according to the laws of this world . . .

In his book, *If This Is a Man*, Primo Levi describes his traumatic experiences from his stay in Auschwitz and says that the need to tell and share with the "others" was essential to human existence in the camps, and rose above other basic needs (Levi, 1991). Laub and Auerhahn (1985) write that the fundamental need of survivors to tell stems from the desire to be recognised and validated in an empathic relationship, as a response to the deletion and annihilation of their human and personal existence.

This chapter describes an analytic group for children of the Holocaust and the second generation as a curative environment for people who have personal and historical backgrounds related to the Holocaust. According to Hopper, in these groups, the participants feel safe and secure to talk about their suffering and sorrow with people that had similar traumatic experiences. The group enables them to use their pains and traumas in a creative way and allows them to connect, build relationships, and identify with the failures and successes of one another (Hopper, 2003).

In this chapter, I discuss the "mutual recognition" concept and elaborate on its contribution to the healing processes in this group of traumatised participants. The group took place at "Amcha" Tel Aviv— a centre for treatment of Holocaust survivors and the second generation. This chapter is dedicated, with great appreciation, to the participants in the group.

The chapter expands these ideas regarding the analytic group as enabling belonging, holding, and social recognition, while restoring and healing personal and collective identity of the post-traumatic individual.

"Mutual recognition": a key concept of interpersonal relationships and its relation to "mirror reactions"

The concept of "mutual recognition" has been developed by Benjamin as the central concept in intersubjective thinking, according to which the other is a separate subject, and right from the beginning we recognise his separation, but need his recognition. This is a reflexive process that includes the approving reaction of the other and the way we experience ourselves in the light of his reaction. The other must gain recognition as a different subject, so that the self can fully experience himself in the presence of the other. The goal of the development is not achieving total separation, but mutual recognition between the growing child and the parent, which will enable mature interdependence (Benjamin, 1988).

Self-expression and recognition by the other becomes essential in the dialogue between the self and the other. The developmental task consists of two poles of one axis: standing up for your rights and recognising the other. It is difficult to maintain the balance between these two conflictual needs (independence *vs.* dependence) over time. Two options are offered to resolve the paradox: the ideal option is that the conflict will continue to exist in a constant and dynamic tension between the poles of recognising the other and the insistence on what is yours, a tension that will return and reach a crisis point out of which it will be rebuilt, time and again, at a higher level. The second, less favourable option, is that it will be impossible to hold the tension and breaking it will create a conflict between the self and the other. In this case, a negative cycle of recognition could be created: the subject erases the other or surrenders to him (Benjamin, 1999).

Foulkes (1984) referred to the "mirror reaction" as a unique and central therapeutic component of group analysis that motivates interpersonal processes in the group and includes a series of reactions that arise in the individual in a group, in response to the behaviours and utterances of the other. This definition combines a set of therapeutic factors, such as identification, reflection, projection, and internalisation. The individual sees repressed and denied parts of himself reflected in interactions between members of the group, and, thus, he can get to know himself.

According to Foulkes, the group serves as a "hall of mirrors", where the individual participant is reflected by many different mirrors and can explore, compare, and observe them. These processes include confirmation, recognition, and visibility that cannot take place without the presence of the other, who sees and recognises. The therapeutic value of the "mirror reaction" relates to the understanding that the other is similar to me with his sufferings and, yet, allows me to identify the repressed parts in me, which are projected on to the other. The mirror's work, according to Foulkes, intensively takes place in the group space, by working on identifications and the release of guilt and anxiety, while building confidence (Foulkes, 1984).

Pines has expanded the concept of "mirror reaction" and considers it to be the cornerstone of group analysis. According to him, this is a process in which the individual acquires information about himself, through social and interpersonal interactions, gets to know himself, becomes understood by others, and, thus, comes to be appreciated. In his words, one can find similarities between the two concepts: "I am like you, you are like me in this aspect of ourselves: I can recognize, re-inspect and re-spect that personality: together, if you accept my perception, or I yours, we can learn more about ourselves" (Pines, 1983, p. 13).

This mirroring reaction enables the participant to meet and expand his unconscious and increase his self-awareness (Weinberg & Todar, 2004). One can see, in a "mirror reaction", the foundation on which mutual recognition processes develop. Through "mirror reaction" processes and mutual recognition in the group, participants can see and show their feelings through others, understand what others do to them, and what they are doing to others, and, thus, become partners in interpersonal and social experiences and gain a sense of belonging (Berger, 2011).

The clinical vignettes that follow illustrate how the process of mutual recognition allows the creation of a sense of belonging and pain relief, with participants in an analytic group for children and the second generation of the Holocaust.

"Recognition of the injustice" or "Tell me I'm not crazy"

For almost twenty years, Rina has never told her mother that she is in therapy. In the group, she describes difficult feelings, including the lack of her own place in the world, and feels that her mother is her "jailor". Her parents, Auschwitz survivors (originally from Belgium), had lost a child in the Holocaust before she was born. She came to Israel from the USA, some time before her father passed away. According to her, "The magnetic and toxic field of my parents drew me to them." Recently, in parallel to group therapy, there are a number of conversations between Rina, her mother, and a couples therapist, during which Rina tells her mother her great secret: that she is in group therapy.

> Rina: My mother stopped talking about her relationship with me and for most of the meetings talked about the war, or her approaching death. I rarely spoke, most of the time I cried . . . Now I'm angry with our therapist, who gave up on us. I'm also angry with another therapist, who,

many years ago, said to my mother that I was the one who needed therapy and everything was fine with her. I don't know what to do . . . I want to talk to these two therapists and tell them they were wrong. It is very difficult for me with my mother, we are constantly fighting, I cannot talk to her at all, we mostly shout at each other.

Amit: It's so annoying—only once I dared to say to my father: "Where were you when I needed you? Where were you when I was left without any support, abandoned and alone? Which father abandons his child? I usually do not speak . . . speechless in regard to what people do to me.

Yael: I understand exactly what you mean, yesterday, when I left my parents, I called my sister and told her that I could not take it any more, that out of despair my curly hair has straightened. I screamed out of anger.

Rina: (crying) I do not have the ability to be like you. I never talked to my mother like Yael, or decided to break away from my parents, like Amit.

Eva: Maybe you need extra help, I will refer you to my friend who often fights with her parents . . . maybe it would help . . .

Therapist: Rina, what do you mean by talking to your mother like Amit or Yael?

Rina: To tell her that I am fed up with this, that she needs to leave me alone and give me some space . . . I cannot do it.

Amit: How can I fix anything now, I've lost everything, I detached myself from my parents and I do not need anything from them, but at the same time I'm not ready to help my sick mother . . . Let them find me now. I have become indifferent.

Rina: We do not get along, my mother and I, we need mediation . . . someone who will help us to speak . . .

Therapist: Perhaps what happens between you and your mother happens here, in the group, as well: you are separating yourself from Amit and Yael, moving them and their advice out of the way, and becoming less attentive to them.

Rina: (hesitates) . . . As soon as I come to visit my mother, I want to leave. I just say a word and immediately there is shouting. I don't even know how to start talking to her . . . and then I try to quickly change the subject and constantly think that she might die, just like that, in the middle of a fight, and we would not manage to work on our relations.

Therapist: And what do you feel?

Rina: Terrible guilt for bringing her to tears, that I'm not a good enough daughter and I don't make her happy, that she is constantly disappointed in me. What kind of a daughter comes to visit her old mother and immediately wants to get away?

Yael: Almost every girl . . . Look what's coming up here, we are frustrated by the relationships with our parents. Eva did not have parents, so it's hard for her to understand. She views it more from a mother's point of view.

Rina: I can't, it's wrong, it's wrong that I feel a lack of love for my mother . . . [smiling]

Therapist: You are smiling. . .

Rina: I feel relieved after saying it.

Therapist: Here, you said it and stayed alive. You even managed to bring your mother to treatment after dreaming about it for so many years. You also succeeded in telling her that you're in group therapy, you found the words for that, you managed to say something that has been "top secret" for so many years. For you, this is recognition that she was a part of your problems.

Rina: . . . Indeed, it's a big change for both of us.

Amit: Now you can dare to say more, you are allowed to, all these fights are not intentional, you were not seen, which is annoying, and now you can begin to see yourself.

Eva: When I hear you, I don't know what to say. All I knew was to miss the mother that I don't remember. Well, there are probably mothers that are not so nice . . .

Therapist: It's time for someone to tell you that you are not guilty. Your parents were busy with themselves and with their pain and didn't see you enough. Not only did they not see you, but they had high expectations of you, and with every expectation you felt even more of a disappointment. You always felt guilty; no room left for any other emotion—not anger, not hatred, only blame—as if you only have one way and it is to suffer instead of telling your mother what you actually feel . . .

Rina: (crying with excitement), That's right; they didn't see me at all . . . I can begin to see myself.

Discussion

Rina expresses a wish for recognition. Her parents, who did not go through the entire process of grieving, remembering, and naming, could not recognise her as a whole and separate human being. Her basic request is to get rid of her label of "problematic". If she gives up her desire, she actually helps the aggressor (the mother) not to accept responsibility for her actions, exempts her from the need to examine herself, and leaves the victim (Rina) hurt, lonely, and guilty. It seems that Rina is trapped in the demand for recognition of the injustice, a trap that became her second home. She moved away from interpersonal relationships, became socially isolated, and the few relationships that she had were characterised by disconnection and avoidance.

In the group, she is very polite, interested in others, and responsive to them, but when it concerns her relationship with her mother she "distinguishes" herself unconsciously from the rest, as if she says to them, "I'm good, you are bad." By recognising this dynamic, while experimenting in the group process, and understanding her part in moving away from people, and the processes of exclusion in which she is involved, she can free herself from her impossible expectation, and yet be recognised in this need. Rina finds it difficult to use the group members as "mirrors" to herself.

As a child, she saw herself reflected in her parent's eyes as "insufficient" and was unable to fill the void left by her dead brother. As a girl, she could not heal the wounded soul of her parents and compensate for the loss of their son. She remained confused and could not cope with the guilt and the "ghost". The faces of her parents stared at her: empty, dull, and guilty. Rina learnt not to show herself or share her feelings and, thus, actually not to learn about herself from others while establishing relationships. One can say that Rina experienced a "malignant mirror", a concept that refers to persecutory mirrors that do not allow proper development (Zinkin, 1983). Or one can say that Rina suffered from "lack of mirror", which is characterised by emotional absence, nothingness, and early developmental deprivation (Weinberg & Todar, 2004).

In the group, Rina is able to observe other mirrors she lacked as a child: compassionate and empathetic mirrors, which validate her feeling of being subject to injustice. In places where she cannot get assistance from her group members—when they can speak ill of their parents and she cannot—she recalls the past, what her parents did to her and co-operates with the lack of recognition. In the group, Rina can begin to deal, with the assistance of the watchful eyes of the group members, with the injury and nullification she experienced in her past and go through the process of mutual recognition between her and the other participants.

This process is the "mirror reaction", in which transformation occurs from a destructive dyadic mirror to triadic and multi-personal dialogue and enables the entry of additional perspectives (Pines, 1983). The members of the group represent the viewpoint of the "other": they are the witness to the crime, recognising the injustice and validating it (Gerson, 2009; Herman, 1992). The group functions as a collective. Being part of it enables fulfilment of the need for recognition, and it provides the injured individual with the necessary repair. Thus, Rina can free herself from her repetitive desire for recognition of the injustice from those who caused it, and being stuck in the position of the victim. Sharing feelings, using mirrors, and identification of the others in the group with what has happened, are the recognition that the event actually happened in the reality of the individual—and the validation of a reality that might be experienced by patients as a private fantasy (Rubenfeld, 2003). As Rina said, "Only in the group I realised I was not crazy, that I just didn't do what my parents expected me to do. I could not fill the holes in their souls—and yet I'm fine."

A transition from a post-traumatic isolation to an interpersonal connection

At this meeting, Eva talks about a trip to Denmark where she visited the family that hosted her for years, as a child after the Holocaust. Arriving this time, she had "come full circle". She talks about the first meeting with the Danish family, at the railway station platform in 1945 after the war. She arrived with a group of Jewish children on a train from France, after a five-day journey. When the train stopped, the little children started to flee, fearing that they were about to be sent to Auschwitz, while the Danes came to meet them with sweets in their hands.

Eva speaks without pause, sometimes associatively; events merge from here and there. Suddenly, she asks the group, "Do you understand this?" She does not wait for an answer, and keeps talking, saying that she decided to look for her brother, since there was no evidence of his death. He was defined "unknown", in contrast to her mother and father, whose murder at Auschwitz had been accurately recorded by the Nazis. She talks unceasingly, in a half-hour monologue (the group is restless).

I ask the group about the meaning of their silence.

Amit: I don't want to ask questions since Eva said it is difficult for her . . .

Eva continues to speak about her experiences in Denmark, her arrival in Israel, her adoption by relatives, and studying at the mission.

No one responds . . .

Again, I ask what happened during the time they were listening to Eva.

Daniel: Now I'll tell you about my trip to the Netherlands . . . but I have something to say first . . . maybe it would be better if I do not say it . . . [hesitates].

Yael: Well, say it.

Daniel: When you were talking I was a little detached. Your experiences are fascinating and painful but I thought about how I wanted to talk about my trip to the Netherlands and how you haven't noticed it. I'm sure everyone wanted to hear me too . . .

Amit: I think that Eva didn't know you were in the Netherlands. She was not here when you said that you were about to travel.

Eva: I apologise, I did not know . . .

Yael: You are a lovely woman, but sometimes you don't really see us. I lost you at some point . . . While you were talking, I remembered how my father was talking and talking and didn't finish from morning to night.

Rina: To me it is just too difficult; I have nothing to say . . .

Therapist: Eva, did you notice that the group was not very attentive to you?

Eva: No, absolutely not. Well, sometimes I think I do not fit in here . . .

Yael: My father never listened to me either, only to himself. He didn't stop talking about the Holocaust until today.

Daniel: Neither does my father but he does not talk about the Holocaust but about other matters. He only talks about himself.

Yael: You said it without any preparation, without checking if we were ready . . .

Daniel starts to talk about his visit to the Netherlands, the purpose of which was to award the "darling of the United Nations" prize to a Dutch woman who rescued his father and hid him and his brother in her attic. She was ninety-one years old and received the award. He tells the group about the impressive ceremony, a meeting with the family of rescuers . . . [the group is attentive to him . . .].

Daniel: I want to get back to you. I was moved by your stories, but it was as if you were in your own world and didn't take us into account.

Yael: Maybe it is difficult for me to listen and to be with you because it immediately reminds me of how I didn't have a place, that Dad took all the space from me at home . . .

Eva: I don't want to constantly remind you of your father.

Yael: He is a very handsome man [laughs].

Therapist: You talked of very difficult experiences, but you didn't notice the reactions of the group members and how it affects them, maybe because it's so hard for you to talk, after years of silence.

Eva: Only in 2000 did I tell my kids that I'm "from the Holocaust". They didn't know and didn't ask, despite my French accent. I was called "orphan" when I was young. I was embarrassed, so I hid it.

Therapist: And you were so accustomed to concealment that now, when you do talk about it, it comes out fluently, in a monologue, and it's hard for you to talk now about your hard experiences from then . . . and then you lose your audience.

Eva is reminded of her visit to Auschwitz and that she did not cry when she was there and did not understand why others have to cry. She did not feel anything. At night, alone in her hotel room, she began to cry and thought to herself, "Did my parents think about me when they were in Auschwitz? Did they worry about me at all?" She starts to cry and the participants start crying with her.

Therapist: How is it to listen to Eva now?

Yael: Completely different, I could just be with you. You aren't making a speech, you are talking with us and not to us about your feelings . . . [Rina, Amit, and Daniel agree].

Discussion

Eva talks about her experiences in a detached way, without checking if the others are interested in listening to her. Her isolation distances the participants even more; the experience of traumatic dissociation recovers itself in the group, takes over the entire space and banishes the "other who recognises". Thus, the chance to transform the traumatic event to a "tale" in the presence of the other is withdrawn from her (Auerhahn et al., 1996). Eva goes through the world and in the group as if her past is irrelevant and is not a unique personal property, which might open a window to interpersonal connection. Her family had disappeared in the middle of the night, when she was two years old. She was given to, and supervised by, acquaintances in a village in southern France, who transferred her to an orphanage, and eventually she was found by her aunt after the war. What was done to her, she now does to herself. She does not value herself, becomes an individual without a past or identity, moves away from personal relationships and does not acknowledge other people as partners for relationship. Eva's trauma was revived in the group through the exclusion process. She brought herself to a state of dissociative detachment, without emotion, in long monologues that do not encourage any dialogue.

Recovery allows understanding of this process and opens a dialogue on the exclusions, using mirrors that the participants provide to each other. The group process enables the revival of unbearable traumas, a willingness to talk about them, and to process and translate them to interpersonal communication. The participants dare to expose and be exposed, with commitment to historical truth, repairing self-esteem, and connection to others. This creates a transitional space in a holding environment (Winnicott, 1986) with inner freedom, based on a tolerant and curious climate that increases the creation of new meaning. The group offers an alternative intergenerational dialogue that seldom existed in the participants' past. This dialogue allows the reparation of the injustice of non-recognition that occurred throughout the process of growth and during which comments such as "You sound just like my mother", or "You talk like my daughter" can be heard. It invites each of the participants to experience a variety of relationships with different characters, while testing the subjective meaning of each interaction for each of its partners, and examining how the inner world of the object relations that every participant brings with him paints the interaction.

Eva talks hesitantly about her past, about the longing for her parents, and the sadness and loneliness she had experienced in her visit to Auschwitz. This slow and cautious process of sharing enables a translation of hidden and implicit communication into a clear, explicit, and meaningful interpersonal communication. The transition from a personal and post-traumatic language, which is the language of symptoms, to an interpersonal common language, frees Eva from isolation and alienation, and achieves reconciliation among the various experience categories throughout her life cycle. These processes correspond to Foulkes' ideas about the value of communication in regulating mental health, according to which the interpersonal experiences in the group assist in translating the language of autistic symptoms to the language of conflict, providing personal experiences with validation and existence through daily language common to all, which is "ego training in action" (Foulkes, 1984).

The area where mutual recognition is given to a traumatic experience is also the area where the relevance and the subjectivity of Eva as an individual is born. Eva begins to see the members of the group as subjects and not just as unidentified objects, a process that enables Yael to say to Eva, "You are talking with us and to us." A dialogue is created between subjects.

Final thoughts

One can watch the analytic group, in which children of the Holocaust and the second generation are brought together, as providing containment and holding to the injured self. The aetiology and recovery, which are related to the trauma, are highly dependent on interpersonal communication and recognition provided by others. Since the result of the trauma is the loss of the safe place of belonging, both inside and outside of the self, the other has the power to connect the person to his past and help him to build his subjective identity (Karniel-Lauer, 2004). In the analytic group, the patients are able to create a communicative matrix that extends the personal resources and validates the subjective experiences and the ability to coexist. The division, about which Benjamin speaks, exists in a group in its full force: either others do to you or you do to others. As the process develops, the group becomes an intersection of transformation in which an attempt is made to link between the inside and outside stories, between the contradictory feelings, between symptom and words, while revealing the difficulty which lies in the ability to see both. The recognition of the existence of hard feelings such as guilt, grief, and despair allows compassion and empathy to enter, and, later, dissociation and traumatic experiences are released.

Note

1.   Yehiel De-Nur, extermination camp survivor, wrote many books about the Holocaust. Commonly known as "K. Tzetnik", he served as a witness at Eichmann's trial.

References

Auerhahn, N. C., Laub, D., & Peskin, H. (1996). Psychotherapy with Holocaust survivors. *Gerontology Journal of Aging Study. Holocaust and Aging*, 72–73: 61–68.

Benjamin, J. (1988). *The Bonds of Love: Psychoanalysis, Feminism and the Problem of Domination*. New York: Pantheon.

Benjamin, J. (1999). Recognition and destruction: an outline of intersubjectivity. In: S. A. Mitchell & L. Aron (Eds.), *Relational Psychoanalysis: The Emergence of a Tradition* (pp. 181–210). New York: Routledge.

Berger, M. (2011). The dynamics of mirror reactions and their impact on the analytic group. In: J. L. Kleinberg (Ed.), *The Wiley-Blackwell Handbook of Group Psychotherapy* (pp. 197–216). Chichester: John Wiley.

Foulkes, S. H. (1984). *Therapeutic Group Analysis*. London: Karnac.

Gerson, S. (2009). When the third is dead: memory, mourning, and witnessing in the aftermath of the Holocaust. *International Journal of Psychoanalysis*, 90(6): 1357–1341.

Herman, J. (1992). *Trauma and Recovery: The Aftermath of Violence—from Domestic Abuse to Political Terror*. New York: Basic Books.

Hopper, E. (2003). *Traumatic Experience in the Unconscious Life of Groups*. London: Jessica Kingsley.

Karniel-Lauer, E. (2004). Post traumatic stress disorder and grief response: their interrelationships, and the contribution of damage to "World assumption" and "Self perception". PhD thesis. Tel Aviv University.

Laub, D., & Auerhahn, N. C. (1985). Prologue. *Psychoanalytic Inquiry, Knowing and Not Knowing the Holocaust, 5*(1): 1–8.

Levi, P. (1991). *If This is a Man* and *the Truce*. London: Little, Brown.

Pines, M. (1983). On mirroring in group psychotherapy. *Group, 7*(2): 3–17.

Rubenfeld, S. (2003). Encouraging personal agency in analytic group therapy. *Group Analysis, 36*: 391–406.

Weinberg, H., & Todar, M. (2004). The hall of mirrors in small, large, and virtual groups. *Group Analysis, 37*: 492–507.

Winnicott, D. W. (1986).Transitional object and transition phenomena. In: P. Buckley (Ed.), *Essential Papers on Object Relations* (pp. 254–271). New York: New York University Press.

Zinkin, L. (1983). Malignant mirroring. *Group Analysis, 16*: 113–126.

CHAPTER TWENTY

The personal, group, and social aspects of dreaming

Gila Ofer

W hen my eldest son, Daniel, was three, he told me a dream he had had the night before: he dreamt about a queen who went on a quest to save the kingdom, accompanied by several knights. Their journey led them through all kinds of adventures: they fought foes, saw all manner of strange beasts, and crossed oceans—quite a caper . . . He paused for a moment, and then continued: then the queen got hungry and they all went to another forest. And the queen got even hungrier and they crossed the stream. Then the queen got even hungrier and they reached a cave and then she got hungrier still . . . and as he continued to tell me about the queen's hunger five times, I understood that he was the hungry one. We sat down to eat and I watched him gobble down everything I made for him.

It is hard to underestimate the magic of dreams, of the entire enchanted world they present. Dreams are some of our most personal experiences: alone at night, bundled up in sleep, the dreamer conjures up wondrous and intricate creations, only a few of which are remembered afterwards, as 95% of dreams are forgotten (Lipmann, 1988). Some dreams can hardly be described in words and remain ineffable even to ourselves. The strange and bewildering images or sceneries are often dumbfounding: we wonder at their beauty or we recoil in fear and terror; we wish to keep them to ourselves or we rush off to tell someone. Dreams exhibit the psyche's extraordinary capacity to delve into the amazing realms of the imagination.

This chapter is devoted to the different aspects of the dream—the personal, the relational, and the social. These are complementary and enriching dimensions, which may be construed in terms of figure/ ground (Foulkes, 1984a), or what Bion referred to as "reversible perspective" or 'binocular vision" (Bion, 1970). The dream is multi-dimensional and can never be observed in its entirety. Every image has a background, every centre its margins, every text its context; we can choose the focus of our gaze and we can shift our perspective, exchanging figure for ground and *vice versa*. In addition, I wish to demonstrate the effect of telling the dream to those involved and what this effect can teach us.

I wish to address the elusive and intricate matter of the dream's shared meaning as it is created and expressed within the therapeutic or social settings. As I see it, working with dreams entails curiosity, emotion, intuition, suggestion, and, naturally, creativity. We might say that this creative activity requires an audience. Working with dreams needs a listener (Friedman, 2008). In individual therapy, this is only the therapist; in group therapy, the therapist and the other members unintentionally become bystanders and witnesses to the unconscious workings of the dream. Interpersonal relations are, therefore, at the very core of the ability to dream.

The construction of meaning requires the presence of the "other", whether this other is the therapist or a good internal object; meaning results from the imaginary interaction with this "other". In the group, the presence of a greater audience allows the enhancement of the process through which meaning is generated.

I shall address three issues:

1. The dream *vis-à-vis* the telling of the dream.
2. The various aspects of the dream and its telling.
3. Comparing the personal dream arising in therapy with the social dreaming matrix.

The dream vis-à-vis its telling

When we talk about dreams, we should distinguish between the dream itself, which is a personal event occurring in sleep, and the telling of the dream. The telling is an interpersonal event, a "public", even social, occurrence, which often seeks to influence an external array of relations, or one's place in relation to others, or to ask for some sort of containment (Friedman, 2008). The opening anecdote is an example of this: Daniel's initial intention in telling his dream was, among other things, to share his fantastic experience with me; when the queen got hungry, his need was no longer for meaning, but for a very particular kind of containing: "I am hungry and want to eat". In the first part, he asked me to allow him to walk with me, like the knights who walked with the queen in imaginary travels. In the second part, the wish for containment becomes also a wish for concrete feeding.

The three aspects of the dream and its telling

Any dream, told to a single listener or to a group, expresses three dimensions: the personal, the group (interpersonal) dimension, and the social dimension. These dimensions parallel, in a way, the different dimensions mentioned by Foulkes: the autocosmos, the microsphere, and the macrosphere (Foulkes, 1984b).

Example: Karen's dream (in my analytic group)

> I am sitting in the group and you are here. Suddenly, three strange Druze show up. I am angry with them, yelling and waving a stick: "Go away, you pigs, what are you doing here?"

This patient had set her mind on individual therapy, but opted for group therapy following my recommendation and for financial reasons. In the group, she spent a long time being silent or confining herself to interpreting others, without sharing herself in any other way. She was the eldest in her family and had three younger brothers. Throughout her life, she had felt unloved and unwanted by her mother.

On the personal level, this dream expresses her own difficulties in her transference relations with me and with her "siblings" in the group: she does not want any.

On the group level, the dream expressed her difficulty as well as that of others in the group. She dreamt it after I announced my intention to introduce new members to the group. This patient, who found it particularly difficult to accept "siblings", had shared a dream that was, in fact, the voice of the entire group: the difficulty in accepting new members, who were experienced as alien, others, and incomprehensible by the group, at this point.

On the social level, the dream expresses a general social atmosphere in Israel, which experiences the Druze and Bedouin Arabs as others, and enemies to be expelled and excluded. Beyond this, the dream attests to a human attribute found in most, if not all of us: xenophobia and the hatred stemming from our fear of the unfamiliar, the other, the different.

As another example of the different aspects of the dream and its telling, I wish to share a short vignette taken from an ongoing group in Turkey, which I conduct in weekend-long blocks. It manifests the different aspects of the unconscious that arise through the dream—the personal, group, and social aspects.

This particular session takes place about two weeks after the mass demonstrations in Istanbul's Taksim Square. The session takes place on the second of three full days with the group. The group is very quiet; some references to the demonstrations are made. All the members are excited and all supposedly support the demands made by the protestors. They are somewhat suspicious of me—unsure if I can truly understand what they are going through. They are not aware of the fact that I was there when it all started. One patient, a thirty-six-year-old psychiatrist, married with one child, comes from an extremely orthodox religious family. Her mother is a devout Muslim and finds it hard to accept that her daughter had strayed away from Islamic tradition after finishing medical school. Despite being quite a lively participant, in this session this patient had remained silent so far. Eventually, she shares a dream she had the previous night.

> In her dream, she is driving to her childhood home, where her mother and two sisters live. She enters her childhood bedroom, looks under her bed, and takes out the thick down quilt she used as a child. She embraces

the quilt, but many flies cling to it and stick to her head. She tries to shoo them away, but cannot seem to get rid of them. She gives her sister the quilt in the hope that she can get rid of the flies, but they still cling to her head. She is very troubled by this, but there is nothing she can do. She goes back to her room and asks her sister what she did with the quilt. The sister answers that she put it back under the bed.

The other patients in the group started offering their associations to it: one of them said that the word quilt reminded her of the word guilt. Another said that she felt like the sister who failed to help the patient; a third said that, for her, the blanket brings back childhood memories— ones she could not get rid of even if she wanted to. After all these associations were shared, the dreamer said that she did indeed feel very guilty towards her mother, who would prefer her to wear a hijab, which she refuses to do, but is still very ambivalent about it. Then she related the process she went through in taking off her hijab. She then answered the patient who said she had felt like her sister, saying that the day before she felt as if her "sisters" in the group did not support her when she brought up a certain problem. The group then went on to discuss the demonstrations and the fact that certain Muslim groups do not support the protestors. The dreamer then mentioned taking part, fifteen years earlier, in demonstrations for the sake of Muslim women, when it was her non-religious "sisters" who failed to support the protest. Another member thanked her, saying that it was quite illuminating for her to understand that those Muslim women back then were, in fact, her sisters, fighting for the same ideals and the same freedom. I then could tell the group how the flies in the dreamer's head are both her guilt feelings and the symbol of her persecuting sisters who also take away from her the calming support of her quilt.

Through this dream and the work the group has done with it, we can observe all the dream aspects the group can engage with *in vivo* as well.

On the personal dimension, the dream expresses her difficulty regarding the secular path that she has chosen, different from her orthodox family, and the guilt feelings involved in it. By working on this dream, members could relate to the guilt feelings they harboured towards their parents.

On the interpersonal and group dimension, the dream relates to the dreamer's relationships and the other members of the group.

On the social level, the dream reflects the political complexity that exists in Turkey, where an entire country is torn between religion and secularism: a rupture manifested both consciously and unconsciously in all members of that and our society as well.

Freud's dream: the importance of the audience to dream-work

I shall now use another example in order to discuss the dream and the process of telling, and to show how the same dream may be considered in the light of all three aspects. I want you to imagine that I am introducing you into a session of a virtual group, a group of people, most of whom have probably never met face to face; a virtual group that has been meeting and persisting for over a century, from the year 1900 to today, sixteen years into the twenty-first century. This session is, in fact, a long journey, but, as our time is short, we will only be "meeting" some of the members. Most of the participants are middle-aged men, distinguished academics and psychoanalysts; few of them are female psychoanalysts. As mentioned, they do not convene in any particular place, but correspond in writing throughout years and decades. As this group is very large, I will refer to only some of these correspondents, which will make apparent the three layers: the personal, group, and social layers.

The most prominent member is, naturally, Sigmund Freud, who was the first to share a personal dream with the group: the Irma dream (Freud, 1900a, p. 107). Although he understood how powerful this dream was and how deeply the other members would be influenced by its telling, I doubt that he had any idea about the extent of the associations and interpretations its telling would eventually merit.

In the year 1885, when he was at his vacation house in the mountains, he had his dream, known as the "specimen dream of psychoanalysis". Freud wrote, when summarising the dream and its analysis, that one day a marble tablet would be placed at his summer home, saying "In This House, on July 24th, 1895, the Secret of Dreams was revealed to Dr. Sigmund Freud". He added that, for the time being, the chances of this were rare.

Freud recounts this dream in 1900, five years after he dreamt it. He provides a great deal of associations to it; as in an archaeological excavation, he suggests who the various characters in the dream might be

in reality, how every interaction, figure, or event is, in fact, a condensation of several interactions, figures, and events. Above all, he
confides that the dream indicates his concealed, unconscious wish to
rid himself of his guilt for his improper and negligent treatment of
Irma (Emma), as well as of another of his patients whose treatment
resulted in death.

Another, less disguised, purpose of telling of this dream is to
demonstrate how to work with dreams through free association, and
to ratify his theory: the dream is the high road to the unconscious and
one should seek out every dream's latent content, which manifests an
unconscious wish. Freud sees the dream as the dramatisation of an
inner wish, analysing it by means of the three fundamental rules he
sets down: condensation, displacement, and reversal. The key process,
according to Freud, is the use of free association.

Freud dreams and tells it to himself. This proves to be insufficient,
and he then tells it to the "group". As often happens in groups, the
group does not respond right away. Many moments pass—and in our
case, these moments are decades long. We are all familiar with the
group's awkward silence; this silence was finally broken in 1949, by
Erik Erikson.

In that year, at a seminar about dream interpretation, Erikson
offers his associations, resonances, and interpretations to the Irma
dream (Erikson, 1954). He seems to be telling Freud: *Regarding our
group of psychoanalysts, it is our duty to keep analysing this dream, time and
again, each time learning more from it about who we are and further developing our group identity.*

On the personal level: The way Freud tells it, the dream is told at an
age when he begins to feel the signs of both old age and illness.
Erikson says that it is a dream that reflects a creative person's mid-life
crisis and we must consider it to be an emblem of the dreamer's
psycho-social stage. The dreamer's life stage is that of creativity *vs.*
stagnation. He turns up at a birthday party in which he is isolated,
where he relinquishes his stubborn autonomy, and allows doubt to
lead him back to a childlike sense of security and trust. Erikson claims
that the Irma dream reveals the struggle between submission to traditional authority (Dr M, the superego), a projection of Freud's self-
value on to his distant and imaginary friend, Fliess (the ego-ideal) and
the recognition that he himself must submit to his own inner impera-
tive to study psychoanalysis in order to attain his integrity.

On the group/interpersonal level: In the Irma dream, Freud is diminishing or disdaining his membership of the dream's population of various doctors, as well as being anxiously and fervently preoccupied with his own isolation and his need to study, discover, and acknowledge the truth.

On the social level: Erikson (1954) mentions the dream's context. The dreamer is a Jew in an anti-Semitic environment, who strives to disseminate a theory against considerable professional resistance. In addition, says Erikson, the dream represents ego syntonic parts of Freud, but also parts that he owes to his nation, the Jewish nation, as well as those aspects for which he is indebted to his people, the Jews. He sees this as an inescapable encounter between Freud and his Jewish identity, Judaism that explores truth and originality.

Twenty years later, in 1975, Anzieu provides his own associations and interpretation for the dream. Anzieu suggests that Freudian theory, as one (oedipal) triangle spreading out into other triangles, matches the dream's formal structure, in which each character appears in sets of three: Freud's associations for the widow are Irma, Irma's friend, and his wife, Martha; his associations for the "Elders" are Breuer, Fleischl, and Emanuel; his associations for his "Equals" are Otto, Leopold, and Fliess. This also explains the (tri-part) trimethylamin formula, which is the chemical counterpart to the dream's formula. Anzieu goes on to claim that this dream actually depicts the founding of psychoanalysis: the secret of dreams is revealed in the dream; the structure of the imaginary is bound with concealed wishes, while the manifest structure of the symbolic entails formal processes (Anzieu, 1986).

Another interesting interpretation to Freud's dream was written by Blum (1996). Blum superimposes the dream on to the interpersonal space between patient and analyst. He argues that Freud's dream exhibits a process of analytic supervision, transference, and countertransference relations. Blum joins the claim that Freud, by trying to reach the dream's latent contents, had, in fact, concealed its other contents from the reader. He dreamt it shortly after Fliess's surgery almost caused Emma's—his patient's—death. While, in his analysis of the dream, Freud claims that he wished to exculpate himself, Blum suggests that, in fact, the dream manifests his struggle with Fliess's influence over him and his attempt to vindicate Fliess for his negligence, which almost led to Emma's death. By publishing the dream,

Freud liberates himself from Fliess's sway, the same way a patient relieves himself of a failed analyst. He is also casting off neurology to become a psychologist, thereby promoting not only his personal benefit, and the professional benefit of the psychoanalytic community, but also that of society at large.

The different aspects of the dream: the personal, the group, and the social

As I have tried to show so far, the individual dream represents the social world as well. The conception and construction of dreams from memory traces entail social meanings that are common to many. In one way or another, our images, recollections, ideas, metaphors, and symbols are all shaped by our nature as social beings.

The contents of our dreams are all derived from the social heritage encoded in our psyches and our brains. Thus, the sleeping individual, as solitary and isolated as she is while dreaming, is simultaneously embedded, in a profound and unconscious way, in the various attributes of her surrounding community, society and family, of her social class, her education, and her cultural tradition, of a certain language, with its particular tropes of thinking and feeling.

The interrelation between personal dreams and social life becomes even more apparent when we take into account dream telling and dream interpretation. Remembering dreams serves, in fact, as a window for external influence, for social commentary and response through associations and interpretation. Might we, therefore, suggest that what little of dreams we remember are actually the result of some mechanism that compels us to share them? As we have seen at the outset of this chapter, children express the desire to share their dreams from an early age, whether these involve adventures, horrors, pleasures, or any other strange experiences. Naturally, there are dreams we wish to keep to ourselves, but both the elements we seek to share and those we seek to hide, in shame or embarrassment, are dependent upon a cultural context.

The effect of telling a dream on the listener is no less intriguing. The dream is often related to as if it were real: the dream feels real to the dreamer, and even the person they dreamed of reacts as if it were true. In one of his papers, Schlapobersky (2000) discusses a dream told in group therapy that was recounted by a male patient, but also indirectly involves another female patient. She attacks him as if he had consciously chosen the contents of his dream in order to personally offend her and is fully responsible for them. What can we garner from this example? That it is only in the interpersonal space that we can study the impact of dream telling on both dreamer and listener (Ofer, 2004) and examine the dreamer's reaction to suggested interpretations.

Dream interpreters have always held great power and sway. In ancient cultures, as well as in many practices that have lasted to this day, these men and women have had the power to explore, heal, punish, and channel the word of god and more. Dream images have been interpreted as divine signs, prophetic intimations, advice and instruction regarding war and peace, interpersonal behaviour, and affairs of state (e.g., in the bible, we find the dreams of Pharaoh and his eunuchs, which Joseph interpreted while imprisoned).

Psychoanalysis grants analysts considerable power as dream interpreters. Nevertheless, as we have seen, dreams can be interpreted in many ways. Even when dealing with a single dream, the Freudian will focus on the unconscious and the working through of infantile sexual wishes; the Jungian will identify the archetypal patterns of the collective unconscious; the Kohutian or self-psychologist will note the representations of the various self-states regulated by the dream; Winnicott (1971) will consider it as a playful transitional space; the relationalists will see it as manifesting the transference–countertransference matrix or current patient–analyst relations, and so on and so forth. The danger inherent in the power of interpretation is ever-present. We must be very careful not to impose interpretations, but to observe dreams in a more open and sharing manner, while relying on the patient's associations to the dream and being mindful of the process of its telling.

The social dreaming matrix

I shall now discuss the study of social dreaming in the context of the social dreaming matrix (SDM), which is a method for working with dreams devised by Lawrence (1998). In it, participants are invited to share the dreams that they had during the previous nights or even weeks, while all the participants are encouraged to provide associations to these dreams, letting them sail through the room seeking resonance to them and witnessing how dreams create images which reveal social processes and the unconscious preoccupations of the participants in the context of the wider society. The idea is that the participants do not claim ownership of their dreams as much as they let their dreams make their own way, meeting other dreams and the associations of all the participants (Lawrence, 1998). Each participant dreams for herself, her groups, the participants in the SDM, their organisation within which these groupings are embedded, and, of course, the wider society as well. As the dreams, rather than the dreamers, are the focus of the work, each dream returns to its dreamer through someone else's dream. Participants in a social dreaming matrix must learn how to surrender their control, and to allow themselves to be surprised by new discoveries through the associations and through discussions of this material. The metaphor of a "casual tourist" in the dreaming space is useful (Lawrence & Biran, 2002). In essence, social dreaming actually liberates people from the need to delve into their personal biographies with respect to their attempts to understand their dreams, thus enabling them to travel along various paths to the unconscious meanings of their dreams.

While its chief purpose is not therapeutic, the SDM is, nevertheless, therapeutically valuable. The richness of its perspectives, the act of listening to other people's dreams, the abundance of associations, all these help the individual relinquish her control and her prominence and reach a different kind of depth.

I conclude with an example taken from such a matrix. I hosted this particular social dreaming matrix in Estonia, at a conference about treating difficult patients (borderline, personality disorders, patients with cancer, patients with criminal records, etc.). The participants were mostly Estonians and Russians. One should keep in mind that the Baltic Estonia was occupied by Soviet Russia. Stalin had meant to settle it with Russians, who were sent there in their hundreds of thousands; for many years, the only official language was Russian. When Estonia gained its independence, about ten years ago, this Russian population found itself trapped—abandoned by "Mother Russia". The official language was changed to Estonian and these people became even more confined. One should also keep in mind that the Estonians are a very peaceful people and their struggle for independence was conducted through song, rather than armed revolt.

Here are some of the dreams brought into the matrix on the first day.

Dream one

> A party takes place with many people dancing, but it is set in the Middle Ages. All the people dancing teach us a well-known dance: everyone should have a magic wand, made of wood. The magic is that inside the wand there is a magnetic wire. We are supposed to gather together, holding our wands to create a culture of skirts. The wands change colour so that they are black on the inside and red on the outside.

Dream two

> This dream is about Cinderella. The scenery is beautiful; much more so than any ordinary landscape. The wind is very strong. At the centre of the field there is a female figure. It is difficult to be there, but I hope that things will turn out for the best. Suddenly, a boy appears, holding a magic wand. The woman says, "We are going to have a new government."

Dream three

> I am looking for a nicer home.

Dream four

> I am looking for a house with my late mother, a house for everyone. She always said we were living in the wrong house.

Dream five

> This dream also seems to take place in the Middle Ages, in a fortress. There is a kitchen with some kind of altar. Four or five people are preparing a meal: diced chicken, peas, and potato casserole. There is plenty to eat. Suddenly, there is a dead body on the floor. We are afraid. We see hunters come in and take the body, saying it was a mistake.

Dream six

> I was working at a morgue, starting to peel off the layers of a body. It was not at all scary. It was interesting.

It is apparent that the dreams shared so far have quite a few common elements: the magic wand, the other-worldly atmosphere, something extra-temporal, losing one's way, women with skirts.

The working assumption (interpretation in the matrix) is that there is a lot of food of a very particular kind (dreams). The "peeling" refers to the different layers of the unconscious. Beyond this, the common element is the feeling that something bad is happening in the country; the house is unsafe. People are afraid that what happened in Russia will happen here as well (fear of Putin). The women want power and receive it through a process in which they have to learn not to wait for a male partner, and to count less on men and more on their relations with the group and themselves, as in wider society.

Working through or interpreting dreams takes place in an area of play. The social dreaming matrix teaches us the degree to which the dream is an extended invitation to observe, study, and play, rather than to restrict ourselves to interpretation and the search for a definite, precise meaning. The difficulty lies in staying long enough with the unknown, the enigmatic, the vague, and the mysterious.

To conclude, the personal and the social are interwoven at every stage of the dream's life: society is situated at the very centre of the psyche. It is fascinating to behold the dream as a manifestation of all these realms, the most intimate private, the relational, and the social context.

References

Anzieu, D. (1986). The place of Germanic language and culture in Freud's discovery of psychoanalysis between 1895 and 1900. *International Journal of Psychoanalysis, 67*: 219–226.

Bion, W. R. (1970). *Attention and Interpretation*. London: Karnac.

Blum, H. (1996). The Irma dream, self-analysis and self-supervision. *Journal of the American Psychoanalytic Association, 44*: 512–532.

Erikson, E. H. (1954). The dream specimen of psychoanalysis. *Journal of the American Psychoanalytic Association, 2*: 5–56.

Foulkes, S. H. (1984a). Similarities and differences between psychoanalytic principles and group analytic principles. In: S. H. Foulkes, *Therapeutic Group Analysis* (pp. 93–100). London: Karnac.

Foulkes, S. H. (1984b). Psychodynamic processes in the light of psy-
    choanalysis and group analysis. In: S. H. Foulkes, *Therapeutic Group
    Analysis* (pp. 108–119). London: Karnac.
Freud, S. (1900a). *The Interpretation of Dreams. S. E., 4–5*. London: Hogarth.
Friedman, R. (2008). Dream telling as a request for containment: three
    uses of dreams in group therapy. *International Journal of Group Psycho-
    therapy, 58*(5): 327–344.
Lawrence, G., & Biran, H. (2002). The complementarity of social dreaming
    and therapeutic dreaming. In: C. Neri, M. Pines, & R. Friedman (Eds.),
    Dreams in Group Psychotherapy (pp. 46–67). London: Jessica Kingsley.
Lawrence, W. G. (Ed.) (1998). *Social Dreaming and Work*. London: Karnac.
Lipmann, P. (1988). On the private and social nature of dreams.
    Contemporary Psychoanalysis, 34: 195–221.
Ofer, G. (2004). The therapist is dreaming: the effect of the therapist's dreams
    on the therapeutic process. In: D. Anastasopoulos & E. Papanicolau
    (Eds.), *The Therapist at Work* (pp. 95–107). London: Karnac.
Schlapobersky, J. (2000). The language of the group: Monologue, dialogue
    and discourse in group analysis. In: D. Brown & L. Zinkin (Eds.), *The
    Psyche and the Social World* (pp. 211–231). London: Jessica Kingsley.
Winnicott, D. W. (1971). *Playing and Reality.* New York: Basic Books.

APPENDIX

The co-creation of the Israeli Institute of Group Analysis: notes from the archives

Avi Berman, Miriam Berger, and Joshua Lavie

T he history of professional group practice in Israel predates the founding of the Israeli Institute of Group Analysis. Sensitivity training groups were imported from the West Coast of the USA, and they flourished with a generation of flower children. More restrained European fun came from Bion's British tradition, which was, ironically, introduced by Itamar Rogovsky and his colleagues from applied psychoanalysis in Argentina. "T Groups" were established in universities, business organisations, and, finally, in the military. In such groups, we experienced for the very first time what it was like to share our emotions and thoughts with other adults who were strangers to each other. Sometimes, we managed to talk about our personal weaknesses and vulnerabilities, and, in turn, to hear the confessions of others. We were often moved by these exchanges.

Those of us who became familiar with Bion's study group legacy were confronted with the challenging and sometimes frightening role of the "leader". We experienced resistances that are still remembered to this day. We learnt how to respond to the appeals of individual members of groups by offering them interpretation of group dynamics. At the same time, we were in the midst of training in mental health professions. We came from different disciplines (psychologists, social workers, and psychotherapists), which focused mainly on the dyadic relationship between therapist and patient. With very few exceptions, our previous trainings did not teach us about the effectiveness of group therapy, or make it possible for us to trust it. Moreover, the leaders of our supervision groups seemed not to understand group processes. We contained this negativity silently, mainly because we were still interns.

In the entire country, we were just a few dozen professionals who believed in the group as a therapeutic modality. Most of us knew each other. Our paths crossed again and again through learning, teaching, and work. While our knowledge of individual psychotherapy deepened, we felt the absence of training in group therapy. We felt that, as a body of knowledge and practice, group therapy should have its own professional place, similar to the way that psychoanalysis had a professional home.

As early as 1965, Foulkes had visited Israel, and stayed for two months (Lavie, 2003). Co-ordinated by Ada Abraham in Jerusalem, this visit was sponsored by UNESCO, and included lectures and supervision sessions for senior professionals. In fact, a lecture given by Foulkes at the Hebrew University of Jerusalem is currently used in our training programme. Ada founded, in Jerusalem, her own Institute of Group Analysis, based on the activities of the Group Analytic Society in London, but this Institute did not survive beyond setting up an introductory Course.

In 1978, two years after the death of Foulkes, several senior group analysts came to Israel in order to train and supervise therapists who wanted to work with groups. Accepting an invitation from Dr Sam Davidson, the Director of Shalvata Mental Health Centre, and with Vivienne Cohen's assistance, Arnon Ben-Tovim, Earl Hopper, Lionel Kreeger, Malcolm Pines, and Meg Sharpe presented lectures and gave seminars and supervision. These colleagues also helped with some of the work with traumatised victims of the Yom Kippur War and of recent terrorist attacks. This special event, which lasted only a fortnight, was highly valued, and, from time to time thereafter, several group analysts from London worked at Shalvata with Dr Davidson.

The 1980s was a productive decade for Israeli group psychotherapy. A few of us participated in the training programmes organised by Benni and Bella Rippa, which focused on the theory of Pichon Rivière and his idea of "the operative group". In 1984, they began to teach the theory of group analysis as well. Later, Beni Rippa supported the initiative to create the Israel Institute for Group Analysis, and he is now an Honorary Member of the Institute. At about the same time, Hanni Biran founded a training programme for group therapists in the school of psychotherapy at Tel Aviv University. Dr M. Ben-Yakar and Dr G. Sheved, backed by the administrative abilities of Dr N. Mi-Bashan, started a training programme for group therapists, which was active for eleven years. The two-year training included practice groups, theory, and operative groups. Many of us worked as teachers in a group leadership training programme in Tel Aviv University, led by Miriam Golan and Ariela Friedman.

In 1990, a group analytic workshop took place at Abarbanel Mental Health Centre, initiated by Dr Alex Aviv, Bracha Hadar, Shimon Kornitzer, Irit Raveh, and Dr Henry Shor, as well as Brenda Fogel from London. The aim of the workshop was to explore the possibility of starting an Introductory Course of Group Analysis in Israel, in affiliation with the Institute of Group Analysis in London. On the basis of the success of this workshop, an Introductory Course was organised in 1991–1992. Brenda Fogel was its convener. The other staff members were Robin Cooper, Levana Marshall, and Marlene Spero. Vivienne Cohen, who immigrated to Israel at that time, served as their consultant.

This Introductory Course gave birth to the idea of a Diploma Course, and Brenda Fogel was its inspiration. Most of the teachers in programmes for group conductors and group therapy, some of whom had already begun to discuss the possibility of starting a formal training in group psychotherapy, wished to participate in the course. The opportunity to belong to an Institute of Group Analysis in Israel and to establish a training programme for group analysis evoked our passion and enthusiasm. Admission criteria for the new course were formulated, including a graduate degree and documented experience in group therapy and teaching.

In January 1995, forty colleagues, many of them had participated in the Introductory Course, met in Bet Levinstein for the new Diploma Course. The plan was for it to be conducted in a setting of "blocks" of five to six long weekends a year. Brenda Fogel chaired a staff team from the IGA in London, consisting of Robin Cooper, Sheila Ernst, and Earl Hopper. A local organising committee, chaired by Shimon Kornitzer, co-ordinated the arrangements between students and teachers. Each weekend block included participation and regular sessions of group analytic small groups, large groups, supervision groups, and theory seminars. Seniority did not excuse an applicant from fulfilling the requirement for participation in group therapy. Thus, we set a positive example that continues to influence the training norms of group therapists in Israel to this day.

These group analytic groups were a very special experience for us: we opened up to them, and they opened up to us. A unique relationship was generated, both between ourselves and between us and our English group conductors. We mumbled in English, which gradually improved. We delved into the personal and collective dynamics of our experience in groups. We became familiar with Foulkes' writings, memorising his long sentences, which contained insights, both familiar and new, both minor and important. His ideas about the primacy of the group and about the mutual influence of people in the group, for example, the matrix, mirroring, resonance, exchange, etc., established our unique professional identity. A spirit of innovation and hope surged in our hearts. These were also times of hope for peace in the Middle East. Yitzhak Rabin and Yasser Arafat signed the Oslo Agreement, and dialogue about a new Middle East was an element in the emerging matrix. We hoped that one day we would establish an Institute of Group Analysis in Israel.

Our joy lasted for about a year. The teaching staff called a meeting and informed us that they were obliged to change certain aspects of the setting of the course. We had to pay more in fees and expenses. Without adequate and proper consultation, several participants were added to the course, some of whom did not meet the existing criteria for acceptance. These new participants included both Jews and Arabs. We had virtually no alternative but to accept these overwhelming changes, because we wanted to continue the course. However, soon after this, another meeting was called, during which we learnt that the course fees failed to meet yet another new financial budget required by the "Overseas Training Committee" of the IGA in London. We realised that our teaching staff were themselves under pressure from the London IGA. In fact, they were in crisis. Some of us learnt that there was a serious health problem in the family of one of the members of staff. In spite of our not having much information about this (and perhaps even *because* we did not have much information), we reacted with anger, disappointment, and anxiety. With the support of most of the participants on the course, some of us initiated a letter, which was sent to the "Castle" (perhaps "Palace" would be more apposite) in London. We asked for an intervention from the IGA in London.

The intervention arrived in the form of a delegation of three people who came to talk to us. However, what might have restored our hopes turned out to be the end of them. We were informed that the IGA had not approved the course in the first place, Brenda Fogel had not been authorised to start it, and therefore, the IGA had decided to close it down. During this meeting our teachers remained silent. We could not understand why the course was closed rather than reorganised and reauthorised. Neither could we understand why our leaders were so "abstinent". Later, we learnt that they, too, were "stunned", and some of them had not known that the course had not been authorised. The delegation caught the next flight back to London. At the same time, Prime Minister Rabin was assassinated. We were speechless and help-less.

There are greater disasters than this, but we were definitely trau-matised by what we experienced as an aggressive, one-sided decision, without dialogue and the offer of negotiation. We were abandoned, both as professional colleagues and as patients. We were extremely disappointed in the organisation, which we had admired and perhaps idealised. We felt that the IGA had violated its own Ethical Code of Conduct. We experienced a failure of appropriate dependency.

Although we were shocked by these events, we began to work through this traumatic experience. As part of the attempts to process what had happened, Bracha Hadar and Gila Ofer, in a paper presen-ted to the Group Analytic Society Conference in 2001 in Budapest, compared what had happened on the course to the events of the British Palestine Mandate, in which there were pronounced ambiva-lence towards Israel and anti-Jewish feelings. After receiving editorial comments from Malcolm Pines, Earl Hopper, and anonymous review-ers, this paper was published in *Group Analysis* in the same year.

After about a year, several students and teachers decided that they could not accept the violent closing of the qualifying course. Monica Tanai went to London in order to meet Levana Marshall to consider alternative possibilities. In turn, Levana discussed this with Robin Cooper, who indicated that he could not bear the IGA's decision. He contacted us and offered to come to Israel and conduct a therapy group in Israel in order to process the rupture. Soon after this, he was joined by Bryan Boswood. Robin and Bryan travelled together, once every two months, for about eighteen months, and conducted a block of therapy sessions during weekends. They met in Eric Moss's and Joshua Lavie's offices in Tel Aviv. To us, they represented the ethical and professional spirit of group analysis, which sought ways to repair the harm caused by unilaterally stopping the course.

Avi Berman, who participated in these sessions, and who was a member of the Management Committee of the Israeli Association of Group Psychotherapy, initiated a proposal to found an independent Israeli Institute of Group Analysis, based on the certification standards and guidelines of the European Group Analytic Training Institutes Network (EGATIN). The new Institute would seek the academic and clinical services of senior European, but not necessarily English, staff who would monitor our certification processes. This was accepted unanimously by the Committee. Haim Weinberg, the Chairman of the Committee, proposed that the Association could provide the funds for the founding of the Institute. We were moved by a spirit of friendship, entrepreneurship, and co-operation.

A steering committee was established, chaired by Avi Berman, who later became the first chairman of the Institute. The committee included Miriam Berger, Robi Friedman, Joshua Lavie, Suzi Shoshani, and Haim Weinberg. Anca Ditroi and Diana Topilsky were members of the steering committee for a period of time. Avi, Robi, and Miriam flew to London to interview candidates who might form the staff of teachers and conductors of the new Institute. All the members of the course that had been cancelled were invited to come to the Institute in order to complete their training. Thirty-three of the original forty-four participants returned. Bryan Boswood was appointed to convene a staff team comprising Robin Cooper, Levana Marshall, and Veronica Muntz (SGAZ Zurich). They became our teachers, supervisors, and therapists.

A short time later, we invited professionals in Israel to join a second course for senior colleagues. Robi Friedman was the co-ordinator of this second course. Tom Hamrogue (IGA London) became the convener of its staff team, which included Beatrice Hook (IGA London), Felix Mendelssohn (IGA Vienna), and Gabrielle Rifkind (IGA London).

Thus, the Israeli Institute of Group Analysis was founded.

Our first years were creative, but also tumultuous. Two events are particularly memorable. The first occurred in the midst of the terrorist attacks on civilians in the cities of Israel, including Tel Aviv (2001–2002). When the Gulf War started in January 2003, the British Foreign Office advised British citizens not to travel to Israel, and the members of the teaching staff decided not to attend the next block. However, we did not want the sessions to be interrupted. The trauma of closing of the Diploma Course was still alive in our memories. In an atmosphere of pain and fear, it seemed to us that our gathering together at the usual designated time and place was necessary for our emotional containment. The management committee decided to hold the block as planned, but it would be self-conducted. In the event, the small therapy groups and the supervision groups were leaderless, and the large group was conducted by members who volunteered for the task. In the large group sessions, members expressed their ambivalence about the Committee's decision to hold the block as planned despite the absence of our staff. It was essential for us to process the tension between our European staff, who expected us to cancel the block, and the Committee, who decided to hold the block. This work was very meaningful for all of us.

The second memorable event was associated with the departure in 2004 of ten participants from the second course upon the completion of their training. They were part of the staff of the Tel Aviv University training programme for group conductors. Their departure was caused by a fierce dispute regarding the nature of the training in the IIGA. They took exception to the requirements of EGATIN that the composition of group analytic small groups must be heterogeneous, and that each group must be conducted by a single conductor. However, the Tel Aviv training programme allowed homogenous groups to be co-conducted. Heated and tense discussions over these issues led to a proposal to allow the staff members from this Tel Aviv University course to be exempted from these EGATIN requirements according to a "Grandfather Clause". Despite the approval of this exception in an assembly of members, these ten participants felt insulted, and left the course after the blocks ended. The IIGA lost good people who continue to be missed.

We have continued to work through the traumatogenic processes that were associated with the foundation of the IIGA. For example, in one way or another, these events have often been discussed in the large groups which are an important part of the meetings of our institute. We have begun to make creative use of these painful experiences. These processes take a very long time.

The IIGA continued to develop. Its first graduates became certified group analysts, after completing all the training requirements and after their final papers (written in English) were read and approved by readers abroad. The IIGA designed its own training programme, appointing teachers, recruiting students, and managing a new course of studies.

Between 2005 and 2010, the Institute was co-chaired by Miriam Berger and Suzi Shoshani. The idea that the position of chairperson could be shared by two people was innovative in psychoanalytic institutes and group analytic institutes. Not only was the position shared by two chairpersons, but they were also women. There were some concerns that without a hierarchy with a single elected chairperson, difficulties in the management of the Institute might emerge. However, the co-chairpersonship proved to be effective and beneficial. The IIGA strengthened its foundations, consolidated its independent course of studies, and established its independent institutional identity.

These tasks, which demanded a huge amount of work, were guided by a vision to create a new training course that would reflect both the spirit of group analysis and the realities of Israeli society. The resources available were mainly our optimism, creativity, and daily work. Miriam's and Suzi's labour of love was supported by an encouraging and committed management committee.

In 2006, Pnina Rappaport and Suzi Shoshani co-chaired a conference that was organised and conducted through co-operation with IIGA in which Jews and Arabs met and worked together in order to develop creative tools to deal with conflicts. It was called "Imagine". Professor Vivian Marcow from Lesley University, USA, facilitated the participation of Palestinian colleagues from Al Kuds University in Jerusalem. The conference was also supported by the Foundation of the American Group Psychotherapy Association. The 350 participants included a group of sixty Palestinians, some of whom were citizens of the Gaza Strip. Building on this successful conference, Pnina and Suzy developed a one-year training programme. Many members of the Israeli Institute of Group Analysis, together with Arab professionals from El Kuds University, volunteered to develop this programme.

In 2009, as part of our desire to expand our connections and to become part of the international professional community, the Institute organised its first international conference in Ein Gedi, named "kNOw hard feelings", co-chaired by Miriam and Suzi. Colleagues from Israel, European and other countries participated in the conference, which laid the ground for fruitful professional relationships with international colleagues, and started a tradition of similar workshops. In 2013, the Institute held a second international conference, located in Gonen, and called "INtouchable". There were 130 participants, thirty of whom were from abroad. In 2015, the Institute organised another international conference, called "The Road not Taken". Pnina Rappaport was the chairwoman of its scientific committee. In 2012, Robi Friedman and Marit Joffe-Milstein organised a conference titled "Away from the Gates of Auschwitz" in Shfeya, Israel. Joining with Dr Regine Scholz and Marita Barthel Rosing, Robi and Marit continued their co-operation and organised two more Israel–German group analytic "Dialogue" conferences, in Nachsholim in 2013, and in Ginosar in 2014, with guests from many countries.

During this period of time, the management committee of the Institute designed a new training programme for group analysts. Nurit Goren initiated and developed this programme, and was appointed as its first convener. Suzi Shoshani was appointed its next convener and Einav Karniel-Lauer its third convener, each of them managing two consecutive courses of four years.

From 2010 to 2013, Robi Friedman was elected the chairman of the Institute. During his tenure, the involvement of the members in various committees increased, and our new graduates joined the staff of the Institute, taking various roles. These processes involved passing the baton of leadership from the founders to the successors. In 2013, Marit Joffe-Milstein, who graduated from the first independent diploma course, and Robi Friedman were elected co-chairs of the Institute. When Robi's tenure ended, Marit was elected the sole chairwoman of the IIGA. In October 2014, the training programme of the IIGA started its fifth class of students.

Today, group analysis in Israel deals with the mutual influence among the various and diverse approaches of psychotherapy and group work in Israel. Our accumulated knowledge is increasingly recognised and absorbed into psychotherapy programmes in universities and in clinics. The IIGA has also started to accept requests for training the staff of outpatient and inpatient clinics in group analysis. The IIGA's group analysts also bring the spirit of group analysis to psychoanalytic institutes, especially to the Tel Aviv Institute of Psychoanalysis, of which four of them are members.

It seems to us that our long journey and the place that we have reached today can be illustrated, both essentially and symbolically, by the fact that, in 2011, Robi Friedman was elected President of the International Group Analytic Society. The writing and publication of *Group Analysis in the Land of Milk and Honey*, co-edited by Robi Friedman and Yael Doron, should also be seen in this context. Certainly, this book was forged out of the dramatic processes of rupture and repair that characterised the conception and birth of the Israeli Institute of Group Analysis. It combines the spirit of group analysis and the Israeli desire to learn and to contribute new perspectives to the growing body of knowledge in group analysis, and represents the diverse professional and national cultures that have been brought together into the dynamic matrix of the Institute and in the foundation matrix of Israel. The clinical and theoretical ideas presented in this book reflect our wish to contribute to the healing process of personal and social trauma in which we are immersed. Israel and our Institute need the core knowledge and core values of group analysis. As in many cases in which dreams "come true", this book offers a productive space for reflecting on the dynamics of our very existence and on the possibilities of a new identity both for group analysis and for Israel itself. The similarities between the creation of the IIGA and the constitution of the State of Israel warrant a separate discussion.

References

Hadar, B., & Ofer, G. (2001). The social unconscious reflected in politics, organizations and groups: a case of overseas group analysis training. *Group Analysis, 34*(3): 375–385.

Lavie, J. (2003). Foulkes in Israel. *Mikbatz—the Israeli Journal of Group Psychotherapy, 8*(1): 79–88.

INDEX